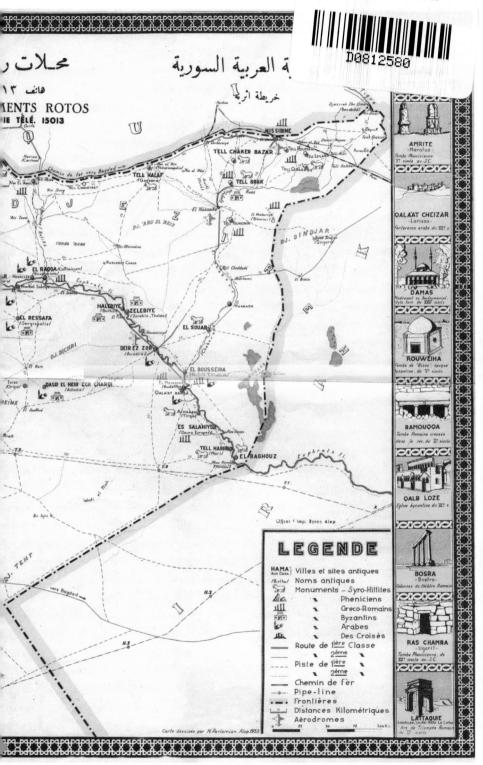

THE MERCHANT OF SYRIA

DIANA DARKE

The Merchant of Syria

A History of Survival

OXFORD
UNIVERSITY PRESS

OXFORD
UNIVERSITY PRESS

Oxford University Press is a department of the
University of Oxford. It furthers the University's objective
of excellence in research, scholarship, and education
by publishing worldwide.

Oxford New York

Auckland Cape Town Dar es Salaam Hong Kong Karachi
Kuala Lumpur Madrid Melbourne Mexico City Nairobi
New Delhi Shanghai Taipei Toronto

With offices in

Argentina Austria Brazil Chile Czech Republic France Greece
Guatemala Hungary Italy Japan Poland Portugal Singapore
South Korea Switzerland Thailand Turkey Ukraine Vietnam

Oxford is a registered trade mark of Oxford University Press
in the UK and certain other countries.

Published in the United States of America by
Oxford University Press
198 Madison Avenue, New York, NY 10016

© Diana Darke, 2018

Library of Congress Cataloging-in-Publication Data is available
Diana Darke
The Merchant of Syria:
A History of Survival
ISBN: 978-0-19087-485-8
Printed in the USA

This book is dedicated to
Syrian friends who have survived
and to dear Ramzi who has not

CONTENTS

LIST OF ILLUSTRATIONS

1. Mohammad Chaker Chamsi-Pasha (later Abu Chaker) aged six, c. 1927, when he attended one of the local Homs church schools and was taught by Syrian Orthodox nuns. Most of the pupils were Muslim, reflecting the two-thirds Muslim, one-third Christian demographic in Homs at that time. Boys and girls sat together in classes of about thirty to forty. Like most young city boys of the time, he wore a fez and a suit made from hard-wearing broadcloth. *(Courtesy of the Chamsi-Pasha private collection.)*

2. Mohammad Chaker Chamsi-Pasha (later Abu Chaker) aged twelve, c. 1933. By this point his father had died and he had left school to take on the responsibilities of head of household, as the only son among many daughters. Still in his fez and broadcloth suit, he is by now also wearing a shirt and tie, the dress code he followed for the rest of his life. The fez was banned by Atatürk in Turkey in 1925, but in the Arab world it was worn for several more decades. Abu Chaker only stopped wearing the fez when his second wife, Rihab al-Atassi, insisted on it as a condition of their marriage. *(Courtesy of the Chamsi-Pasha private collection.)*

3. Abu Chaker in London in the 1990s, as a wealthy man in his seventies. He smoked heavily all his life – cigarettes, cigars and the *arghile* (water-pipe) yet lived to the age of ninety-two. He never drank alcohol. *(Courtesy of the Chamsi-Pasha private collection.)*

4. A portrait of Abu Chaker aged sixty, taken in 1981 after his acquisition of the Bradford-based Yorkshire textile manufacturers, Hield Brothers. Today the portrait hangs in the Library of Yew Tree Mills, headquarters of Moxon Huddersfield Ltd, also owned by the Chamsi-Pasha family. *(Courtesy of the Chamsi-Pasha private collection.)*

5. A second-century altar dedicated to the haloed Roman sun god Sol, worshipped as Sol Sanctissimus (also Sol Invictus) and often identified with Bel (also Baal), the chief Palmyrene deity. Following a succession of high-profile predictions, his status rose to be that of one overarching god on a higher level than other gods, his cult preparing the ground for monotheism and Christianity. The city of ancient Emessa (modern Homs) was key in this evolution, as home of the famous sun temple with its cult object, a conical black stone, and whose high priestess, Julia Domna, married Roman Emperor Septimius Severus in 183. *(Public domain, photo taken by Jean-Pol Grandmont, 2011, reproduced under the terms of https://creativecommons.org/licenses/by/3.0/legalcode. Source: https://commons.wikimedia.org/wiki/File:0_Autel_d%C3%A9di%C3%A9_au_dieu_Malakb%C3%AAl_et_aux_dieux_de_Palmyra_-_Musei_Capitolini_(2).JPG, last accessed 21 December 2017.)*

6. An eighteenth-century astrolabe, disassembled. The astrolabe is a complex navigational and measuring instrument, which enabled Islamic societies to develop the world's most advanced maps and navigational techniques, to reach new markets and to establish the *qibla*, the correct direction of prayer towards Mecca. First invented by the Greeks, then further developed by Muslim astronomers of the eighth to thirteenth centuries, it worked by locating and predicting the positions of the Sun, Moon, planets and stars. *(Public domain, photo taken by Austin Evan, reproduced under the terms of https://creativecommons.org/licenses/by/2.0/legalcode. Source: https://commons.wikimedia.org/wiki/File:Astrolabe,_18th_century,_disassembled.jpg, last accessed 21 December 2017.)*

LIST OF ILLUSTRATIONS

7. Palmyra, the merchant trading city that grew up beside Syria's largest natural oasis in the desert, halfway between Homs (ancient Emessa) and the Euphrates river. Through the cross-fertilisation that followed in the wake of trade, Palmyra developed its own unique multicultural society, with its own language, tax system, architecture, dress style and even jewellery. *(Public domain, photo taken by Ed Brambley, 2010, reproduced under the terms of https://creativecommons.org/licenses/by-sa/2.0/ legalcode. Source: https://commons.wikimedia.org/wiki/File:Palmyra_Ruins_-_Flickr_-_edbrambley.jpg, last accessed 21 December 2017.)*

8. An original drawing of the castellated Homs citadel as it looked in the eighteenth century, by Louis-François Cassus, landscape painter, archaeologist and architect, who accompanied the French ambassador to the Ottoman Empire on a tour of the Middle East in 1784–87. The artist depicts himself in the foreground, sketching the citadel, surrounded by his own guards and intrigued residents of Homs. Very few structures have been found on the citadel mound today, in use by the military since the 1960s, despite joint Syrian–British excavations carried out on the site from 1995 to 2001. A chance find of an altar to the local sun god on the mound in the 1970s seemed to confirm it as the possible site of the famous sun temple. *(Public domain. Source: https://commons.wikimedia.org/wiki/File:18th_century_original_drawing_of_the_castle_of_Hims_by_Cassas.jpg, last accessed 21 December 2017.)*

9. Annual departure from Damascus of the *Hajj* pilgrims to Mecca, guarded by uniformed soldiers, while the women watch from the rooftops, c. 1900. Half the taxes collected by the Ottoman state for the treasury in Damascus were earmarked for financing the *Hajj*, itself a great river of commerce leading to and from Mecca. Pilgrims would buy gifts to take back to their relatives – gifts which frequently included the high-quality cloth made by Hield, a brand which enjoyed high recognition in the region. *(Reproduced with kind permission of Badr el-Hage.)*

10. Aerial view of the Şemsi Pasha Mosque on the Asian shore of the Bosphorus, Istanbul. The mosque, built by Sinan, was

commissioned by Şemsi Ahmet Pasha (the Ottoman ancestor of Mohammad Chaker Chamsi-Pasha) in 1580, the year of his death. Şemsi served under three sultans, including as Grand Vizier to Süleyman the Magnificent. He was a poet, chief falconer, chief hunter and commander (*agha*) of the military cavalry who also served as governor of Damascus in the 1550s, where he first began the broadcloth trade that was to be passed down through later generations of his family. He died in Istanbul, aged eighty-eight, and is buried in this mosque. (© *Reha Günay.*)

21. An early photo, thought to have been taken in the 1950s, of Briggella Mills, Little Horton Lane, Bradford, West Yorkshire, as featured on the Hield website. Built in the mid-1800s on a 5.5 acre site one mile south of the city centre, the mill has served as the headquarters of Hield Brothers since 1922. The company was bought in 1981 by the Chamsi-Pasha family of Homs, Syria, to save it from a hostile takeover and to secure their supply of high quality British cloth for their overseas markets. In 2008 before the financial crash Forbes magazine listed a $21,000 set of seven Hield suits as one of "the best ways to blow your bonus". The mill and site may soon be redeveloped for social housing and light industrial projects. *(Courtesy of the Chamsi-Pasha private collection.)*

22. Tree-planting ceremony at Briggella Mills in 1981, to mark the Chamsi-Pasha takeover. Abu Chaker and the Lady Mayoress of Bradford are both pictured with shovel in hand. *(Courtesy of the Chamsi-Pasha private collection.)*

Endpapers: Map of Syria drawn by N. Partamian in 1953, showing both Banias in the southwestern Golan Heights and Antioch in the northwest within Syrian borders. Banias was occupied by Israel in the 1967 Six Day War, then unilaterally annexed to Israel in 1981, while Antioch, modern Antakya, was given by the French Mandate authorities to Turkey in 1936. *(Noubar Partamian, 1953, as purchased by the author at the Avicenne bookshop, Damascus, in 2005).*

Every effort has been made to trace the copyright holders and obtain permission to reproduce this material. Please do get in touch with any enquiries or any information relating to an image or the rights holders.

PREFACE

Set against the backdrop of a socio-economic history of Syria, *The Merchant of Syria* tells the story of Abu Chaker, a Syrian textile merchant from the city of Homs who lived from 1921 to 2013. His father died young, leaving him suddenly alone to support his mother and sisters. He lost everything—twice—through political instability and war, before moving to England in the 1970s. Despite being barely literate, he succeeded in building up a vast commercial empire based ultimately on little more than trust. Deeply religious, he gave away a great deal in charity without ever flaunting his wealth. The climax of his tumultuous life was to buy and save a Yorkshire wool mill, the same mill that still serves today as the headquarters of Hield, the textile manufacturing company he and his sons turned into a global brand.

As a reflection on the vagaries and complexities of globalisation and migration, the book seeks to build a bridge between the cultures of Syria and Britain, a bridge that I hope may draw others in too. It is a plea for multiculturalism, for it is my sincere belief that we can retain the best of our own culture while still adapting to another. The textile merchant and I crossed over into each other's country and culture. He brought with him to England his business ethic, founded on faith and trust in humanity. I took with me to Syria my natural independence and freedom as a Western woman. He was not seduced by the West's materialism, and saw it as his duty to share his wealth, discreetly. I considered it the norm to challenge corruption, and saw it as my duty to evict the war profiteers who stole my house in Damascus. When the bridge is strong, everyone benefits.

The instinctive Syrian sense of community and empathy for one another, even for those who are outside the family, is something we in the West lost a while ago, without even noticing or seeming to care. In Damascus I was welcomed, accepted and respected, even as a foreigner. The contrast between Syrian and British attitudes to outsiders is summed up in their approach to refugees. In summer 2006, I witnessed Syrian friends driving to the Lebanese border without hesitation to collect total strangers fleeing the war between Israel and Hezbollah in south Lebanon. In a spontaneous act of humanity, they brought these Lebanese refugees back to Damascus and housed them till it was safe for them to return.

The pull to return to Syria is strong for all those who have been displaced. Once the war had forced his final departure, the merchant tried his best to maintain a connection to his beloved Homs through simple, everyday acts that formed invisible links—feeding his favourite aubergine dishes to his many guests in London, watering the plants on his balcony in remembrance of his Syrian farm. It is a connection I understand and share every time I feel the touch of Syrian cloth or soap on my skin, every time I tend the vine on my London terrace in remembrance of the vine in my Damascus courtyard. "It was cut at the wrong time," said a Syrian friend, on my last visit there during the war, "and its soul went out."

But the sap rose again and the dying vine regenerated.

INTRODUCTION

In the boardroom of a mill in Bradford hangs a picture of a white-haired man with piercing blue eyes. Dressed in a suit and tie, he is clean-shaven. His expression betrays the slightest of smiles. But it is the eyes that haunt you—wherever you stand in the room, he is watching you. "He was the only man I ever knew who was fluent in five languages without ever saying a word," joked one of his oldest friends.

Bradford, boomtown of the Industrial Revolution, once boasted thirty-eight mills. Two thirds of Britain's wool production was centred here at the heart of Yorkshire's prestigious wool trade. In a city dubbed "wool capital of the world", Bradford's thundering mill machinery worked flat out to meet an apparently insatiable demand for Britain's famous top-quality worsted. Today these huge industrial powerhouses have fallen silent. Some have been converted to flats, some are art galleries, others have mysteriously burnt down—all bar one.

Briggella Mills is still alive. Standing on Little Horton Lane, halfway up the hill, it continues to function discreetly as the headquarters of Hield Brothers, manufacturers of the finest-quality English cloth. Some of its looms clatter on. When the world wool market collapsed under competition from jeans from the USA and synthetics from the Far East, how did this one brand not only survive, but even transform itself into an international business, selling its products to luxury-end global markets, from the USA to Japan?

Hield Brothers, established in 1922 by British entrepreneurs David and Hugh Hield, had been a publicly listed company, twice awarded the prestigious Queen's Award for Export. The story of its takeover made headlines in 1981, but has long since disappeared from local memory.

The Bradford daily newspaper the *Telegraph & Argus* ran an article on 17 June 1981, which read:

Syrian firm gets Hields

The long takeover battle for control of the Hield Brothers worsted cloth concern has been won by Gamma Beta Investments, representing Hield's main customers, the Chamsi Bacha family of Syria...

Company chairman George Park said today: "We are all very pleased at the outcome. It means we can now get down to our real business of making cloth and making a profit."

There were powerful drivers behind why this Syrian entrepreneur needed to secure his supply of cloth, and why he repeatedly pushed himself out of his comfort zone. He had grown up in an unstable Syria under the French Mandate, experienced personal tragedy, lived through the fragile early years of Syrian independence, the disastrous union with Egypt, the rise of the Assads' Ba'ath Party and the descent of his country into its most destructive war ever. How had such a man saved the last working mill in Bradford?

Based on scores of interviews conducted between 2013 and 2017 in Syria, Lebanon and Britain with his family, friends and colleagues, this account touches on many of today's most pressing issues—poverty, family tragedy, Islamic beliefs, religious coexistence, refugees and economic migrants, displacement, multiculturalism, political unrest and war. The merchant was eighty-four when I first met him at his home in Homs in summer 2005, and I knew him for the remaining eight years of his life.

The chapters in the book alternate between two parallel narratives. The odd-numbered chapters give the bigger picture as a socio-economic history of Syria up to the present day, providing vital context and an illuminating backdrop to this story. The even-numbered chapters narrate the life of one man who lived through these turbulent times, the true story of Mohammad Chaker Chamsi-Pasha—the man with the striking blue eyes—and his survival against the odds. In the final chapter the parallel strands are woven together, seeking an answer to a question that is crucial to Syria's future. After seven years of war, in which over half of Syria's population has been displaced, exports and international banking transactions have been blocked by sanctions, and the currency has lost 90 per cent of its 2011 value, how can Syria survive?

1

THE MERCANTILE TRADITION

Experimentation is the greatest science.

(Arab proverb)

"Everybody feels the government is going to fall"—these were the words of a chorus of respected economists from the Institute of International Finance, a US-based global banking association with branches in Damascus. That was in 2012, when the Syrian state's foreign reserves had dwindled, according to official estimates, from $20 billion to just $2 billion. Crippled by international sanctions, starved of foreign investment, in a culture where tax evasion is endemic and where water and electricity run for just a few hours a day, Syria's economy must surely be heading for bankruptcy.

***

Syria has always been an outward-looking nation built on trade. One glance at the map is enough to see how the country's geographical location at the eastern extremity of the Mediterranean has put it at the natural junction of trade routes, running both east–west between Europe and the Orient and north–south between Anatolia and

Egypt. Its dynamic landscape of snow-covered mountains, forests, rivers and desert have shaped its inhabitants, and in the broad arc of land known as the "Fertile Crescent" that follows the curve of the Tigris and Euphrates river valleys, the world's first settled societies developed from around 8000 BC: the Babylonians, the Assyrians and the Phoenicians. A land of such abundant resources would inevitably provoke conflict, and for millennia Syrian territory has been a battlefield criss-crossed by a multicultural maelstrom of peoples— Akkadians, Egyptians, Hittites, Persians, Greeks, Romans, Byzantines, Arabs, Frankish Crusaders, Mongols, Turks, and others. All of them have left their mark on Syrian identity, but none more so than the Semitic Arabs, who spilled out in waves at roughly one-thousand-year intervals, whenever their population reached the limits of what the Arabian Peninsula could sustain. In the final and most important of these waves they brought with them a new religion and philosophy, which went on to shape the region and which, together with the Arabic language, continues to dominate today.

Islam provided a new and unifying battle-cry, but it was economic necessity and not fanaticism that drove the Bedouin Arabs of the seventh century north from their harsh, arid environment to greener, better-watered lands. The ninth-century Syrian poet Abu Tammam, born in Dera'a, summed it up in his famous anthology, *Hamasah*:

No, not for Paradise didst thou the nomad life forsake;

Rather, I believe, it was thy yearning after bread and dates.

The Prophet Mohammad chose green—the very antithesis of the desert—for the colour of his banner, as his armies surged north. When these Muslim newcomers conquered his land, Byzantine Emperor Heraclius was recorded by Arab historian Al-Baladhuri to have cried out: "Farewell, O Syria, and what an excellent country this is for the enemy!"

The majority of the indigenous people in the conquered territories did not convert to Islam immediately. When they did, over the course of several centuries, it was generally to escape payment of taxes or to gain the benefits of identification with the ruling class. Centuries of continuous social interaction between the various communities created a multi-ethnic, multi-religious society that was surprisingly cohesive, held together, at its very core, by the glue of commerce.

The art of the deal, in many ways, began here. The native Phoenicians, astute navigators and merchants, set sail in their celebrated cedar wood boats in search of fortune, founding new colonies like Carthage on the Mediterranean and Cadiz on the Atlantic. They invented the phonetic alphabet over 3,000 years ago to record their complex business transactions, and in Ugarit on Syria's coast, thousands of clay tablets in the palace archives provided documentary evidence of their administrative records, listing detailed cargoes of ships. Textiles like silks, wools and cottons featured prominently. Their local manufacture and trade was exceptionally important, employing more people than any other occupation. Even then, fine woollen garments made from Syrian sheep were famous—often dyed purple from Tyre's coastal murex shell. Here in the Fertile Crescent grew the wild cereals that are the predecessors of early European wheat and barley, while the sheep that roamed the steppeland from Anatolia to Iran were the forebears of domesticated European sheep.

It is no accident that so many of the world's greatest innovations originated in this melting pot of civilisations, where the blend of diverse ethnicities, cultures and religions led to a uniquely stimulating cross-fertilisation of ideas. In medieval times while Europe was in its Dark Ages, this region was experiencing a scientific and cultural renaissance. Greek, Persian and Indian philosophy, science and literature were translated into Arabic, leading to new inventions whose Arabic names are now a common part of the English language: magazine and camera; caravan and traffic; algebra, algorithm and zero; zenith and nadir; mattress, divan and sofa, to name just a few.

Creativity is built into the DNA in this part of the world, a direct result of the multicultural ambiance where three continents meet and where trade and competition drive enterprise and build prosperity. Embedded in the regional mindset is the belief that for every problem there must be a solution, a view that has taken root not least where rulers and governments have shown themselves to be neither capable or reliable. Many innovations—like soap, carpets, quilts, the three-course meal, alcohol and coffee (from *al-kuhoul* and *qahwa,* both Arabic words)—have heavily influenced the Western lifestyle, yet our debt to these imports from Muslim culture goes largely unacknowledged.

The concept of debt itself was born here, in answer to a problem that was common in trade. A merchant had a willing buyer, but that buyer did not have the immediate means to pay. Rather than lose the sale, it was in the merchant's interest to facilitate the transaction, and so the Arabs invented "*saqq*", from which we get our word "cheque". *Saqq* was a written vow to pay for goods when they were delivered, and was developed partly to avoid cash having to be transported across dangerous terrain. As early as the ninth century, a Muslim businessman could cash a cheque in China drawn on his bank in Baghdad. This concept then evolved into bills of exchange, letters of credit and promissory notes, such as those now widely used to finance commerce and international trade.

Many more innovations originated in this part of the world, among them weights and measures, essential for fixing quantities of products to be traded; the seven-day week; the numeral system on which our numbers are based; the decimal point; and the division of time into sixty minutes and sixty seconds. The need to measure time precisely so that mosques could accurately announce the five daily calls to prayer provided the incentive to develop advanced time-keeping instruments like the astrolabe, described by an American astrophysicist as "the most important astronomical calculating device before the invention of digital computers." The tenth-century observatory at Damascus had a sextant the length of ten cars end to end. Such early measuring devices enabled Muslim societies to develop the world's most advanced maps and navigation techniques, essential for reaching new trade markets and for establishing the *qibla,* or the direction of prayer towards Mecca. The Syrian astronomer Al-Battani (858–929), working in Damascus and Raqqa, calculated the length of the solar year to an accuracy of within two minutes and was quoted as a major source by Copernicus over 600 years later.

Syrian cities like Palmyra, built beside a huge oasis in the Syrian desert, developed a unique civilisation that blended local traditions with elements of Graeco-Roman, Aramean, Persian, Parthian, Mesopotamian, and Egyptian culture—a fusion that manifested itself not only in architecture but also in language, fashion, jewellery and even hairstyles. Priests could be identified from their tall cylindrical fez-like hats, while women toyed with their veils in a Roman symbol of modesty or raised their palms outward in the typical Semitic gesture to ward off evil spirits. Their clothing and jewellery declared their social status. The city thrived on trade, and wealthy merchants were immortalised in statues on the city's column plinths during their lifetime, and in funerary busts that graced their tombs after their death. Even the tombs themselves were commercial ventures, their Palmyrene Aramaic inscriptions detailing how the multi-storey burial spaces were to be sold on in later generations to other families, like high-rise blocks of flats. Wars between the Romans and the Parthians disrupted trade a little, but ambitious construction projects continued unabated, only coming to a standstill when trade routes changed because of altered political alliances.

The relics of many civilisations are strewn across the Syrian countryside, among them the 800 early Byzantine "Forgotten Cities" or "Dead Cities" scattered over the hillsides southwest of Aleppo. Their prosperity was built on the production and trading of wine and olive oil, ideally suited to the limestone terrain. Olives were the sole source of oil in the ancient world, used not only in cooking, cosmetics, perfumes, medicines and religious anointing, but above all in lighting. Olive oil was the equivalent of today's hydrocarbon oil, and demand was staggering across the Roman Empire. When the Romans lost their North African province in 439 AD, and with it the empire's traditional source of olive oil, these Byzantine cities of northwest Syria were the beneficiaries, and their prosperity boomed from 450 onwards. Repeated wars with the Sassanid Persians then disrupted their trade routes, forcing these early Christians to become economic migrants and move from the mountains to the coast in search of other trading opportunities.

The arrival of the Muslim armies in the seventh century added further layers of complexity, but they rarely clashed with the indigenous Syrian Christians. In Palmyra the four churches within the Episcopal quarter continued to be used, and bishops continued to be ordained, even as a mosque was constructed in the centre of the city. The Muslim newcomers built a market of fifty shops along the Great Colonnade, bringing about a resurgence in trade. The inclusive syncretism of early Islamic civilisation accounted for the great speed and success of its spread, as it absorbed elements of Christian and Hellenistic cultures together with their architectural and artistic influences. As late as the twelfth century Palmyra had a Jewish community with three rabbis.

In Damascus the sacred space at the heart of the city—originally a pagan temple under the Arameans, Greeks and Romans—was converted into the Cathedral of John the Baptist, then shared by the Muslim conquerors for nearly a century, with both sets of worshippers entering through the same door. When the population expanded beyond the capacity of the cathedral, the Muslim rulers decided in the early eighth century to build a new central mosque on the site, and compensated the Christians with land to build four new churches in what eventually became the Christian quarter of the walled Old City.

This mosque, known as the Damascus Umayyad Mosque, incorporated echoes of church architecture in the triple window of its main facade as well as classical themes in its columns and capitals. The iconography of its extensive courtyard wall mosaics, created by Byzantine craftsmen, depicted Islamic visions of Paradise in heavenly images of buildings, bridges, trees and rivers. Its minarets evolved from the towers of the earlier Roman temple of Jupiter on the same site; the most famous of them today is the Jesus Minaret, from which local tradition holds that Christ will descend on the Day of

Judgement. Sacred to both Sunni and Shi'a Muslims, it is the fourth holiest site in Islam, after the Ka'aba in Mecca, the Prophet's Mosque in Medina and Jerusalem's Al-Aqsa Mosque. In Homs and Hama there are similar buildings at the spiritual centres of their respective Old Cities, which likewise evolved over the centuries from pagan temples to cathedrals to mosques.

There was an immediate affinity between the local Syrian Christians and the Muslim newcomers. Islam recognised Jesus as a major prophet and the Prophet Mohammad had himself been a merchant. In his tribe, the Quraysh, merchants were considered the elite—well-travelled, wise and wealthy. The first verses of the Qur'an were revealed to him in Arabic via the Archangel Gabriel in a cave near Mecca, but during the twenty-year period of revelation the Prophet made many journeys out of Arabia. He had once even visited the outskirts of Damascus while accompanying a camel caravan owned by his wife Khadija, a Meccan merchant who was wealthy in her own right. As Mohammad stood on Mount Qassioun looking down over the prosperous city and its well-watered lavish gardens, legend has it, he proclaimed that since he could not enter Paradise twice, he would go no further.

The architectural layout of all Syria's major Muslim trading cities today reflects their deep mercantile tradition. First there was the mosque, always the heart of the city, and beside it the souks (markets), functioning like the city's stomach and labyrinthine intestines. Religion and commerce—the mosque and the market— were both central to Muslim urban life, offering spiritual and material sustenance side by side in a tradition that stretched right back to pagan shrines and their accompanying fairs in pre-Islamic Arabia.

Ancient Islamic cities have an overwhelmingly organic feel, as though they evolved biologically to best meet the needs of their inhabitants. The streets are the bones giving the city its structure; the water channels are the veins bringing life-blood to the public and private buildings. Every resident of such a city understands this instinctively, by virtue of having grown up in a tightly knit community where everything is interlinked and interdependent.

Aleppo's souks are the earliest, dating back to the medieval times of the Mamluks. The rest of Syria's cities, like Damascus, Homs, Hama and Deir ez-Zour, all have souks dating from the sixteenth century onwards, the four centuries of Ottoman rule that ended with World War One. In the West the Ottoman Empire in its later stages is mainly remembered as the "sick man of Europe", yet it was also one of the largest and longest-lasting empires in history and deserves credit, especially in its early centuries, for its remarkable success holding people from a variety of faiths and ethnic backgrounds together under one system of governance.

Over the last fourteen centuries since Islam became the dominant religion in the region, a handful of enlightened rulers have sought to foster an inclusive, multicultural approach, embracing minorities, while despotic rulers have sought to ostracise them, imposing restrictions and harsh laws on those they did not favour. The results have been predictable. The periods of tolerant rule led to increased trade and prosperity, while the periods marked by exclusion and discrimination resulted instead in wars, uprisings and disputes that thwarted commerce, bringing deprivation and hardship to the population. Aleppo's commercial activity soared when in the thirteenth century the Ayyubids, a Sunni dynasty founded by Saladin, encouraged coexistence among its diverse communities, through such acts as restoring Shi'a shrines and even adding inscriptions in praise of Shi'a imams.

More than three thousand archaeological sites in Syria testify to the land's cultural richness. These are only those sites that fall within the country's modern borders of today, and say nothing of the far bigger area of Ottoman Greater Syria (in Arabic: *Bilad al-Sham*) that predated the Sykes-Picot agreement of 1916 and encompassed what is today divided between Israel, Palestine, Jordan and Lebanon, as well as Syria itself. The absence of borders across the Ottoman Empire simplified and encouraged trade, with minimal requirements for documentation or regulation. It was a gigantic "single market". The Ottoman system of taxation was certainly convoluted, with over fifty different types of taxes and fees recorded, for example, in the

Hama court of the late eighteenth and early nineteenth centuries. But once the sums were remitted to the treasury in Damascus, about half was sent to support office-holders in Istanbul while the other half was earmarked for financing the annual pilgrimage (*Hajj*), itself a great river of commerce leading to and from Mecca.

The Ottomans favoured the "Circle of Justice" system—an equitable social interdependence whose origins can be traced right back to Hammurabi's Code in ancient Mesopotamia—where the Sultan, the army and the people all relied on each other. Fairness was a guiding principle of government and there was an acknowledgement that the survival of the state depended on the prosperity of its subjects, particularly the peasantry. The Sultan, granted the divine mandate to rule, was protected by a strong army, which in turn had to protect the peasants from invasion and banditry, so that agricultural productivity could generate food and taxes. Rates of taxation therefore reflected the relative prosperity of villages, so Turkoman villages closer to steppe and desert areas, for instance, paid reduced rates to reflect the fact that their agricultural land yielded poorer returns. Richer villages situated on the fertile banks of the Orontes river around Homs and Hama could benefit from irrigation by waterwheels, so were charged a higher tax rate. 'Alawi villages in the mountains had a heavier tax burden because their dominance of the commercial tobacco trade, along with their wine production and distribution, brought in much wealth, especially at its peak in the eighteenth century.

The Ottoman authorities' consistent guiding principle was to maximise tax revenues from all subjects, but if areas were in need of economic revival, taxes were frequently forgiven, to give subjects the chance to restore their own and their government's future fortunes. Ottoman court records make it clear that 'Alawis were not, contrary to the much-repeated narrative, persecuted as an extremist brand of Shi'ism, but were simply seen as members of the Syrian variant of Iran's "Twelver" style of Shi'a Islam, which had spread into northern Syria and the coastal highlands under the patronage of the tenth-century Shi'a Hamdanid dynasty of Aleppo.

Christians and Jews, as "People of the Book", were obliged to pay the *jizya* tax stipulated in the Qur'an, because of their protected, albeit subordinate, status, but the rates were not high. Some predominantly Christian villages, for example, were obliged to pay an extra 2 per cent over and above the total tax amount due, showing they were treated with relative clemency. Tax rates on religious endowments (known in Arabic as *waqf*), vital for the upkeep of mosques and other religious and public facilities like hospitals and baths, were also often given preferential low tax rates. Only the *'askeri* class—the military—did not pay taxes.

Across the centuries this dominance of commerce also affected the mentality of local people, who learnt to welcome trade as one of life's constants in a region rife with the vagaries of political upheaval, wars, invasions, earthquakes, fires and plagues.

When the Ottomans entered Aleppo in 1516 after defeating the Mamluks at the battle of Marj Dabiq, prayers were said in the Aleppo Great Mosque recognising the Ottoman Sultan Selim the Grim as the new Sunni Muslim ruler. The people of Aleppo, weary of the 250-year Mamluk rule, had welcomed the Ottoman advance, offering no resistance. Selim referred to himself as "world conqueror" and took on the title of "Caliph", and with it the responsibility to protect the holy cities of Mecca and Medina and the pilgrims performing the annual *Hajj*. His successors demonstrated their commitment to this responsibility by building a series of caravanserais starting at Khan Tuman, 12 miles south of Aleppo, from where the route passed through Hama and Homs to Damascus and onwards into what is now Jordan and Saudi Arabia along the route to Mecca. These caravanserais imitated the style of Roman forts, built around open enclosures, offering protection, accommodation, stabling and sustenance to the pilgrim caravans, as well as to traders. They operated all year round so that Muslims performing the *'Umra*, or non-mandatory lesser pilgrimage, which could be undertaken at any time, were also able to use their services. This land route was used till the early twentieth century when rail and then bus and air travel rendered it obsolete.

Even when the Ottomans were engaged in their frequent wars against the Persian Safavids, merchants of all stripes—Sunni, Shi'a, Christian or Jewish—continued their caravan traffic in both directions unabated. Vasco da Gama's discovery of the sea route to India in 1498 caused barely a blip to the overland caravan trade. Much more significant and disruptive to the commercial flows were local factors like banditry, shipwreck or plague, which resulted in massive trade fluctuations when certain commodities simply disappeared off the market, sometimes for an entire season. Merchants learnt to be adaptive and switch commodity according to availability. The Ottoman authorities did not attempt to constrain or restrict the regulation of trade. Although their interpretation of Islamic law might have been expected to favour Sunni Muslim traders, the realities on the ground meant that Shi'a, Christian and Jewish merchants were all able to thrive under the loose Ottoman administration.

When Selim the Grim had stayed in Damascus for four months after his winter campaign of 1517–18, he had not built an imperial mosque near the centre. Instead he ordered a mosque complex to be constructed high on the slopes overlooking the city, beside the tomb of Ibn 'Arabi, a highly revered and much-loved Sufi mystic. He had found Ibn 'Arabi's tomb severely neglected by "bigoted fanatics" who had seen the mystic's open-minded and inclusive teachings as heretical. It was also a mark of thanks to the Sufi shaikh whose writings had supposedly foretold Selim's conquest of Syria. The Ottoman links with the Sufis were strong throughout the centuries of their rule, bringing them much popularity among the rural peasantry and the urban poor, and Selim's complex in honour of Ibn 'Arabi included a hospice for the needy with a kitchen, a bakery, and a pantry for the residents of the Salihiyya district. Its architectural style was non-intrusive, built by local Damascene craftsmen.

When it came to establishing Ottoman dominion symbolically over Damascus, Selim's son Süleyman the Magnificent, also known as Süleyman the Legislator, three decades later ordered the construction of the Tekiyye Süleymaniye, designed by his chief court architect, the famous maestro Sinan. It was the stamp of an unmistakeably Ottoman presence, with its full domes and slender minarets, but it also incorporated and blended local features, like the typically Damascene *ablaq* stonework in alternating black and white stripes, and the polychrome marble panelling. Concession to local preferences was also clear in the large rectangular pool in the courtyard of the Tekkiye, which had a central fountain and water-spouts on each of the four rims. This was to comply with different ablution styles practised by the different law schools.

There are four schools of Islamic law that are recognised by mainstream Sunni Muslims; all four were developed in the eighth and ninth centuries. Most Syrians, before the arrival of the Ottomans, belonged to the Shafi'i school of Islamic law, which has a preference for performing ablutions from still water in large basins. The Ottomans however were of the more liberal Hanafi school, which prefers to perform ablutions under running water, a tradition continued by today's Muslim Turks—the modern Arabic word for "tap" is *hanafia*, and derives from the Hanafis' love of running water. The pool design of the Tekkiye catered to both schools. This was a deliberate decision, reflecting the Ottomans' inclusive approach, which allowed local traditions to continue to be practised alongside those imported from Istanbul. Likewise, while in Istanbul only Hanafis could be appointed as imams and professors, in Damascus the governor-generals permitted the appointment of either Hanafis or Shafi'is, to accommodate local preferences.

Such policies reflected an instinctive acknowledgement of the diversity of practices within Islam, without any attempt to impose a hierarchy of which type was "better" or more favoured than another. In Syria today most Sunni Muslims are of the Hanafi school, with sizeable Shafi'i and Hanbali minorities. The fourth school, the Malikis, are hardly found in Syria, but are concentrated across North Africa and were the dominant school throughout Muslim Spain and Sicily. In practice the differences between the four schools are not great, and it was even accepted practice to switch school according to whichever one a plaintiff felt would deliver the most favourable judgement. The Hanbali school was considered by some to be the best for commercial transactions, though all the schools gave rulings on what constituted fair exchange of goods. Trade across the Islamic world was governed by a well-developed body of legislation governing contracts, exchanges, loans and market conduct in recognition of the major part that commerce played in Islamic life. The Damascus Umayyad Mosque contains four prayer niches (*mihrabs*), each representing one of the four schools, to show that all were embraced as equal. The Hanafis, predominant under the Ottomans, today have the largest worldwide following of the Islamic law schools, comprising over a third of all Sunni Muslims.

The location of Süleyman's Tekkiye complex was set apart from the Old City at a respectful distance from the Great Umayyad Mosque, on the edge of the city amid fields and gardens beside the Barada river. Sinan had himself camped in these fields when he had accompanied Selim the Grim on his Syria campaign. Their intention was to build a gathering place for pilgrims about to set off to Mecca for the annual pilgrimage, as the last safe staging post before the difficult and dangerous journey across the desert. Turkish explorer Evliya Çelebi, writing in the seventeenth century, describes the Tekkiye complex as having the atmosphere of a resort or country retreat, popular for fishing and evening strolls.

Upwards of 20,000 pilgrims would arrive from the northern parts of the Ottoman Empire and from Iran and set up camp in the fields, waiting for the official escorted caravan to Mecca. Their needs had to be served by local traders. It was in these fields where crowds of pilgrims awaited the departure of their caravan that the first ever coffee shops grew up along the banks of the river, the precursors to the coffee chains that have become ubiquitous today in cities all across the globe. An integral part of the mosque complex was the souk in front of it; shops ranged all round the courtyard of the adjoining theological college where pilgrims and students alike would stock up with goods in readiness for the *Hajj*. It was a merchant's dream.

In the imperial geography of the Ottoman Empire, Damascus held pride of place in Syria, despite Aleppo's unquestioned superiority as a commercial centre. As the former capital of Syria, and as the chosen seat first of the Umayyad caliphs and then of other subsequent Sunni dynasties, like the Ayyubids under Saladin, Damascus enjoyed a higher status under its Ottoman masters than any other Syrian city, and this was reinforced by contemporary literature that spoke of the great city's "virtues". Jerusalem was regarded as a dependency of Damascus and the Ottoman province of Damascus extended into what is today Israel, Occupied Palestine and Jordan. Süleyman and subsequent sultans were keen to boost their popularity and legitimacy as religious rulers of Sunni Islam through their religious and charitable endowments, which is why only Damascus can boast an Ottoman complex such as the Tekkiye Süleymaniye.

As with all such foundations, the upkeep of the Tekkiye complex was ensured by the extremely careful and clever integration of adjoining souks, shops and bathhouses. The income from these commercial businesses, as stipulated in the *waqfiyya*, or religious endowment deed, was used to pay the salaries of the imam and professors at the theological colleges and for the ongoing maintenance of the buildings, a set-up that bound Islam inextricably to the life of the surrounding community. Any wealthy person could set up a *waqf* (religious endowment), not just the Sultan or a government official: all they had to do was endow an amount of accumulated wealth and set out the purpose and conditions of management in a deed that was then submitted to the authorities, often the Ministry of Awqaf (plural of *waqf*). In this way the sum of money became God's property. The deed specified exactly how the annual revenue of the *waqf* should be spent—it could either be allocated to a religious purpose or to a group of beneficiaries, such as the offspring of the *waqf* founder, to give them an income stream throughout their lives. This was especially the case in lending financial support to female relatives, provision for whom was generally problematic under the terms of Islamic inheritance law.

Waqfs offered more than just a means of ensuring continued income streams for mosques. They also stipulated how the income was to be earned and distributed and thereby enabled the religious authorities to intervene and make sure the terms of the *waqf* were respected. Scholars have recently traced the origins of such systems back to Sassanid Iranian laws, but Islam adopted them and developed them further. They represented the perfect balance between altruism and ambition. *Waqf* systems are not directly specified in the Qur'an, though there are numerous references strongly encouraging wealth redistribution, such as:

Should a debtor be in straitened circumstances, then grant him respite, in respect of the capital sum, till a time of ease. But if, in such a case, you remit the capital sum also as charity, it will be the better for you, if only you knew. (Qur'an 2:280)

Wealth creation is also encouraged in the Qur'an, as long as it is not hoarded but is circulated, so that there is more for the family, for the community and for *zakat* (obligatory alms): "Woe to the loose-tongued slanderer, who heaps up riches and counts them again and again. He thinks that riches have made him immortal. On the contrary, he will surely soon be cast into the realms of damnation." (104:2–5) The Qur'an enjoins Muslims to "be benevolent towards parents, relations, orphans, the needy, the neighbour who is related to you and the neighbour who is not related to you, to your associates and to the traveller and to those who are under your control." (4:37) Marriage is obligatory for those that can afford it (24:33) with children the hoped-for blessing. The monasticism of Christianity is specifically disapproved of as something not laid down by God, but as self-imposed by Christians seeking God's favour (57:28).

Waqfs were widely used in early Islam, encouraged by several sayings (known collectively as the *Hadith*) of the Prophet Mohammad, such as:

Make the property inalienable and give the profit from it to charity.

When a man dies, only three deeds will survive him: continuing alms, profitable knowledge and a child praying for him.

The institution of the *waqf* ensured ongoing recurrent charity for years, even centuries after the founder's death. By financing colleges, it also supported the work of scholars whose books would go on to benefit mankind for generations to come. The offspring of the founder could be entrusted with the management of the *waqf*, thereby ensuring careful, loyal management and guaranteeing that descendants were not destitute. Property could be protected that way, since without such provision, it would automatically be divided under Islamic law among all inheritors according to fixed rules. Modern legislation has reinforced the sound structures of the *waqf* and to this day it is often used as a way of protecting inheritance, especially for daughters, to whom a father can only bequeath a maximum of a third of his estate under Shari'a law. If there are also male heirs, daughters can only ever receive half the amount passed down to them. Yet the rules are complex, so complex that the medieval mathematician Al-Khawarizmi (from whose name the word "algorithm" derives) devoted the longest chapter of his classic textbook on algebra to solving problems of Islamic inheritance, using linear equations.

In Syria research has shown that cash *waqfs* were frequently set up by wealthy people for charitable purposes, such as to fund orphanages or to support the poor in certain specified areas. People would borrow from the cash in the *waqf* and pay interest of about 10–20 per cent on the loan. Incredibly, the archives record the almost total absence of default in payment of the loan. This striking finding was attributed to the nature of Muslim society where families were collectively responsible, so if one member defaulted, another family member would automatically step in to support them, for anything up to fifteen years after the debt was originally contracted. If there were no family members left to help pay the debt, there was a further fallback system, under which, if the debtor was known to be a decent and honourable person, the residents of their *mahalla*, or quarter, would collectively take on the debt in order to stop the debtor being sent to jail. In Aleppo one such case records that on 31 July 1718 the Muslim residents of a *mahalla* together paid off the debt of a

Christian. Such a system of collective debt repayment persists to modern times and is another example of how Islam's essential concerns are for society, while Christianity tends to focus more on the individual. Islam's severe criminal code (*hudud*) punishments, like amputation of hands for theft, also reinforce this emphasis on protecting and benefiting society by creating deterrents, rather than focusing on the criminal or their reform.

The remarkable thing about the *waqf* system is that it provides a wealth of essential services to society, such as education, health, public baths, shops, and so on, at no cost whatsoever to the government. The result is that government has a massive reduction in its spending requirement, therefore having to borrow less and impose fewer taxes. On top of that, it ensures a better distribution of income in the economy since the well-to-do donate privately accumulated capital to endow and finance all sorts of social services.

One of the consequences is that taxation takes on a secondary role, and the lower tax burden means people have more disposable income. This in turn helps prices stay low and creates the right conditions for non-inflationary growth. All the services provided under the *waqf* system are available to everyone, never restricted to any particular segment of society, and *waqfs* by definition never compete with each other as they do not exist to make profit. The *waqf* systems put in place under Islam and maintained by the Ottomans have lasted centuries and are directly responsible for why Syria's historic city centres have survived and been maintained across the centuries.

In addition to the *waqf* system, giving alms to the poor—*zakat*—is one of the Five Pillars of Islam, along with the declaration of faith (*shahada*), performing ritual prayers (*salat*), fasting in Ramadan (*sawm*) and the pilgrimage to Mecca (*Hajj*). It is therefore at the very core of Islam, an essential religious duty for every Muslim, performed discreetly and without fuss.

These things taken together—the injunctions in the Qur'an and the *Hadith* and the *waqf* system of endowments—reveal a major contrast between Islam's general approach to wealth distribution and that of Christianity, where riches generally accrue to the church and its priesthood. "The wealth of the Maronites is for their priests," jokes the Lebanese proverb, the Maronites being the largest Christian denomination in Lebanon. They are followers of the fourth-century St Maron of Antioch, Eastern Syriac Catholics in communion with Rome, who welcomed the conquering Christians of the First Crusade.

In more ways than one, Islam exhibits a different value system. This can be seen in the lack of ceremony enjoined in funeral rites: the body of the deceased is traditionally washed, wrapped in a cloth and buried in a simple grave within twenty-four hours. Ostentatious funerals and lavish headstones are discouraged. Far more important is how a person shared their wealth while alive.

Most striking of all perhaps is a difference that lies at the very core of both religions and that is reflected in surprising ways. Christianity has a strict hierarchy of priests, starting from the head of the church, archbishops, bishops, deans, and so on, and finally reaching the congregation or the"flock" at the bottom of the heap. Sunni Islam, to which 90 per cent of Muslims worldwide adhere, has no such hierarchy. There is no priesthood, as each Muslim is considered to have an unmediated relationship with God that does not require intercession from other human beings. The Prophet Mohammad was not thought to be divine but was simply the "messenger" of God, and in Sunni Islam his successors, the caliphs, were in no way ordained but were chosen by consensus, respected for being wise and devout. While Catholicism has the confessional where the priest acts as an intermediary, in Sunni Islam a believer communicates directly with God. Faith is personal and all-embracing, not delivered or dictated from the pulpit. Shi'a Islam, on the other hand, whose followers account for about 10 per cent of the world's Muslim population and which is mainly practised in Iran, Iraq and parts of Lebanon, does have clerics who mediate between man and God, like the Ayatollahs and the mullahs. This system is more comparable with that of the Catholic Church, though a Shi'a can choose their spiritual guide while a Catholic must follow the Pope.

This fundamental absence of hierarchy in mainstream Sunni Islam by contrast with Christianity is manifest even in the way the holy books of the two religions are formed. Early Bibles are bound via a mechanical process and designed to lie flat, which may reflect the "linear" process whereby the words of the books are delivered by the priest to the congregation. Much church architecture reflects this linear approach, with long straight naves, and a clear sense of division between the altar, the chancel, the choir and the congregation, furthest away from the altar.

Through her work on both Christian and Islamic early texts, senior conservator at Dublin's Chester Beatty Library Kristine Rose has observed a fundamental difference in how Qur'ans are made. Instead of being part of a production chain like early Bibles, worked on by teams of monks and craftsmen, all of whom had an allotted task, early Qur'ans have a much more organic feel, evolving as objects of beauty in their own right, each one the work of one individual and as such representing a reflection of that individual's deep, almost mystical connection with God. The early Ottomans banned all printing, making it a crime punishable by death, and it was only in the 1720s with the start of the more outward-looking Tulip Age that Sultan Ahmed III approved the printing of maps. This was followed a decade or two later by the first printing in Arabic characters of such texts as Ottoman chronicles, grammar books and dictionaries for translation between Arabic, Ottoman, Persian and French, but printing of religious material remained forbidden. The Qur'an after all is held by Muslims to be the very word of God and those who could read it—as well as those who could not—enjoyed experiencing the sensual touch of a created manuscript. The artistic patterns used to decorate the pages are frequently circular, conveying inclusivity, embracing the believer, welcoming them into the fold of God, so that they can sense it, absorb it, even feel that they have become part of it. Calligraphers speak of their art as inducing a trance-like communion with God. Qur'ans are designed not to lie flat but to be part-open in Qur'an holders, which can be balanced in front of the worshipper and shared with a group of believers, generally sitting in a circle around them.

Mosque architecture reflects this too, in that there are no divisions of hierarchy. There is no furniture, no special pews or seating, but simply an empty carpeted space for worshippers to arrange themselves in rows at prayer times. Architectural decoration focuses on the prayer niche or *mihrab*, indicating the direction of prayer, and the *minbar*, the pulpit from which an imam, any recognised Islamic scholar, can be seen or heard when he delivers his sermon at Friday noon prayers. Many mosques are centred around domes, gathering the congregation into one shared and open space, embracing everyone together without preference.

Where Christianity has followed this model, as in Sir Christopher Wren's grand masterpiece, St Paul's Cathedral—whose design he freely admitted was heavily influenced by what he called "Saracen" Islamic architecture—a marked difference can be felt in the nature of the religious space, where the main congregation is gathered in the circular space beneath the dome, and the aisles are the overspill. Christianity often puts a divine figure into that central dome, such as painted representations of Christ Pantokrator, Ruler of All, whereas in Islamic art, God's presence is implied, never represented, often through architectural devices conveying infinity, such as *muqarnas,* where a series of vaulted shapes recede into the dome, blending the transition between the earthly and the divine. Wren, after careful study and thorough research, pronounced himself in his *Discussion of the Islamic Origin of the Gothic Style* a great admirer of Arab architecture, with its "extravagant imagination... as extraordinary as their thoughts."

An important characteristic of Ottoman rule in Syria was the way in which the powerful leading families were allowed much latitude in their affairs, provided that all military and financial obligations were met and that there were no local disturbances. Shared economic interests lay at the heart of this relationship, and the Syrian "notables" (in Arabic: *a'yan*) were careful to appear politically ambiguous, neither as enemies of the state nor as colluders with the state authorities. The term *"a'yan"* was first used in this way under the Ottomans to mean the landowning-bureaucratic class, whom the Arab historian Philip Khoury describes as "a fairly well-integrated network of propertied and office-holding urban families".

These notables were permitted to maintain huge economic power, and it was tacitly understood that they would curb the stirrings of any political discontent among their feudal poor. They tended to live in vast courtyard houses in urban centres like Damascus and supported activities in the neighbourhood from youth clubs to Sufi orders, to trade and craft guilds, a role that gave them powers as landlords, employers, protectors, contract guarantors, moneylenders and arbiters of disputes.

But if there was an unacceptable level of self-aggrandisement among those appointed to positions of power and influence, Istanbul would act, in extreme cases by sending an army and having the governor killed, as happened in the case of Nasuh Pasha in 1713, who had appointed most of his family to sub-governorships in Damascus. The famous 'Azem family were probably the most successful at striking the right balance between nepotism and good management, holding the governorship of Damascus several times during the eighteenth century, and whilst they did benefit financially from the role, often institutionalising corruption on a massive scale, this was never so blatant as to incur the wrath of their Ottoman masters in Istanbul.

As long as the annual remittance due to the central treasury in Istanbul was paid promptly and all other formalities of the relationship with the sultan were observed, the Ottoman rulers allowed the local governors control over regional revenues, most of which were based on trade in grains and in textiles: cotton and silk. Whenever there was a trade blockade however, the trade in Iranian silk would shrink as relations worsened, leading to critical shortages that damaged both the Ottoman and the Persian Safavid economies. One of Süleyman the Magnificent's first acts, Ottoman historian Caroline Finkel tells us, was to compensate Iranian merchants at Bursa whose silk his father Selim had confiscated. He "sought to contain Iran, not conquer it", and ruled for forty-six years, longer than any other sultan, styling himself among many other extravagant titles "Conqueror of the Lands of the Orient and the Occident" and "Sultan of the Sultans of the Arabs and the Persians".

Much of the commercial profit from trade was directed into the development of towns and cities of the province, with *waqf* endowments for mosques, souks, public fountains and bathhouses. Thus the local population tended to remain content, as long as they could see where the bulk of the money was going.

The Bedouin tribes of the Syrian Badia or semi-steppe were also given a stake in the stability of the times, by being employed under the Ottomans to guard the treacherous pilgrim routes across the desert to Mecca. Guaranteeing the safety of pilgrims on their annual *Hajj* to Mecca was regarded by the Ottoman rulers in Istanbul as one of their key duties, since it conferred on them the religious legitimacy they sought. Rather than raiding the caravan, as their custom had been before, the Bedouin were now paid by the authorities to protect it instead.

This was the start of a major change that began to erode the power of the tribes, making them increasingly subject to a central authority as the Ottomans started to exert more control over the desert regions of eastern Syria. Some semi-settled tribes were given land grants—fertile farming land along the Euphrates and Khabour rivers—in return for which their sons were exempted from military service. They even agreed to pay a percentage of their harvest to the state in taxation, ordinarily a complete anathema to the nomadic tradition. The Ottoman rulers gradually established police stations and forts in areas where nomadic tribes had previously roamed freely, and started lending out their troops to one shaikh or another for use in settling intertribal feuds. Once tribal leaders started to become clients of the state in this way, their own internal unity and independence was weakened. In their scramble to win Ottoman patronage, they could be played off against each other, losing the respect and allegiance of their own tribal members.

But the ethos of Ottoman rule was to change forever, with the rise in the late eighteenth century of a puritanical Islamic sect in the heart of the Arabian Peninsula. Founded by Mohammad bin 'Abd al-Wahhab, this movement rejected what it considered the un-Islamic practices that had grown up under the Ottomans over the centuries—mysticism, dervishes, cults of holy men and shrines and superstition.

By the time he died in 1792, 'Abd al-Wahhab's doctrines had found new supporters, leading over the next few years to a new tribal leader, 'Abd al-'Aziz bin Mohammad bin Sa'ud, and laying the foundations of a new state. Saudi Arabia was born without the Ottomans, who were so far away in Istanbul, even realising its significance. The Sherif of Mecca who had been ruling the Hijaz in western Arabia in the name of the sultan appealed for help from the governors of Syria and Iraq, but was ignored.

The Wahhabi fanatics, more convinced than ever, after Ottoman Egypt was lost to the "infidel" Napoleon in 1798, that it was their duty to salvage Islam in its pure form, captured the Shi'a pilgrimage city of Kerbala in Iraq. The Ottomans failed to send troops and supplies in sufficient quantity to pose a serious challenge, and by 1806 the Saudis had taken Mecca and sacked Medina. The following year they closed the Hijaz to Ottoman pilgrim caravans, and the Saudi leader substituted his own name for the sultan's in Friday prayers. The Ottomans had lost control of the holy cities at the heart of Islam, and any claim of the sultan in Istanbul to be the supreme Islamic ruler disappeared at a stroke. It was the beginning of the long Ottoman decline.

The subsequent amalgamation in the late nineteenth century of the three Syrian provinces of Damascus, Tripoli and Sidon into a single "super-province" created an unusual degree of cohesion and a feeling of 'Syrianness' based not on denominational factors but on geographic and linguistic realities. These were widely regarded as the basis for Syria's natural borders.

The Ottoman reorganisational reforms of the 1850s (known as the Tanzimât) had more success in Syria than in other provinces, in that they encouraged people to think of themselves as Syrians rather than identifying themselves first and foremost as members of a particular religion. The Reform Edict of 1856 promised equal civil and political rights for Muslims and non-Muslims alike, and the wearing of the fez as a headdress across the board, irrespective of religion, aimed to consolidate and reinforce such a process. Most, especially non-Muslims, were keen to adopt the fez, since it made them indistinguishable from Muslims. Only clerics refused to shed their turbans. When Atatürk in modern Turkey later went on to ban the wearing of the fez, it was as a deliberate rejection of the Ottoman imperial past.

In Syria the fez lingered on much longer, as did many other social customs that became firmly rooted under Ottoman culture. Syrians acquired a taste for drinking Turkish coffee and smoking a hookah (or water-pipe, known in Syria as the *arghile*), along with a taste for sweets like baklava, trays of which used to be offered in a special ceremony by the sultan to his elite Janissary troops halfway through the fasting month of Ramadan. Refined Ottoman cuisine was developed in the imperial kitchens of the Topkapı Palace in Istanbul, based around fresh vegetables and fruits. One such example was the aubergine dish called Imam Bayıldı, whose name translates as "the imam fainted", presumably from ecstasy upon tasting it. Many such delicacies found their way to Syria with similar approval ratings.

2

AN OTTOMAN INHERITANCE

Success depends on a man's reputation, not on his soul.

(Turkish proverb)

Mohammad Chaker Chamsi-Pasha, our Syrian merchant, was known universally as Abu Chaker (pronounced Abu Shaaker). The Ottoman ancestor from whom he took his surname was Şemsi (Turkish spelling of Shamsi) Ahmet Pasha, who had served as Grand Vizier to the Ottoman Sultan Süleyman the Magnificent from 1556 to 1565. "Pasha" was an honorary title granted to him, as a high-ranking dignatory, by the sultan, in the same way that peerages were granted by monarchs in Britain.

As an old man, Abu Chaker had once visited his ancestor's tomb out of curiosity. It still stands on Istanbul's Asian waterfront among a tiny complex of buildings attached to the Şemsi Ahmet Pasha Mosque. Like the Tekkiye Süleymaniye in Damascus, the complex was designed by the Ottoman master architect Sinan. Built on an asymmetrical plot directly on the Bosphorus, it is a gem of architectural creativity, beautifully adapted to the natural landscape. Its irregular courtyard is bordered by a wall whose iron-grilled windows yield glimpses over the water.

Abu Chaker passed through the small gateway into the miniature walled garden of red roses, where he rested on a bench to look at the white marble graves of Şemsi Ahmet Pasha's family, with their Ottoman inscribed headstones. At prayer-time he entered the mosque, ignoring the pair of fundamentalist preachers on the porch trying to convert passers-by. They were offering fresh fruit as bait— scarlet strawberries and crimson cherries spread out on white cloths—but their pushiness offended Abu Chaker's natural reserve. After prayers he sat at one of the shaded waterfront cafés to enjoy a tea and a water-pipe. He kept his own counsel, his bright blue eyes intently fixed on the fishermen casting their lines and the water splashing up onto the quay, or watching the ever-changing parade of families in modern and traditional attire, a kaleidoscope of identities. He was an observer, blending into the scene.

When Şemsi Ahmet Pasha was asked why he chose to live in Üsküdar, in a modest palace beside the mosque on the fringes of the capital, instead of in the thick of political intrigue in the Topkapı Palace area with the other viziers, he had replied: "Üsküdar is a way-station of mankind, a place where countless people come with business from the lands of Anatolia, Damascus, Aleppo, and especially Egypt and Iraq." Situated on the Asian side of the Bosphorus, his was the first port of call for those arriving from the East, before they crossed to the "lofty capital" opposite, on the European banks. As a result, "I receive the cream of the gifts." By holding himself aloof from the palace feuds and infighting, Şemsi Pasha succeeded in remaining in favour with three consecutive Ottoman sultans, a powerful testament to his discretion and tact.

He was quick-witted, to judge from an anecdote about his skilful handling of a Persian delegation of 700 diplomats and 1700 fine horsemen that arrived in Istanbul after the death of Süleyman the Magnificent. Delegations from all over the world came bearing gifts for Süleyman's son, the new Sultan Selim II. The Persians, however, as the second world power after the Ottomans were enemies of the empire, and so Selim II ordered Şemsi Pasha to go and receive them at the head of a large army. Şemsi immediately gathered hundreds of soldiers, dressed them in great finery, with silver and gold weaponry, and led them in a splendid military parade to meet the Persians. The Persian emir greeted him sarcastically, saying, "Is this a military parade or a wedding party?" Without hesitation Şemsi answered, "It is indeed a wedding party and these are the bridegrooms of Çaldıran"—Çaldıran being the battle in which the Persians had suffered a crushing defeat at the hands of the Ottomans in 1514. The emir was taken aback at the speed and sharpness of his reply. The parade over, he declared his delegation was coming to make a truce.

Harvard academic Gülru Necipoğlu cites archival material that describes Şemsi as "hunting companion" to Süleyman the Magnificent, "drinking and carousing comrade" to Sultan Selim II and "confidant in matters of state and religion" to Sultan Murad III. Only Sinan himself was able to achieve this same level of patronage—and from the same three Ottoman sultans. Many of Şemsi's peers, viziers like Sokullu Mehmet and Rüstem Pasha, fell foul of court intrigues and met with undignified ends. Şemsi, on the other hand, was cut from a different cloth, and was careful to keep himself untainted by political affiliation. While political masters came and went, commerce was a necessary constant.

The *waqfiyya* for the Şemsi Pasha Mosque recorded in 1580–81 how "he built near his palace along the seashore an agreeable Friday mosque whose heart-ravishing silver dome is a bubble on the lip of the sea, and each of whose polished polychrome marble panels is a world-illuminating mirror of the eight paradises." Beside his mosque, the Pasha "of sun-like countenance" (Şemsi means "of the sun", from Arabic *shams*) also built a theological college. The L-shaped madrasa was designed by Sinan to complement the mosque and enhance the waterfront location, with twelve cells for students, each under its own tiny dome, and a separate spacious classroom under its own larger dome. Today this college has been carefully restored and renovated into a magnificent religious library.

In Istanbul there are other buildings that have significance for Abu Chaker's Ottoman merchant heritage. The head of each artisanal guild had a small mosque or *masjid* built for him by the office of chief architect, Sinan. A *masjid* was a small mosque, not used for Friday prayers, and therefore construction did not require the sultan's permission. Royal approval was necessary only for a *cami*, a mosque in which Friday prayers were held. In his autobiography Sinan claims to have built eighty to a hundred Friday mosques across the empire, roughly half of them in Istanbul, commissioned by the sultans, the royal family and the highest ranking officials. He additionally lists over four hundred *masjids* scattered region-wide, about fifty of them in the imperial capital, discreetly located, usually outside the city walls. Even so, their sheer number is revealing. *Masjids* tended to be relatively modest, each with its own imam who represented the local neighbourhood (*mahalla*) in its dealings with the state. The imam and the *muezzin* (caller to prayer) of the *masjid* had their salaries paid for by the *waqf*, and were chosen by petitions from the residents of the *mahalla*, who were therefore in some ways semi-autonomous and self-administered. For the purposes of tax collection, however, they were brought under the umbrella of the state. They tended to be spread at roughly 200-metre intervals across the city, often with independent elementary schools or dervish convents attached.

Beyond these *masjids* for the heads of the artisanal guilds, there were just two Friday mosques designed by Sinan that were not for the tax-exempt ruling elite of Istanbul in the mid-1580s—in both cases the patrons were merchants: the master butcher (*kasap ustası*) and the chief merchant, the *bezirganbaşı*.

The master butcher's Friday mosque is in Yedikule close to the city walls, near the slaughterhouses and tanneries, and is named after him, Evhadüddin Cami, graced with its own Halveti Sufi convent, a bathhouse, two public fountains and a cemetery garden. An inscription on the mosque gate reads:

Hacı Evhad, who built this decorated Friday mosque,

Expended money for the sake of God.

It is befitting to that patron of charitable works, if

I call him the most generous butcher of the world.

The second is the Friday mosque and mausoleum of Hacı (in Arabic: *Hajji*, or pilgrim) Hüsrev, the chief merchant. Attached to it was a "joy-giving" convent (*tekkiye*) for the Halveti dervishes, whose founder, Ramazan Efendi, was known as the spiritual guide of the "illiterate" (the *ümmi*). Illiterate himself, Ramazan Efendi encouraged his disciples to burn like "torches" with longing for God. The floral Iznik tiles inside the mosque bear no inscriptions, but with their palmettes, rosettes, saz leaves, naturalistic flowers and spring blossoms they suggest the eternally blooming garden of Paradise.

The *waqfiyya* document explains that Hacı Hüsrev, the "pride of merchants", with the permission of the Sultan, built the Friday mosque in the garden of his own residence in the suburb of Kocamustafapaşa, with ten adjoining cells for the Sufis. Outside the mosque courtyard were eighty-four rooms integral to the *waqf* foundation, one of which was for the imam, two for the *muezzins* and one for the janitor. The remaining eighty rooms were to be rented out to married couples in order to finance the salaries of these employees. Hacı Hüsrev was to administer the *waqf* during his lifetime, after which the responsibility would pass to his freed slaves and their descendants over the generations.

Both complexes give an indication of the high esteem in which merchants and highly skilled tradesmen were held in the Ottoman world order, in recognition of their value to society, and of course to the treasury through the revenue they generated.

Another area in which merchants could compare with sultans and court officials was in their endowment of public drinking fountains. In a culture where the life-giving and cleansing properties of water were highly valued, this was the greatest gift a ruler or important man could bestow. Best of all in the eyes of the Hanafi Ottomans was running water, since it was used to perform the ritual ablutions before prayer.

When Sinan was appointed chief court architect in 1538, he became responsible for the maintenance of existing dams, cisterns, aqueducts and water supply systems feeding Istanbul's mosques, madrasas, hammams and palaces. The position of inspector of waterworks (*Suyolu Nazırı*) was vitally important, and was held by all three of Sinan's successors before they became court architect. Over ten years Sinan doubled the supply of water in Istanbul, bringing the number of wells up from 300 to 590—something that would have greatly enhanced the city's reputation, as one of the measures of a city's wealth was how many wells or bathhouses it could afford. These wells in turn supplied the public drinking fountains around the city, providing neighbourhoods with both the blessing of water and a focal point for gathering. Sinan's own triple-courtyarded residence had three pools, two wells, two bathhouses and five toilets. His tomb, alongside a public drinking fountain, carries an inscription, part of which reads:

With the sultan's orders he exerted great effort on water channels

Like Hizir*, he made the water of life flow to the people.

[*The miracle-working Saint Khidr (whose name translates to "the green one"), discoverer of the fountain of life.]

Water was always central to Ottoman culture. Osman, founder of the dynasty, had a dream where:

A tree sprouted from his navel and its shade compassed the world. Beneath this shade there were mountains, and streams flowed forth from the foot of each mountain. Some people drank from these running waters, others watered gardens, while yet others caused fountains to flow.

Small wonder that the Ottomans quickly chose Istanbul, with its profusion of waterways, to be their capital for four and a half centuries.

According to the *waqfiyya* of the Şemsi Pasha Mosque, Şemsi's mother was an Ottoman princess called Şahnısa Sultan, the daughter of Bayezid II's son Prince Abdullah, while his father was the son of Mirza Mehmed Beg of the Kızıl Ahmedli (İsfendiyaroğlu) dynasty of Kastamonu. Mirza Mehmed Beg, who was referred to as Mirza Pasha al-Khalidi, was a nobleman who traced his ancestry back to Khalid ibn al-Walid, a companion of the Prophet Mohammad and the military commander who had masterminded the Muslim conquest of Syria.

This genealogy is questionable, since the Meccan Sharif's envoy to Istanbul wrote in 1557 that according to *Hadith* experts Khalid ibn al-Walid left behind no descendants, a pity since it would otherwise very conveniently provide the first direct link from the Chamsi-Pashas of Istanbul to Homs, the city where Khalid ibn al-Walid was buried and where our merchant of Syria was born. But genealogy aside, Şemsi Ahmad Pasha was evidently rewarded for his services and loyalty to his Ottoman masters with land and money in Syria.

Homs (the ancient Roman Emessa) was, then as now, Syria's third largest city after Damascus and Aleppo, strategically located at an altitude of 500 metres on a natural trade crossroads where the north–south corridor between those two cities intersects with the "Homs Gap", the only break in the Ansariyeh mountain chain between Turkey and Palestine. This key location ensured not just a milder climate and cooling breezes from the sea, but also the city's great importance as a commercial centre at the start of the Silk Road, along the east–west passage from Palmyra in the Syrian desert to the Mediterranean coast, a journey of five days by camel. Guarded by Syria's largest and strongest citadel, Homs' fortunes waxed and waned in accordance with Palmyra's. The strategic location also made it the natural centre for livestock trade, where flocks of sheep and goats from Aleppo met camels and cattle from Damascus. First settled in 2300 BC, it has been identified as Zobah in the Bible, and Christianity was well-established in Homs by the fifth century. It was famous throughout its history for silk and wool weaving, especially for the *homsiyye,* a heavy silk run through with gold and silver threads. Used for local women's scarves, and sometimes exported to Constantinople, it may well be the reason why the women of Homs were so celebrated for their beauty.

Homs surrendered to Khalid ibn al-Walid after a two-month siege in 636, just four years after the Prophet Mohammad's death. The Arab historian Al-Baladhuri records that the people of Homs welcomed him with the declaration: "We like your rule and justice far better than the state of (Byzantine) oppression and tyranny under which we have been living," a sentiment that seems to have been representative of most indigenous Syrians. Their new Muslim rulers offered them the same terms as Damascus, Baalbek and Hama, all of which had been likewise abandoned by the Byzantine garrison:

> In the name of God, the compassionate, the merciful. This is what Khalid ibn al-Walid would grant to the inhabitants... he promises to give them security for their lives, property and churches. Their city wall shall not be demolished, neither shall any Muslim be quartered in their houses. Thereunto we give them the pact of God and the protection of His Prophet, the caliphs and the believers. So long as they pay the poll tax, nothing but good shall befall them.

Al-Baladhuri tells us the poll tax was one dinar and one measure of wheat on every head, a relatively modest demand.

The Khalid ibn al-Walid Mosque, a landmark in Homs and significant centre of pilgrimage, stands on the northern edge of the Old City in the Khaldieh district, which was named after him. It was completely rebuilt in Ottoman style in 1913, in the final years of their rule, on the site of an earlier Ayyubid mosque. Khalid's tomb inside was engraved with a list of his fifty major victorious battles. Some 500 of the Prophet Mohammad's companions were said to have been settled in Homs after the Arab conquest, giving the city a reputation for more religious fervour than the capital Damascus, where the more pragmatic Umayyad court held sway. Homs was probably the first city in Syria to have a sizeable Muslim population.

In its era under the Byzantines, Homs had previously been the seat of residence of the Emperor Heraclius, but after his forces were routed by Khalid ibn al-Walid's army, both his daughter and his son-in-law were captured. Appealing to Khalid's sense of honour, Heraclius sent an ambassador with a letter that read:

> I have come to know what you have done to my army. You have killed my son-in-law and captured my daughter. You have won and got away safely. I now ask you for my daughter. Either return her to me on payment of ransom or give her to me as a gift, for honour is a strong element in your character.

Khalid replied to the ambassador: "Take her as a gift, there shall be no ransom."

The sheer speed of the Islamic conquest is testament to how superficial the hold of the Graeco-Roman rulers was on the Near East. Use of the Greek language vanished almost overnight. It had been used predominantly by the rulers not the ruled, especially on inscriptions carved into fine buildings to commemorate their achievements, an early use of propaganda, akin to control of the media today. Hardly a trace of the Greek language can still be detected today in Semitic languages.

Khalid's military prowess and leadership also accelerated the spread of early Islam. Even today his reputation lives on in unlikely places. The video game *Civilization IV*, which seeks to include real figures from history, features Khalid as a "Great General" in its 2006 *Warlords* expansion pack. Local tradition holds that the Mongol chieftain Tamerlane spared Homs from destruction during his raids on Syria in the early fifteenth century because of its associations with Khalid ibn al-Walid, whom he held in high esteem as conqueror of Byzantine Syria and companion to the Prophet Mohammad.

Abu Chaker's ancestor Şemsi Ahmet Pasha wrote an autobiographical history in which he explained that his own ancestors were skilled in falconry and fighting, like Khalid ibn al-Walid, and that they had accompanied Ottoman sultans on hunts and wars. The posts he held in Istanbul included chief falconer, chief hunter and *agha* (honorific title for a military commander) of the cavalry troops. During hunts as the companion to Süleyman the Magnificent, he would entertain the sultan by telling stories and reciting poems he had composed himself.

In a further connection to Syria, Şemsi Ahmet Pasha had, earlier in his career during the 1550s, served as governor-general to Damascus, where his residence stood on the site of what is today known as the *Qasr al-Adl* (Palais de Justice) on Al-Nasr Street, the highest court in the land. He endowed a small mosque and *tekkiye* in his own name, in a garden with a pool just south of the Souk al-Hamadiyyeh, main market thoroughfare of the Old City of

Damascus. Its foundation deed is from 1554, a date that coincides with the foundation of the Tekkiye Süleymaniye in Damascus outside the Old City along the banks of the Barada river, and he would almost certainly have used the same local craftsmen, trained by a specially established Ottoman workshop. As a *tekkiye*, or dervish convent, the centre would have provided food to the poor.

Sultan Süleyman was at that time suffering inconsolable grief from the deaths of his two sons, one of them at his own command. Some scholars have speculated that his construction of the charitable foundation of the Tekkiye Süleymaniye may even have been an attempt to salve his conscience, since the complex was started soon after he had ordered his son Mustafa's execution. As a distraction, his doctors had prescribed regular hunting expeditions to try to cure him of his depression. It was as a reward for Şemsi's companionship on these hunting trips that Süleyman appointed Şemsi to the position of governor-general of Damascus, a considerable promotion from the post of *agha* of the Cavalry Troops, which he had held before. He remained governor-general for three years, from December 1552 to November 1555, during which time he oversaw the building of the Tekkiye Süleymaniye. Şemsi himself even composed the foundation inscription:

> Sultan Süleyman, son of Selim, built such a hospice that
>
> Meals in Damascus became submerged in benefaction.
>
> The Friday mosque of the Sultan of Rum gave new life to Damascus.

As well as the Şemsi Pasha Mosque itself, two other buildings in the city were commissioned by Şemsi, both of which hold significance for our mercantile story since they are commercial buildings. The first is discreetly tucked beside the Souk al-Khayateen (Tailors' Souk), and is called the Khan al-Joukhiye (Broadcloth *Khan*). The inscription above its fine arched *ablaq* entrance says it was built in 960 AH (1552/3 AD), the year before the Şemsi Pasha Mosque. It is the first ever covered *khan*, with a pair of stone domes, which must have been thought necessary in order to protect the highly valuable cloth inside from exposure to the elements, fire and theft. Domed *khans* are found nowhere else in the Ottoman Empire and therefore represent another unique local blending. The fact that Şemsi, as governor of Damascus, built this *khan* suggests he was probably involved in the broadcloth trade himself and had a stake in promoting it. By the mid-sixteenth century English exports of broadcloth were booming, reaching as far afield as Syria. Since the custom in Syrian families was for a trade to be handed down from one generation to the next, it is not unreasonable to suppose that *joukh*, the broadcloth historically made from English wool and so valued for its hardwearing quality and warmth, had been the Chamsi-Pasha family business since the 1550s. The Khan al-Joukhiye is the oldest surviving Ottoman *khan* in Damascus and is still in use today, though its two original domes have long since fallen in.

The second of Şemsi's commercial buildings was just south of the main thoroughfare of the Souk al-Hamidiyya, and was called the Souk al-Arwam (*arwam*, plural of *roum*, Turks from Anatolia), also known as Souk al-Sibahiyya (*sepahis*, or Ottoman cavalry viewed as a kind of military aristocracy), which tallies with Şemsi having been *agha* of the Cavalry Troops before he became governor. It was built in 1554/5, the first ever two-storyed *bedestan* or covered market hall built in Syria. It was like a kind of lock-up shopping mall, roofed with stone vaulting to protect the valuable goods, usually fabrics, especially from fire, as earlier wooden gabled roofs had easily caught alight, the blaze spreading fast with disastrous losses. When the commodity at stake was this precious, architecture adapted to reflect the need. German architectural historian Stefan Weber tells us that the Souk al-Arwam is the oldest dated commercial building in Damascus to be preserved in its original structure to the present day, explaining how these stone-domed *khans* and *bedestans* multiplied as the city's wealth grew, becoming "veritable cathedrals of commerce" by the eighteenth century.

As "drinking and carousing comrade" to Sultan Selim II, Süleyman the Magnificent's, also known as Selim the Sot, Şemsi learnt to adapt himself to a totally different master who, by his own admission, preferred to remain permanently drunk on wine than face the administrative tedium of running an empire. His rule marks the beginning of the Ottoman decline. He largely handed over affairs of state to his ministers, and devoted his energy instead to domestic affairs. His Venetian wife gave him four daughters and seven sons, the eldest of whom grew up to be Sultan Murad III.

Following Selim II's unfortunate death from slipping in a state of inebriation on a marble bathhouse floor, Şemsi took up his role in service of Murad III as the sultan's "confidant in matters of state and religion". As such, he would almost certainly have been privy to the correspondence sent by Queen Elizabeth I of England to the Ottoman court in 1578, in what British historian Jonathan Freedland calls an "Elizabethan Brexit", seeking new trade relations beyond Europe.

Most Imperial and Most Invincible Emperor,

We have received the letters of your Mighty Highness written to us from Constantinople whereby we understand how graciously and how favourably the humble petition of one William Harebroom was granted to him and his company. We desire of Your Highness that the commendation of such singular courtesy may be enlarged to all our subjects in general.

Elizabeth was asking for free access to the markets of the Islamic world through the gateway of Constantinople. At the time any European ruler who traded with the Islamic world would automatically be cast out of the Catholic Church, but since Elizabeth had already been excommunicated for her rejection of papal authority over the Church of England, she had nothing to lose and everything to gain by reaching out to the world's other trading superpower, bypassing her enemy in Europe, Philip II of Spain. As part of the diplomatic wooing process, she sent the Sultan exotic English gifts, like a clockwork organ complete with its Lancastrian manufacturer to turn the handle, which delighted and fascinated Murad III. In return, he and the Sultana sent back perfumes, soaps and silks. They established mutually beneficial trading links, in which the main items sent east to the Ottomans from England were not only the woollen cloth for which Yorkshire was even then famous, but also tin and lead, stripped from Catholic churches and monasteries. These materials were recycled by the Ottomans to manufacture the guns and bullets with which they then fought against Catholic Spain, an irony that would not have been lost on Elizabeth and the English court.

Archives show that English trading relations soon reached as far afield as Baghdad and Raqqa, after the so-called "Capitulation" treaties extended preferential terms for Christians operating within the Ottoman Empire, allowing them to establish privileged trading communities. When military dominance later shifted in Europe's favour, Western merchants exploited and abused these treaties, rousing much hostility from local merchants whose trading terms were less favourable.

Where did Abu Chaker and his Ottoman ancestors fit into this heritage? It is clear that Şemsi Ahmet Pasha's immediate offspring would have slotted naturally into the governor's military entourage, but at some point, later generations of Chamsi-Pashas drew closer to the religious and mercantile elites, as did many notable families of Syria. The move might even have started with Şemsi's links to the broadcloth trade, if he perhaps left behind some family members to run the Khan al-Joukhiye and set up a few shops in the adjacent Tailors' Souk and the Souk al-Arwam.

Abu Chaker's father and grandfather before him were never involved in politics. The family had been textile traders for generations, but even they might not have been aware of just how ancient this tradition was. Textiles had for centuries played a central role in the commercial life of Homs, just as in Palmyra, the ancient desert caravan city situated on the Silk Road some 160 kilometres to the east. Over 2,000 fragments of cloth were found in the Palmyrene tower tombs. The cloth, often made of silk, was used to wrap mummies placed in the cavities of the mass graves, and was remarkably preserved thanks to being high above ground in the dry air—by comparison, no textiles were found in the underground tombs as they had rotted long ago. All restoration work on the ancient textiles, dating from the first century BC to the second century AD, was carried out in Syria. They consisted of local linen, wool and cotton, together with imported silk from India and China. The quality was excellent, and they were clearly used only for the highest aristocracy of Palmyra, with sophisticated designs of floral arabesque patterns that can be traced to architectural patterns found in the classical stone-carved capitals.

These funerary traditions were continued by the Byzantines and the Copts, both of whom used fine silks to wrap the bodies of the deceased. The pre-Islamic textile factories of the region were then taken over by the Muslims. Funerary silks used by the Persian Buyid dynasty, whose empire spread into Syria from their capital Shiraz in the tenth century, show the continuation of the tradition, displaying plant and animal designs that revived ancient Persian Sassanid symbols, as well as poetic texts. At its greatest extent, the Buyid dynasty incorporated the modern states of what are now Iran, Iraq, Syria and Kuwait. Like the majority of Iranians today, the Buyids were Twelver Shi'a and believed in the "Occultation" of the last of the Twelve Imams, held to be the rightful successors to the Prophet Mohammad—a politically attractive option, which left them free to conduct themselves according to the demands of the times. They did not impose their own religion on their subjects, and occasionally even appointed Christians to high rank in order to dispel Sunni–Shi'a rivalry and to ease sectarian jealousies, a model that led to great stability and prosperity.

One of the earliest British consuls in Damascus who travelled to Homs and Hama in the mid-nineteenth century was astonished to find over 5,000 looms at work in the private homes of both Muslim and Christian families. He dubbed it "the Manchester of Syria."

The Homs of the early twentieth century had long been a city where Muslims and Christians had lived together and shared a long history. The Ottomans had made it the capital of the *sanjak* (administrative district) of Homs, attached to the Province of Tripoli, a port city and Homs' former rival. The Roman walls of the

Old City and its seven gates were to a large extent demolished or destroyed in earlier conflicts—the inevitable corollary of its central location at the crossroads of competing interests—but one gate survives, Bab al-Masdud in the west, along with some fragments of the ancient walls, especially in the Christian quarter, where three major churches still stand in Bustan al-Diwan.

The oldest, Umm al-Zinnar (Church of the Virgin's Belt), dates back to the fifth century. Beneath it runs a spring of holy water, from which Muslims and Christians alike drink freely to gain its spiritual blessing. This was the site of an underground church built in 59 AD to escape Roman persecution, making it one of the oldest churches in the world. Homs served as the centre of the Syriac Orthodox Patriarchate from 1933 to 1959, after which the Church's headquarters moved to Damascus. Today the church is still part of a complex that serves as the seat of the Syriac Orthodox archbishopric, and has been restored after heavy shelling damage in 2012. It is named after a lengthy textile belt discovered under the altar in 1953 by Patriarch Ignatius Aphrem I Barsoum. The relic is believed to be the Virgin Mary's girdle that was sent down from the heavens as a sign to Thomas the Apostle, who, late to return from India, had missed the occasion of the Assumption. On his death it was kept in India until 394, when it was transported to Urfa with the other relics of St Thomas. From there it was taken to Homs by a monk and buried inside the altar in a metal pot to keep it safe.

The nearby Mar Elian (Church of St Julian) is another Syrian Orthodox church of fifth-century origins. It contains beautiful early murals, which had been hidden under later plaster, some even thought to date to the sixth century making them possibly the oldest church murals in Syria. Julian was the son of a local Roman officer who was martyred in 284 for refusing to renounce Christianity; his sarcophagus is still in its martyrium. The newest of the three Bustan al-Diwan churches is the Church of the Forty Martyrs. There are still twenty-seven churches in the archdiocese of Homs and Hama, as well as a Bishop of Homs.

The presence of churches and monasteries was a part of the landscape. Al-Nouri, the oldest mosque in Homs, had, like the Great Umayyad Mosque in Damascus, previously been a Church of St John, with its rectangular courtyard orientated east–west like all early basilicas. When the Muslims arrived they shared the great church with the resident Christians, just as they had in Damascus. But while the church in Damascus was converted into a mosque after a hundred years, in Homs the two communities of worshippers shared the space for four hundred years. The arrangement only came to an end during the Crusades, when the tolerance of early Islamic rulers wore thin after truces with the Christian "Franks" were repeatedly broken.

Under the Roman Empire, before the advent of Christianity, the building had been a colossal pagan temple famed throughout antiquity, with a lavish sanctuary dedicated to Shams, the Mesopotamian name of the sun god El-Gabal, hence the temple's orientation towards the rising sun. The kings of Emessa (Homs) ruled as high priests over their subjects. British historian Warwick Ball tells us that the first historical mention of the Emesenes records them as a nomadic Arab tribe who settled and built the city of Emessa in the first century BC, after they discovered it was more lucrative to control the trading caravans than to raid them. They struck a deal with the Roman general Pompey, who incorporated them into the Seleucid state in 64 BC in exchange for recognition of their tribal shaikh Shamsigeramus (*shamsi* meaning "of the sun" and *geram* from the Arabic root *k-r-m,* meaning "to venerate") as phylarch or king of the Emesenes. They thus became the first of Rome's Arab client kingdoms on the fringes of the Syrian desert, since Pompey had realised that if he was to control Syria, he would have to do so with the help of the local communities. He restored their damaged and destroyed settlements and guaranteed their independence, especially along Rome's potentially vulnerable frontiers, granting Shamsigeramus dynastic power over Emessa and Arethusa (Al-Rastan) to the north, both on the Orontes river. In 72–78 AD Emessa was integrated into the territory of Palmyra.

Much to the bafflement of the Romans, the cult object itself, representing the sun god Shams, was not a statue of a god in human form as they would have worshipped in their own temples, but a large conical black stone, presumed to be volcanic or meteoric. In Arab and Jewish Semitic cultures such abstractions of the divine were common—the pre-Islamic black stone at the Ka'aba in Mecca, and the Nabatean stone blocks in Petra, for instance. The temple was generously endowed by neighbouring rulers, and coins minted in the third century depict its full grandeur, with its vast columns and gable enshrining the altar, the stone flanked by parasols (an Eastern symbol of royalty) and an eagle in front—another representation of the sun god, as found in Palmyra on the cella ceiling of the Temple of Bel, destroyed by so-called Islamic State in summer 2015.

By the fourth century Emessa had grown to outrank Tyre, Sidon, Beirut and Damascus in splendour because of the famous Temple of the Sun, decorated, according to Herodotus, with gold, silver and precious stones. Of this ancient wealth, only a pair of dazzling gold funeral masks have survived, unearthed in the remains of the royal necropolis. Located at the crossroads of numerous invading armies across the centuries, Emessa is perhaps the most thoroughly destroyed ancient city in Syria. Just a handful of ancient blocks can still be detected in the courtyard of Al-Nouri Mosque.

The mosque has survived till today, and one of its entrances still gives directly onto the extensive medieval souk. Built under the Ayyubids in the thirteenth century, the souk was restored by the Mamluks and the Ottomans, destroyed in the 2011–2018 war, and has now been rebuilt—commerce and religion, forever side by side in the heart of the city. On the same site the Temple of the Sun would also have attracted thousands of pilgrims, buying gifts and in need of food and accommodation while they sought the god's blessings. The surrounding souks would have been humming with activity to service their needs. All these Homsi buildings—mosques, churches and souks—were built from the same black basalt, a rugged volcanic stone found in abundance locally. A few volcanic cones, all now extinct, can still be seen across the landscape, in places like Qala'at Shmeis a few kilometres to the northeast near Salamiyeh.

Chaker Chamsi-Pasha, Abu Chaker's father, had been born in Homs in 1885. Photos show him in his fez, clean-shaven and wearing a suit and tie. He was fully literate, like other men of his class in society. The fez was worn by both Christian and Muslim professionals, a mark of status, not of creed. Though banned in Turkey by Atatürk in 1925 to dissociate Turks from their Ottoman heritage, in Syria and the wider region it remained the norm for all respectable men who considered themselves of a certain level in society—doctors, teachers, lawyers, accountants and merchants. In this part of the world to be a merchant was high status, the same profession as the Prophet Mohammad, carrying none of the British class connotations of "trade".

Chaker Chamsi-Pasha was from an elite family of urban-based landowners, who had for more generations than anyone could recall owned farming land north of Homs, around the villages of Al-Qusour and Qarabees, bestowed by an earlier ruler in gratitude for services rendered. In addition to the weaving tradition, Homs and its surrounding land was known for its fertility, based as it was in the Orontes river valley. It was famous for its olive orchards, together with presses to make the oil; for its fruit and nut orchards, especially its almonds; for wheat and sesame, together with water mills for the grinding; for grapes and for rice grown in the marshlands. Some of the Chamsi-Pasha land was used as vineyards, the grapes harvested not just for their own sake, but also to be sold to Christians to make wine, a common practice among Muslims who owned vineyards. The Chamsi-Pasha family income was based on revenues from this land, plus the profits of the textile shop that Abu Chaker's father, as head of the family, owned and ran in the souk. He had the reputation of being a strong, honourable and kindly man who doted on his son, buying sweets for him everyday and teaching him how to ride a horse.

In Arab societies the family name has always been extremely important and the study of the family *nasab*, the ancestral lineage—

unlike in Western societies where the trend today is almost in the opposite direction—continues to be highly valued. It is still the way many people know to place each other in a pecking order of importance and social standing, making the vital assessment of whether or not they are from a "good" family. "Ah, you are a Droubi from Homs!" or "Ah, you are an 'Azem from Hama!" conveys levels of meaning and information to Syrians that outsiders cannot begin to fathom. Even towns themselves take on specific associations: "Never trust anyone from Deir-ez-Zour, even if he is a Christian!" Aleppo had no single pre-eminent family, relying instead on factional alliances between many families as they vied with one another for control of local resources and revenues, a reflection perhaps of the city's more cosmopolitan commercial drive.

Unquestionably, to be a Chamsi-Pasha from Homs was highly respectable, as landowners who were securely amongst the social class of people known as "the notables". "You are a very fine old family," Abu Chaker's sons remember being told, "but you are few in number." The big landowning Homs families were the Atassi, Droubi, Raslan, Jundi, Siba'i, Jandali, Suwaydan and Dandashi families, mostly absentee landowners resident in the city itself. Between them, they owned nearly 55 per cent of the surrounding land and 110 villages, together with the most fertile land, especially fruit farms irrigated by the Orontes.

Abu Chaker's mother, Fatima, was a Jandali, born in 1901 (died 1988). The Jandali family owned whole villages as well as land, and were known to be a branch of the Rifa'i and hence direct descendants of the Prophet Mohammad. Fatima would recall how, when she was young, they could ride for two days without ever leaving Jandali land. She spoke Ottoman Turkish, like most of her generation of the landed elite, as well as Arabic. Coming from a traditional Muslim family, she was not sent to one of the Christian missionary schools in her area. Instead she occasionally attended a *kuttab*, a Qur'an school, and may also have been schooled a little at home, since she was able to read and write to a basic level.

She was short in stature but strongly built, an extremely able woman who married very young, aged just fourteen. By sixteen she had her first child, giving birth to seven children in all, some of whom died in childhood, which was quite common for the time. Even so, these early child-rearing years evidently had a toughening effect, as she lived to eighty-seven, far past the average life expectancy of her generation, which was closer to fifty. She came from a deeply conservative religious background, and wore a headscarf that she would pull across her face when men passed in the street. She never shook hands with men, whatever the context. In addition to bringing up her own children, she also raised her husband's older daughters from his previous marriage, all of whom were below the age of ten yet still only a few years younger than she was herself. Any land that she owned in her own right would have remained hers after marriage, just as her name remained Jandali. Taking a husband's name is not the practice in Syria, for Muslims or for Christians, and is regarded as an odd Western habit, implying loss of identity and the severance of ties with one's own family.

Fatima's grandchildren, Abu Chaker's sons, have clear memories of her as an old lady, her personality strong as ever, donning a white headscarf and dressed in any of a range of coloured, sometimes floral-patterned, full-length gowns. They still keep one of her triangular white headscarves, along with a colourfully patterned square scarf that would have been worn over the white one, and her heavy-rimmed old spectacles.

The Chamsi-Pashas were comfortably off as a family. Abu Chaker's father was born into privilege in one of the biggest houses of the neighbourhood, in a milieu where having domestic servants was the norm. They lived in a district called Bab Dreib, which lay within the perimeter of the Old City. While most houses had a single courtyard, the Chamsi-Pasha house had two: the inner courtyard (*jawwani*) and the outer courtyard (*barrani*), each with a central water fountain. The house was designed following the age-old "inside-out" pattern whereby the starting point was the courtyard around which all the rooms were individually arranged, each accessible only from the courtyard, never linking to each other by adjoining doors. No windows gave onto the street but only onto the central courtyard, so from the outside the main entrance alone was visible, usually an unobtrusive door set into a blank undecorated wall. The stables for the horses adjoined the back walls to help with heat insulation. Every morning the groom would bring Abu Chaker's father his favourite white mare for him to ride to his textile shop nearby. He would be wearing a smart suit and tie, a white shirt and red fez, as befitted a man of his standing. If you were from an important family, you were expected to dress the part.

Privacy was always the guiding principle in the courtyard design of these houses, keeping the women and the children safe from prying eyes in the street, giving them a haven where they could relax and feel at ease. Only the rooms upstairs, accessed by a staircase in the courtyard, were linked by a corridor. This floor was even further removed from the main street entrance than the downstairs rooms, and therefore was often where the family slept. This organic circular layout built the warmth of an embrace into the foundations of a house, as no other design could so intimately reflect the needs of the family and its hierarchies. The notion of family as sacrosanct is enshrined in the courtyard house plan, and though the design first emerged in Mesopotamia centuries before the advent of Islam, the space perfectly suited the requirements of local cultural practice by minimising the risk of strangers seeing into the house from the street or from neighbouring buildings. The relative size of the rooms also reveals a great deal about the priorities of the family. Kitchens and bathrooms were always very small compared to the living and sleeping areas. These principles were the same in Muslim, Jewish and Christian households, as can be seen in their strikingly similar house layouts.

The evolution of each house reflected its social order, completely removed from and uninfluenced by any concept of urban planning. Domestic life and public life were strongly segregated, a fact that inevitably enabled the continuance of the patriarchal system. The women of the household spent most of their daily lives within the privacy of the inner courtyard and did not often venture out of the home. All family life took place in the courtyard, as did all movement between the rooms. Whilst the courtyard house was therefore in some ways a mirror to the traditional principles and morals of Islam, keeping women and family secluded from outdoor life and maintaining utmost privacy, houses in the Christian quarter and the Jewish quarter were very similar and shared many of the same features. The design was therefore a reflection less of religion than of the cultural climate and milieu.

Each house had an additional layer of privacy as the residential alleyways outside the house belonged to their own residential quarter (in Arabic: *hara*), which were themselves then also enclosed by walls and gates. Every *hara* had its own headman (in Arabic: *mukhtar*, literally meaning "chosen man") who was agreed on by consensus among the respected elders of the neighbourhood, and who in turn depended on a small nucleus of other men to help him agree on how best to run the quarter. The *mukhtar* was historically chosen because of his high social status, and his home had to be constantly open to guests and callers wanting help with solving problems. He was also the administrative reference point for any communications with the authorities, something that inevitably laid him open to financial inducements from them if, as was sometimes the case, their interests were in danger of diverging from his. Each *mukhtar* was funded by the wealthier members of the group, generally merchants with a steady income from their shops in the nearby souk or those with small local businesses like barbers, bakers or smithies. Together they then decided how much money was given to charities for the poor, how much was used for public renovations such as drinking water fountains and even how much should be set aside for emergencies. Women were never involved in such decisions.

In many ways, each *hara* was like a village, and the interdependence of members of the community was apparent in all forms of social activity. A birth would therefore be attended not only by the midwife and close female relatives of the mother-to-be, but by as many women of the *hara* as could find a pretext for being there. Once word went out that labour was starting, they would begin to assemble in the house and stay there till the baby was born, in order to congratulate the parents if it was a boy or discreetly condole with them if it was a girl. Weddings would be attended by the entire *hara* population. Deaths would be followed by visits to the bereaved family by every other family in the *hara*: the men would visit the men and offer help with the funeral arrangements and extra funds if the death had left the family short of income, while the women would visit the grieving women to support them in running the household and help with the preparation of funeral food. Newcomers to the *hara* would be brought food by the neighbours throughout the first week to help them settle in, and every family would then ceremonially come to call on them to welcome them into the community. Another striking aspect of this traditional Islamic society was its egalitarianism, where rich lived alongside poor and where servants often mixed with their masters. Girls brought in from the countryside to work as maids would serve guests with deference, but when there were no guests, they would sit down with the family, sometimes eat with them and converse with them as equals, sharing in the life and interests of their employers, who would in turn feel responsible for their welfare, as if they were part of the family. Sometimes, perhaps inevitably, such intimacy crossed a boundary, with maids becoming mistresses to their employers—the US historian Daniel Pipes has estimated that up to 25 per cent of the 'Alawi children born in the 1930s and 1940s had Sunni fathers.

The dramas of these local neighbourhoods, and their conflicts both in the public sphere with the governments of the time and in the private sphere within their families and communities, continue to fascinate modern audiences, as demonstrated by the historical soap operas that attract millions of viewers every year during Ramadan. In some ways reminiscent of the British ITV drama "Downton Abbey", many of these immensely popular television series are set against the backdrop of a typical urban courtyard house, and the extensive casts of characters often include the *mukhtar* and his helpers. Part of the attraction lies in nostalgia, harking back to an idealised time when Syrian society seemed to be simpler. Relics of that world exist even today, as the *mukhtar* system continues in all Syrian cities, in both Muslim and Christian areas, and a female *mukhtar* remains unheard of.

3

THE PATRIARCHAL SOCIETY

A woman's word is wind in the wind; a man's word is a rock in the wall.

(Arab proverb)

Look in the index of any book about Ottoman Syria and there are no women to be found. They might as well have been invisible. Historical accounts of Syria under Ottoman times were populated entirely by men: rulers, notables, judges, merchants—people in authority were uniformly male. Women were only ever mentioned in the context of whether or not, based on the prominence of their families, they were good matches for marriage, like chattels to be bought and then bred from, in the hope they would produce male heirs. Failure to bear a son was grounds for divorce or for taking a second wife.

The only exceptions were in Ottoman Istanbul, not in Syria. In the Ottoman capital there were a few women who sponsored social works, but even their power only came through their powerful male relations. Roxelana, a slave of Russian origin who married the Ottoman sultan Süleyman the Magnificent, had a huge budget at her disposal, which she used to build pilgrimage inns along the difficult route to Mecca, in Jerusalem, Syria and Egypt, just as

Zubayda, wife of the Abbasid Caliph Harun al-Rashid had done for pilgrims starting out from Baghdad seven centuries earlier. Princess Mihrimah, Roxelana and Süleyman's favourite daughter, controlled such vast wealth that she was reputed to be the richest woman in the world in the sixteenth century, and commissioned mosques, madrasas and many public works.

Today many in the West unquestioningly blame Islam for all such patriarchal views and customs, including the traditional preference for sons over daughters. And yet the Qur'an itself explicitly rejects the pre-Islamic cultural practice of killing unwanted girls at birth:

> When the news is brought to one of them of the birth of a female child, his face darkens, and he is filled with inward grief. With shame he hides himself from his people because of the bad news he has had. Shall he retain it or bury it in the dust? Ah, what an evil judgement he makes! (Qur'an 16:58–9)

The Prophet Mohammad reinforced the same message, saying, "One to whom a daughter is born and who does not bury her alive, does not humiliate her nor prefers a son to a daughter, will be sent to Paradise."

Research by Dr Hatoun al-Fassi, a Saudi academic working at King Saud University, has discovered that women in Middle Eastern societies may not always have had such subservient roles to men. Through her detailed study of inscriptions found in the Hijaz in northern Arabia, she has found evidence of how women belonging to the early Nabatean culture had independent legal rights, enjoying the power to strike contracts on their own without male involvement. Best known to us through their capital Raqmu (today's Petra in Jordan), the Nabateans were an essentially trading people, their commercial caravan networks based on strings of oases that they loosely controlled. The remains still extant at Petra show how they cultivated grapes, made wine and devised ingenious water systems to garner the flash floods common to the region's climate. They spoke and wrote in Aramaic, but their distinct culture was eroded and gradually disappeared after they were annexed to the Roman Empire by Emperor Trajan in the first century AD. Al-Fassi concludes that Arab women were divested of many rights when the Nabateans were assimilated into the Greek and Roman orbit, where the role of women was more constrained.

Julia Domna of Emessa (Homs), the wife of Roman Emperor Septimius Severus, was a rare exception to this pattern and enjoyed a level of political influence that was out of the ordinary for women of her era. Nonetheless, even her power was only gleaned through her husband and later her sons, two of whom also became joint emperors: Caracalla and Geta. Between them, Julia Domna and her sister Julia Maesa mothered four Roman emperors, all of whom were therefore ethnically Syrian—it is easy to forget that from the second century onwards many Caesars were not from Rome but from the provinces. It was said that pressure from Julia Domna played a part in Caracalla's famous decree in 212 to extend Roman citizenship to all free citizens of the empire, thereby sweeping away all distinctions between Romans and provincials. In some ways the Roman Empire was one of history's most successful melting pots, generally tolerant of foreign cultures and religions, with no apparent prejudice according to race or skin colour so long as the empire's subjects did not challenge its rule.

Youngest daughter of the high priest of Emessa, Julia Domna met Septimius Severus (originally from Leptis Magna, in modern Libya) in around 182, when he was stationed in Syria as commander of a legion. An oracle had told her she would marry a king, but at the time he was still married to his first wife Marciana. When Marciana died during his subsequent posting in Lyons, Septimius sent for Julia Domna, and they were married in 183. Whether or not his choice was, as the eighteenth-century English historian Edward Gibbon puts it, due to "the fruitful offspring of his superstition or his policy", it is indisputable that her family was exceptionally wealthy, thanks to the fame of Emessa's Temple of the Sun, which drew in many worshippers, bringing with them gifts and trade. Septimius Severus was marrying into one of the richest, oldest and most aristocratic families in Syria. Gibbon also describes Julia

Domna as deserving "all that the stars could promise her," as she possessed, he explains, "the attractions of beauty, and united to a lively imagination a firmness of mind, and strength of judgement, seldom bestowed on her sex."

Julia Domna remains a popular figure in Syrian folklore, remembered for her reputation as a strong wife and mother. She accompanied her husband Septimius on all his campaigns and was with him when he died in York in 211. Even today her legacy is memorialised in the names of businesses in Syria and in Britain alike. Alongside statues of Roman general Scipio and the Greek philosopher Socrates, a life-size figure of Julia Domna stands majestically on a pedestal in the Great Hall of Syon House in west London near Heathrow Airport. This magnificent hall formed part of the eighteenth-century neoclassical revival, inspired by detailed drawings of Palmyra brought back to London by the early travellers Robert Wood and James Dawkins. The ceiling at nearby Osterley Park is likewise modelled on the stone-carved zodiac ceiling in Palmyra's Temple of Bel, as are ceilings all over Britain in homes of the landed aristocracy, like Dumfries House and Blair Castle.

Julia Domna was known to have a circle of protégés, especially philosophers, the most prominent of whom was Philostratus, a disciple of the mystic Apollonius. Fascinated by his teachings, she commissioned him to write his famous *Life of Apollonius*, sometimes viewed as the Graeco-Roman challenge to the Gospels. The work was highly influential in spreading the philosophy of Apollonius, a mystic from Cappadocia who preached extreme asceticism, warning against the evils of alcohol, meat, wool, hot baths or any other luxury. He believed in reincarnation, venerated birds and animals and even claimed to speak their languages. By the early 300s, Apollonius' cult following rivalled that of Christ, and some scholars believe that Julia Domna's patronage played a key role in preparing the ground for Christianity to become the dominant religion in the Roman Empire.

Septimius was himself of Phoenician blood and thus accustomed to the idea of an abstract deity, as well as the concepts of rebirth and resurrection. Christianity spread from the East first to cities like Carthage in North Africa, and from there to other Phoenician trading settlements like Cadiz in Spain, Sicily, Malta and Sardinia. Through Septimius, other Phoenicians of North African origin were given important posts throughout the empire. As a descendant of priests of the sun god, Julia Domna was also very familiar with the idea of a single all-powerful god, its attendant rituals of sacrifice and the concept of the daily resurrection in the East where the sun rose. Syrians had always been open to religious experimentation and syncretism, and the eventual local blending of abstract sun gods into one omnipotent god merged virtually seamlessly into the cult of Christ, which early on was commonly associated with the sun. Since modern notions of Arab or Syrian nationalism had not yet developed, citizens of the empire subscribed to an all-embracing Roman identity, which made it easy for ideas to spread. The first state to proclaim Christianity as its state religion, the Kingdom of Edessa (now modern Urfa in Turkey, the reputed birthplace of Abraham) was under Septimius' inclusive rule. The third-century Roman emperor known as Philip the Arab (ruled 244–249), from Shahba in southern Syria, first allowed Christians to worship in public. Some scholars even claim he was the first Christian emperor.

The most prominent Syrian figure to break the patriarchal mould in the later years of the third century was Queen Zenobia, last ruler of the Palmyrene Empire. Roman historians describe her as the woman who knew how to rule in an age of incompetent men. Zenobia was famed not only for her beauty but also for her intellectual accomplishments and bravery, both in battle and when hunting wild beasts. Sometimes likened to Cleopatra, she defied the authority of Rome by conducting her own trade agreements, negotiating with the Persian Sassanids, and bringing new territories under her sway without consulting Rome or its interests. Coins minted in her name and image have survived to this day. At its peak Zenobia's trade-based empire extended from modern-day Iraq, south through Egypt and north into Turkey. Today she is the namesake of Syria's main sanitary ware company, whose logo is the

Zenobia crown, and of countless other smaller businesses. She has provided the inspiration for at least eight operas.

Zenobia's armies conquered a significant portion of the Eastern Roman Empire before being defeated by Emperor Aurelian in 273. Aurelian attributed his victory to the sun god, whose support he had prayed for at the famous Emessa temple before continuing on to Palmyra. After a brief siege Aurelian let loose his mercenary troops—a mix of Celts, Goths, Moors and tribal desert Arabs—on the city, which was pillaged and plundered and its citizens brutally clubbed. Aurelian kept the finest treasures from the Temple of Bel, some of which hailed from as far afield as India and China, and carried them back to Rome, where he used them to adorn his new Sun Temple, built to show his gratitude to the obliging god. The temple's dedication ceremony (*natalis*) to Sol Invictus (Unconquered Sun) took place on 25 December 274. Emperor Aurelian went on to promote the cult of Sol Invictus as an official Roman national cult, elevating the status of the sun god to one of the most powerful deities in the empire and not just another god in the pantheon.

The Roman sun god would later find another fervid supplicant in Constantine, who became emperor in 306. During his reign the cult of Sol Invictus as the empire's premier deity unfolded into the beginnings of monotheism. After Constantine's conversion to Christianity, sun temples were adapted to Christian practices, continuing their orientation to the east, and the day of the sun—Sunday—was decreed as the official day of rest. The advent of Christianity was not a momentous revolution, but a gradual transition, adopting many elements from the Eastern Syrian sun cult, building on foundations put in place and encouraged by the Emperor Septimius and his Homsi wife, Julia Domna.

Julia Domna's proactive example may have inspired other kinds of social change. In a unique third-century mosaic found in a villa near Hama, an all-female orchestra led by a conductress is depicted, the ensemble performing onstage with an organ, a harp, a flute and a set of eight bowls filled with water to different levels to produce the eight notes of an octave. Nothing similar has been found in the rest of the Roman world. The world's first ever musical melody was found in Syria, on a 3,400-year-old clay tablet unearthed at Ugarit. It is known as the Hurrian Hymn, and sings the praises of Niqqal, the goddess of the orchards, asking her to grant fertility to both crops and women:

The sterile may they make fertile

Grain may they bring forth

May she who has not yet borne children bear them.

When played as a tune today by Syrian musician Malek Jandali, the song sounds remarkably modern.

The matriarchal Aramaic and Arab tribal traditions remained strong in the Homs and Palmyra region throughout the Roman era. Palmyra's role as a strategic military bastion of the Eastern Roman Empire, coupled with the need for caravan trade as the economic life-blood of the city, guaranteed the high status that women enjoyed in the political and social life of the oasis. The large number of distinctive Palmyrene statues and funerary portraits that are still to be found, not only in Syrian museums but also in museums across Britain, show women immortalised alongside men as their equals, staring straight at us with startlingly direct gazes. Not only were women active in the indigenous textile industries of the region, but they also owned property, were involved in the political and economic affairs of the city, and through carefully orchestrated marriages guaranteed wealth and access to Silk Road trade routes via clan alliances with regions as far away as India.

Funerary genealogies found in Palmyra's tombs seem to indicate that some Palmyrene women practised a traditional tribal matriarchal marriage arrangement called the *mut'a* marriage, by which a woman would choose a male spouse for a specified period of time in order to produce children for her clan or tribe. This could well be the origin of the *mut'a* temporary marriage contract in Shi'a Islam, sometimes seen as a kind of licensed prostitution whereby a man marries a girl or woman "for pleasure" for a set period, after which time the marriage expires. In the Palmyrene *mut'a*, the marriage was also short-term, and the resultant children belonged to the woman and her associated clan, not to the male partner. This meant that certain women had the potential to become the founders of their own clans and families, granting them more control over economic, military and cultural affairs. Queen Zenobia, for example, was widely praised in Arab sources for her chastity, refusing to sleep with her husband except to procreate; inscriptions found at Palmyra suggest that her marriage to her warrior-husband, Odainat, was of the *mut'a* type.

The style and bequeathal of women's headdresses, which were passed down through the female members of an extended family, and the motifs decorating their textiles also appear to embody the matriarchal tradition. Surviving specimens of fine mixed textiles from the ancient Near East, woven of silken warp and woollen weft, all originated in Palmyra. Portraits found in the tombs of Palmyra show that textile production was an important aspect of the work of women of the city. On the earliest extant funerary stelae from the late second century BC the distaff and spindle regularly feature in the hands of deceased Palmyrene women. Atargatis, the great pagan female deity of Syria described by the Roman author Lucian in *De Dea Syria*, was depicted in sculpture with a distaff, indicating her powers to weave cosmic destiny and control Fate. Weaving in Palmyra was viewed as an economic necessity, but also carried with it cosmic associations with the roles of these powerful female deities.

Atagartis was a blended deity, taking on the faces and characteristics of Athena, Aphrodite, Artemis, Selene, Nemesis and the Fates, just as her Syrian male equivalent Hadad was a composite Zeus-style ruler of the cosmos. Such a spirit of religious compromise helped Palmyra's rulers reconcile the competing interests of neighbouring powers, giving them all a stake in the city. Each deity had its own feast days, with the major cults staging grand processions to draw crowds. The famous temples became pilgrimage centres which in turn kept the markets busy, supplying mementoes and votive objects for sacrifice. The Atagartis Temple at Hierapolis (modern-day Membij) even started a tattoo parlour so that pilgrims could have their necks or wrists tattooed to show that they had completed the pilgrimage, giving them a shared sense of community and identity.

As a caravan city that had grown up around a desert oasis on the Silk Road route from the Mediterranean to the Euphrates river, Palmyra's civilisation represented a unique culture founded on trade. The entire central area of the city was a hub of commercial and administrative activity, based around a massive agora or marketplace with eleven entrances built to avoid congestion. Beside it was the Tariff Court (from Arabic *ta'rif*, meaning "notification" or "information") where a huge stone block in Greek and Palmyrene Aramaic, the two languages of the bilingual city, detailed the rates of tax payments for goods passing through the city and its territories, such as slaves, purple-dyed wool, perfumed oils, salted fish from Lake Tiberias and livestock like cattle. Listed separately were the tariffs on goods exchanged within the town, such as garments, pine nuts, camels, bronze statues and the services of prostitutes. This Palmyrene Tariff generated huge wealth for the merchants of the city, be they men or women, with items like perfumes commanding particularly high tariffs. Ironically, the Tariff stone itself languished for two years in the port of Odessa because of unpaid import taxes, after it was given as a gift in 1901 to the Russian Tsar by the Ottoman sultan. Today it sits in St Petersburg's State Hermitage Museum.

The position of women in Palmyra was not typical of women in the Roman Empire, who were generally regarded as subservient to men. Under Roman law women were not allowed to vote, stand for office or be active in politics. As a result most were not deemed worthy of education, so very few were in a position to write their own stories. Roman women were expected to perform their role as dignified wives and good mothers with no power beyond managing the domestic arrangements of the household. Spinning, weaving and making clothes from wool or linen were traditionally their responsibilities, though rich women who frequently dressed in expensive imported fabrics like Chinese silk or Indian cotton had their clothes sewn for them by their servants. Throughout their lives they were subject to the authority of men, their fathers before marriage and later their husbands, who always had the legal rights over their children. Female slaves were common, as maids, agricultural labourers and occasionally even as gladiators. Only a wealthy widow could be independent and act for herself, sometimes even starting up a business. The only other route to independence was to become a priestess or a vestal virgin.

After the Muslim conquest of Syria, much Roman law relating to women seems to have been absorbed into Islam and some modern scholars consider that it forms a major part of the Shari'a law still being practised today—a theory that is highly controversial for those who believe the Shari'a cannot have man-made origins, since it is based on the Qur'an and the *Hadith*. In the pre-Islamic Arabian Peninsula the norm for most women had been that they enjoyed no legal status under customary tribal law. They were sold by their male guardians into marriage, and their husbands could terminate the marriage at will. Both female infanticide and unlimited polygamy were common in pre-Islamic Arabia. On the whole, women could not own or inherit property. Customs did however seem to vary from tribe to tribe and a small number of women, such as the Prophet Mohammad's first wife Khadija, even ran successful businesses and were powerful figures in their own right.

Khadija's story can shed light on the ways in which many injunctions relating to women actually improved under Islam: polygamy, for example, was restricted under Islam to four wives, and then only if the husband guaranteed that all four were kept in equal conditions. The Qur'an stipulated that women were entitled to keep their dowry as a safeguard in the event of divorce, and gave them rights of inheritance and property ownership, albeit not on the same level as men, but higher nevertheless than anything that had previously been afforded them. In other cultures, including in the West, women did not obtain such rights till centuries later.

Khadija had inherited her wealth from her rich merchant father, whose business she then managed from her base at Mecca after his death. Twice widowed, she had three sons from her first marriage and three daughters from her second. Both husbands were killed in the wars that were widespread in Arabia at the time. She had not planned to marry a third time, but decided to propose to Mohammad, having identified him as a trustworthy young man after he had worked for her over the course of several years, accompanying her trade caravans. She herself did not travel with the caravans, but stayed in Mecca running the business. Mohammad, a distant cousin, was recommended to Khadija as an agent, and she promised him twice the usual commission if he made a successful trip. He returned with profits that far exceeded her expectations and impressed her with his honesty and integrity. His caravan would have carried items like hides, raisins, perfumes, dates, silver and herbs, and he would have purchased in return whatever she had instructed him to buy—items not available locally, such as more luxurious manufactured goods and clothes made by Syrian craftsmen—for her onward sale to wealthy Meccan families.

At the time of their marriage, Khadija was forty and Mohammad was twenty-five, and he came to live in her house beside the blacksmiths' market off the main Meccan souk. He did not take another wife until after her death, sixteen years later. Their daughter Fatima, who later married 'Ali, the fourth caliph, survived both her parents and is known as one of Islam's "perfect women". Khadija and Mohammad had three other daughters and two sons before Fatima, both of whom died in infancy. Unusually for her time, even before marrying Mohammad, it was recorded that Khadija did not believe in worshipping idols.

One of the most revolutionary innovations in the Qur'an was the recognition of spiritual equality between men and women:

> For men who submit themselves wholly to God, and women who submit themselves wholly to Him, and men who believe and women who believe, and men who are obedient and women who are obedient, and men who are truthful and women who are truthful, and men who are steadfast and women who are steadfast, and men who are humble and women who are humble, and men who give alms and women who give alms, and men who fast and women who fast, and men who guard

their chastity and women who guard their chastity, and men who remember God much and women who remember Him, God has prepared forgiveness and a great reward. (Qur'an 33:36)

During the *Hajj*, to this day, women and men perform exactly the same rituals, not segregated as they are in mosques, but side by side. They walk together seven times around the Ka'aba, climb together to the top of Mount Arafat, and throw stones together at Jumarat, the three pillars representing the devil. The only gender difference is vestiary—men wear two unstitched white sheets with nothing underneath, while women have no specific dress requirement, except that they dress modestly. They are not supposed to cover their faces, though today some do, not with a *niqab*, or full-face covering, which is forbidden, but with a scarf that can be pulled across the face. At the end of the pilgrimage men shave their heads while women simply cut a lock of their hair. Women need to be accompanied by a *mahram* or male guardian, but rules have been relaxed to allow women over the age of forty-five to go instead with an older female companion.

Cases of sexual abuse and molestation of women, not only whilst mingling with men on the pilgrimage but also in public places generally, were extremely rare in previous eras, but in recent years have been on the increase. The rise of Wahhabism and the resurgence in the wearing of the veil, both the *hijab* (headscarf) and the *niqab*, far from leading to men to behave more respectfully towards women seem to have had the opposite effect. Women today have even reported being groped by the religious police in Mecca during the *Hajj*. Sexual violence and rape, used the world over as weapons of war and means of control and humiliation throughout history, are no less practised in Muslim societies than elsewhere. Yet in early Islam the Prophet Mohammad is recorded as saying, whilst making his final pilgrimage, "Treat your women well and be kind to them. It is true that you have certain rights with regard to your women, but they also have rights over you." It is hard to convey how revolutionary such thoughts were for the time.

In the *Hadith* of Al-Bukhari the second Caliph 'Umar is reported to have said, "We never used to give significance to ladies in the days of the pre-Islamic period of ignorance, but when Islam came and God mentioned their rights, we used to give them their rights, but did not allow them to interfere in our affairs." Even sexual equality between men and women is implied in the Qur'an: "It is made lawful for you to consort with your wives during the nights of the fast. They are as a garment for you and you are as a garment for them." (2:188) For all the respect granted to women in the Qur'an and by the Prophet Mohammad, and the injunction to treat both parents kindly, the predominant culture in all religions across the Middle East—Christianity, Islam and Judaism—most definitely displayed a bias towards the senior male of the household. It was with him that the ultimate power resided. In sub-Saharan Africa and parts of south Asia, such a bias was arguably even more pronounced—it was never a specifically Arab or Islamic characteristic, but rather a cultural one.

Turkish academic Deniz Kandiyoti called this allocation of power and respect the "patriarchal bargain". Foreign male rulers controlled the public sphere and entered a social contract with the male notables of the region, under whom they in turn were permitted to control the local sphere. In Ottoman times the governors sent out from Istanbul were often unfamiliar with local customs and were only rarely Arabic speakers. As a result they had to rely on powerful notables resident in the big cities to fill the gaps in their local knowledge and to help ensure they had sufficient military backing to exercise direct control over their province.

The notables whom these governors had to depend on were not guaranteed their status by virtue of their birth or wealth. They earned their position thanks to their skill in performing a delicate balancing act: they could never be seen directly to oppose the Ottoman governor, or appear to betray the interests of their local clientele. Sometimes they were leaders of the great religious families, members of the *'ulema* (religious scholars) and the *ashraf* (direct descendants of the Prophet Mohammad via Fatima). They tended to live in the walled old cities of Damascus, Aleppo and Homs, close to the cathedral-turned-mosque and the main souks, where they enjoyed strong links with the traditional commercial activities of trade and manufacturing.

By later Ottoman times these families were also often the most prominent commercially, their wealth coming not only from control of the religious trusts but also from their control of trade and production, together with income from hereditary tax farms around the cities. The practice of tax farming, where private citizens were responsible for collecting tax revenues, was widespread not just in Syria but also in Egypt, Rome, Greece and even seventeenth-century Great Britain. It was not necessarily an abuse of power, but a type of privatisation for managing agrarian revenues and a form of borrowing to finance government programs. French colonialists used it in Algeria in the 1850s. The practice was launched in Ottoman lands by Mehmet the Conqueror in the fifteenth century and then abolished in the 1856 Tanzimât reforms. A tax farm, known as an *iltizam,* would typically be an annual agreement that the Ottoman authorities would sell to the highest bidder from among the wealthy notables (usually Sunni Muslims but sometimes also Christians or 'Alawis), who would then collect up to five times the amount they had paid for the land from taxes levied on the peasant farmers and from the agricultural produce itself. Tax farmers in early Islamic times in Egypt were recorded as sometimes being Coptic Christians and even wealthy women, probably because it had always been their land: most Islamic schools of law regarded the conquered land of non-Muslims as state land so it was in a sense compulsorily purchased. Muslim tax farmers were later granted the right to hold tax farm contracts for life and to pass them on to male heirs, a very effective way of reinforcing loyalty to the Ottoman state, via their own self-interest.

The 1858 Ottoman land law reforms were designed to maximise tax revenues, and urban notables with legal know-how and greater resources were able to manipulate the land registration process to consolidate their holdings. Peasants and the rural poor on the other hand rarely registered their land, for fear of greater taxation and military conscription. By the end of the nineteenth century the Ottomans had built roads and railways, opened telegraph offices, postal services and local schools. Most rural inhabitants, however, were suspicious of these new institutions, understanding all too well that telegraphs conveyed intelligence, roads brought government agents and police, and school rosters recorded names of children who could later be taxed and perhaps conscripted for distant and possibly fatal military service. A new class of enterprising peasants and lower-level merchants deeply resented efforts to conscript their sons and tax their agriculture. They felt they had earned the right of relative independence from the state. Real power, in their view, should reside within their own patriarchal societies, not within the state—experience had taught them that the state rarely, if ever, had their interests at heart.

The other powerful figures in society were the commanders-in-chief of the local Janissary garrisons, known as *aghas*, who tended to live outside the city walls in the suburbs. In Damascus many lived in the suburb of Midan to the south; in Aleppo the equivalent was the suburb of Bab al-Nayrab. These suburbs were much less homogeneous than the walled city centres, and were generally inhabited by a mix of immigrants of one sort or another—uprooted peasants, semi-sedentarised tribes who came in for the winter season, non-Arab ethnic groups like Turkmens, Kurds, Druze and Jews, and the poor, none of whom could afford to live inside the city walls. The *aghas* derived their power from protecting these segments of society, sometimes integrating them into their paramilitary organisations. Because many grain merchants and livestock traders tended to live in the outer suburbs, the *aghas* also managed to dominate the grain and livestock trade with the cities.

Since their interests frequently clashed, the *aghas* often came into conflict with the urbanised religious establishment, who feared their influence, resented their disruptive protests and despised their lower social status. The *aghas* had the power to hold entire cities to ransom by blockading grain and livestock supplies, while the religious and mercantile elites saw it in their interest to maintain the status quo since they had far more to lose. They preferred to use subtler methods of pressuring the Ottoman governor, rather than resorting to open urban revolt.

Syrian society in the mid-nineteenth century mirrored both the powerful military entourage and the religious and mercantile elites. Yet a range of factors would soon combine to make it in the interests of these two rival urban groups to merge into a single elite with a largely unified class base. This same class base would go on to dominate Syrian political life virtually unchallenged until World War Two.

In such an arrangement women had no power or say at all, their voices relegated to the background. Moreover, whenever war broke out, inevitably leading to the celebration of physical strength and the rife sexual exploitation of women, this status quo played naturally into the hands of men. Weapons throughout history have overwhelmingly been wielded by men, and the physical abuse of women—and occasionally of male prisoners—has itself been used as a very powerful weapon of war. Women were frequently detained and used as bargaining chips in hostage exchanges. In captivity, rape then as now was assumed to have taken place, so that even on release, the stigma was such that men would divorce their wives and society would reject them. One such woman, a Yazidi traded by so-called Islamic State in the Raqqa slave market, said to the media on her escape in 2015: "I felt as though I was being raped again with every look of pity and contempt. The pain from the wounds that tore my body was nothing compared to the pain of the repeated rejection of society."

Female independence was often feared, with men justifying their controlling behaviour by reiterating the need to ensure that they would not unwittingly raise another man's child. This is the logic used to justify the *mahram* system of male guardianship under which a woman cannot, even to this day in some conservative households, leave her home unchaperoned. It is a system that implies a lack of trust of both men and women. Left to their own devices, the thinking goes, people will stray and behave immorally, the women more so than the men. The same logic lies behind the ritual of female genital mutilation, a cultural practice that predates Islam but is still endemic in some societies today amongst both Muslims and Christians. Nothing in the Qur'an or the sayings of the Prophet Mohammad condones the practice, but weak arguments are sometimes made by ill-informed Islamic jurists in its favour. Ottoman scholars and sultans outlawed such barbaric traditions in the 1850s, and banned punishments such as amputation of hands for stealing and stoning to death for adultery, only to have them re-introduced by literalist, fundamentalist Muslim-majority countries like Saudi Arabia and Iran in the twentieth and twenty-first centuries.

One Ottoman governor in the late eighteenth century who typified the patriarchal system so prevalent in the region was Ahmad al-Jazzar, originally a Christian Bosnian slave, whose surname meant "The Butcher". Such an epithet was routinely used as a mark of respect for those who had slaughtered Bedouin raiders. Al-Jazzar was originally appointed governor of Sidon (in today's Lebanon), the natural port for Damascus, and succeeded on four separate occasions in extending his authority to act as governor of Damascus at the same time. With the help of the British Navy he defended Acre from the forces of Napoleon Bonaparte, forcing the French general to withdraw in disarray, a feat for which he earned much prestige, even in Europe. A heavy drinker for most of his life, he reformed himself and practised total abstinence from alcohol after participating in the *Hajj* in 1791.

Al-Jazzar described himself thus:

> In order to govern the people of this land, one cannot be too severe. But if I strike with one hand, I recompense with the other. That is how I maintained for thirty years, in spite of everybody, complete possession of all the land between the Orontes and the estuary of the Jordan.

He is reputed to have walked around with a portable gallows in case anyone displeased him, and kept the doors of his prisons open so that anyone could view those detained before their torture or execution. He maintained equal treatment of all religions, imprisoning Muslim scholars, Christian priests, Jewish rabbis and Druze elders alike. His generosity to the poor was likewise consistent; large kitchens would provide rice and money was distributed regularly, irrespective of religion, on his orders.

Ironically, but perhaps predictably, Al-Jazzar's reign brought with it a high degree of economic prosperity thanks to its relative domestic stability, a stability that was quickly upturned by his successors in later decades who, whilst sharing his brutality and corruption, possessed neither his talent, his cunning nor his stamina. The secret of his success was his understanding that he needed a solid commercial foundation to maintain his political and military dominance in Syria. By suppressing marauding Bedouin tribes he increased security and maintained law and order in his territories. This in turn increased trade from Palestine and bolstered prosperity in coastal cities like Acre, Sidon and Beirut. Al-Jazzar expelled the French cotton traders from Acre and Jaffa and strengthened his own monopolies on cotton and grain. His architectural legacy reflected his interest in commerce, with several surviving monuments in Acre, including a caravanserai and a souk. He supported via a *waqf* one of the finest public baths (hammams) in the region, built of granite, porphyry, marble and painted tiles. He even built an aqueduct to supply the city with fresh water, subsequently destroyed by Napoleon's forces during the siege.

Al-Jazzar derived his income from trade, supplemented with tax deals that he struck with local communities. He even sought to attract immigrants, often Christians and Jews, to settle in his domains, to replace those that had emigrated to neighbouring regions in search of lesser tax burdens as part of a centuries-old pattern of movement in the quest for a better life elsewhere.

As the economy withered under a succession of subsequent incompetent rulers, entire villages in northeast Syria depopulated or disappeared altogether. Gradually the population reduced to a third of what it had been under the Romans. Ottoman rule in some parts of Greater Syria as the centuries wore on frequently disintegrated into a catalogue of mismanagement and exploitation.

Occasionally an exceptional leader would appear, such as the diminutive Druze Ma'ani prince Fakhr al-Din II, "lord of Arabistan from Aleppo to Gaza". A visionary ruler, his base was in the Chouf Mountains southeast of Beirut in the part of Greater Syria that is now Lebanon, from where he united the people of Lebanon against the Ottomans, even forging a secret military alliance in 1608 with the Italian Grand Duchy of Tuscany. The Ottomans had him publicly strangled in 1635, but his thirty-year rule had brought with it a rare period of economic and cultural prosperity. He introduced silk industries to the country and encouraged Christians to migrate from their Mount Lebanon heartlands to the Chouf mountains in order to direct its agricultural production. He built bridges and caravanserais such as the Khan al-Franj in Sidon to facilitate trade with European cities like Venice, Florence and Marseille. He entered into a series of alliances with the influential Medici family in Tuscany, invited engineers and agricultural experts from Italy and allowed European Catholic missions to settle under his patronage. What he lacked in stature, he made up for in ambition.

Another rare prince, Bashir II al-Shihabi, was a Sunni convert to Maronite Catholicism who ruled for fifty-two years in the early nineteenth century. His reign is widely regarded as the starting point of the sectarian politics which beleague Lebanon to this day, as a time that saw numerous battles fought to combat Druze hegemony and the preferential championing of the Maronite heartland of Mount Lebanon. Yet Bashir's legacy also marked a period of intellectual flourishing. The tax farming system he introduced brought prosperity and security to the mountainous Christian region, prompting the saying: "Happy is he who owns but a goat's enclosure in Mount Lebanon." His province (in Arabic: *mutasarrafiyya*) of Mount Lebanon survived right through till World War One, and his magnificent nineteenth-century palace of Beiteddine, still a highlight of any visit to Lebanon's Chouf Mountains, featured both a chapel and a mosque.

THE MERCHANT OF SYRIA

Midhat Pasha (1822–1883), whose name lives on as the modern name for the biblical "Street Called Straight", was one of the very few enlightened Damascus governors whose rule was not for self-interest. A great Ottoman statesman of the late Tanzimât period, he was progressive and liberal-minded, even launching a revolutionary programme of public works which he encouraged the notables to finance. He appointed many local Arabs to positions of responsibility, as well as some minorities, and also encouraged education and freedom of the press. Under him the number of local newspapers rose to twelve, far more than exist today. He resigned after three years because he felt his masters in Istanbul were not supporting him sufficiently in his reform attempts.

Apart from the military, Syrian society up to then had consisted of just two classes: the rich, or the well-to-do or aristocratic landowners, and the poor, who were peasants, farmers and manual workers. Anything in between did not matter. Families continued to follow the old extended patriarchal model, dominated by the grandfather or the oldest male member. Such education as existed was almost entirely the domain of a religious elite, often Christian. The first printing presses in the region had been acquired by Maronite monasteries like Qozhaya in Lebanon as early as 1584. Manufacturing functioned on the lowest domestic level, with local craftsmen using looms and simple hand tools to make only what their neighbours or at most their fellow townsmen needed. The average farmer grew only what was necessary for his family and to pay his rent. Business partnerships were limited largely to members of the same family. The typical city merchant was his own buyer, salesman and bookkeeper.

Ironically the first impetus for change came as a direct consequence of inter-communal conflict, which had begun in Mount Lebanon between the Maronite Christians and the Druze. After simmering and spreading into southern Syria the disputes reached their climax in the 1860 Damascus massacre of thousands of Christians. Across the country 380 Christian villages and 560 churches were destroyed. Yet the origins of this conflict lay not in religious differences but in the silk industry and in the social and economic grievances of the peasantry against exploitation by the wealthy elite.

In Damascus the predominantly Catholic wealthy quarter in the Old City was burnt and looted by a mix of impoverished Druze and Bedouin, while the mostly Orthodox and therefore indigenous Christians of poverty-stricken Midan outside the walls to the south were protected by their Muslim neighbours. The Catholics, who were commercially closest to the French, lived in self-contained and socially isolated grandeur, rich from the privileges awarded them by Western powers seeking to gain new markets at a time of European recession. As the Ottoman grip on its empire weakened, a feeding frenzy began in its provinces, with foreign interests competing for the spoils. The result was not only the ensuing inter-confessional violence among communities which had lived together largely peacefully up to that point, but also the complete undermining of the regional silk industry, as it was gradually bought out by foreigners, mainly Catholic, leading more and more local people to lose their livelihoods.

The 1860 war, like the war that rages today in Syria, is often called a civil war. However as with all wars, far from solving the root causes of the grievances, it only exacerbated them, deepening foreign interference in Greater Syria. The French intervened militarily to help their fellow Catholics and public sympathy was stirred in Europe. Educational and philanthropic agencies began to arrive, often run by Catholic missionaries, founding orphanages, boarding schools and dispensaries. Together with the opening of the Suez Canal to world traffic, the region was now exposed to outside cultural influences. A French company in 1895 built the first railway in the region, from Beirut to Damascus, later connected to Turkey, Iraq and Egypt.

During these late Ottoman times many women would have worn the şalvar, wide baggy trousers which were also worn by men, something which the first European women to travel to Ottoman territories regarded as hugely liberating and much more egalitarian, accustomed as they were to confinement in tight skirts and dresses while their menfolk enjoyed the freedom of trousers and shirts. Early wives of British ambassadors marvelled in their diaries that Ottoman women "possessed legal property rights and protections that far surpassed the rights of Western women". The şalvar even went on to be adopted by early feminists as a mark of emancipation, with some aristocratic English ladies in the 1920s and 1930s wearing them as a symbol of "their refusal of traditional British standards and sexual differences." These loose trousers then spread beyond Europe to America where, thanks to women's rights advocate Amelia Jenks Bloomer, they were renamed "bloomers".

Layering, that is dressing in layers, was another Ottoman habit borrowed by women in the West. Ottoman women commonly wore several layers of chemises and shawls, a fashion that conveyed class and status in the display of many sumptuous fabrics. Sometimes the layers themselves had significance—in Islamic art for example, different patterns worn in different layers were not simply thrown together at random, but were carefully planned to relay a religious message, like a spiritual metaphor of the divine order, infused with many levels of meaning. No one, man or woman, went outdoors in the region without a head-covering of some sort, unprotected from the heat and dust. Early photos reveal that Christian women very often wore head-coverings or scarves that were indistinguishable from those of Muslim women. Women's head-coverings could be remarkably similar to those worn by men, and both sexes always dressed in loose, long-sleeved, ankle-length garments to protect themselves from the sun.

The improved sea and land transport led to the arrival of ever more foreign merchants, who introduced items previously unknown in the region: factory-made textiles from Bradford and Manchester, machine-made items from Paris and industrialised commodities from New York and Detroit. The traditional markets were invaded, and local populations gradually developed a taste for fashionable Western clothes, alcoholic drinks, cigars and cigarettes, and sweets and bonbons, all of which the indigenous market was incapable of producing. Those with the acumen and vision to recognise these new possibilities thrived and prospered, becoming part of the nouveau-riche class, who began to wear tailored French clothes, bedeck their wives and daughters in expensive jewellery, and eat and drink exotic new concoctions.

Many of the wealthy merchants, allied to the conservative religious establishment and less adaptable to change—indeed often resistant to modernisation—turned to land as a more secure investment, especially as agriculture too started to become a profitable commercial enterprise in its own right. They wanted their ownership of the land registered officially in title deeds. The Ottoman administrators soon realised that deeded private property led to more efficiently taxed property, so they instituted a new legal system, fully aware that the additional revenue could in turn help pay for state modernisation schemes.

By the 1870s land ownership and political power began to go hand in hand, a state of affairs which continued in Syria and across much of the Middle East till as late as the 1950s. The military *aghas* cum grain merchants however had less of a stake in the old order, so they adapted more quickly to the new administrative system. Suddenly they were useful to the old notable families, who now saw an advantage in doing what had previously been unthinkable—intermarrying with the *aghas*, an arrangement which brought the *aghas* social status and brought the notables access to government and wealth through land.

By the turn of the twentieth century the two groups, previously rivals, had merged into a single urban elite with a common economic land base and shared access to the power networks of the Ottoman administration. Together they now became the key players in the large cities of Syria and across the wider Fertile Crescent, adopting a distinctive Ottoman aristocratic behaviour and style. As citizens of Greater Syria they spoke Arabic, but also polite Turkish, and adopted the Ottoman dress-coat and fez.

4

A BRIEF CHILDHOOD

What is learnt in youth is carved in stone.

(Arab proverb)

The chaotic world into which Abu Chaker was born on 20 March 1921 in Homs was the same strictly patriarchal milieu that it had been in Ottoman times. In this environment, imagine the consternation of Abu Chaker's father when his first wife gave birth to three daughters, and his second wife four more. The birth of his only son was met with huge relief: this boy was Mohammad Chaker Chamsi-Pasha, and from the start he was guaranteed unconditional devotion and a key position in the family hierarchy. Abu Chaker's birth was not registered until 1922, since formalities of this sort were often lax under the Ottoman authorities. His first official identity document, which his family still has in its possession, was therefore issued by the French Mandate. This is the reason that the family name is still spelt using French phonetic transliteration, where "ch" represents the sound "sh".

As a child, Abu Chaker lived an unremarkable but privileged life. Despite being born into a traditional conservative Sunni Muslim household, at the age of six he was sent to a Christian primary school run by Syrian Orthodox nuns, where he learnt the basics of reading and writing. Homs at that time was roughly two-thirds Muslim, one-third Christian, so most children at the school were Muslim. Boys and girls sat together in large classes of about thirty or forty. It was only at secondary level that schools became single sex, though Muslim and Christians of all ethnic backgrounds stayed together at the same schools, be they Arab, Kurdish, Jewish, Turkmen, Circassian or Armenian.

To be sent to a Christian school was usual for many Muslim children at the time, at least for those who could afford the fees, since it was the Christian schools that offered the best education. The urban elites sent their sons to be educated at schools set up by French, British and American missionaries, none of whom were permitted to use their institutions to attempt to proselytise their predominantly Muslim students. Still, it would be naive to imagine that their motives in setting up these schools were disinterested. By learning foreign languages at such institutions, Syrian pupils could become equipped to later earn positions as translators or commercial representatives for the businesses of Western Catholics, a service for which they might be awarded diplomatic immunity or even nationality. The cleverest were even sent to universities like the Sorbonne in France and entered the class of the educated elite— some of whom, ironically, went on to become politicians in the fight for Syria's independence.

In Homs the best and most prestigious secondary school was Al-Yassouiea, a Jesuit school, which also had the highest fees. Orthodox children felt like second-class citizens there, and some were withdrawn by their parents for that reason. Next door, in the neighbourhood of Bustan al-Diwan, was the second-best school, Al-Ghassanieh, run by the Melkite *mutran* (bishop). The school was co-located in the precinct with the Church of the Forty Martyrs. These schools were big, with three parallel classes in each year group, and even attracted Lebanese children from wealthy backgrounds, for whom Homs was closer than Beirut. The sister school for girls was close by, part of the same establishment.

The same principles applied to universities in the region, where the best university was, and still is, the American University of Beirut, founded in 1866 as the Syrian Protestant College. Christians and Muslims studied there together and thereby learnt to accept each other's differences. This kind of two-way exchange was common in Syria in all kinds of social interaction; Christians and Muslims would, for instance, routinely visit each other's houses. At funerals and memorial services, they would likewise pay each other respects, with Muslims often attending special services in churches—especially at Christmas and Easter—where they were always welcome. Christians would come and pay their respects to Muslim deceased in special tents set up outside mosques, and the standard greeting, used by both Christians and Muslims, was: *Qaddar Allahu sa'iykum* (may God value your efforts), to which the standard reply was: *Barak Allahu fadlakum* (may God bless your generosity). The Armenian community in Homs did not have very good Arabic, often mixing up the masculine and feminine, which meant that their slightly garbled version would translate instead as "God takes the good, and leaves the crap." The mistake was the source of much hilarity among the Muslim and Orthodox communities and led to many jokes at the Armenians' expense.

Christian women would offer prayers at Muslim holy sites, and Muslim women were often found praying at statues of the Virgin Mary in church courtyards. It was Muslim women who would wash the paving stones in the street around the Orthodox Umm al-Zinnar church. At the graves of Christian loved ones Muslims would lay myrtle leaves (*'aas*), while Christians would lay flowers where Muslim friends were buried—many continued to visit their friends' resting places for years, until their own deaths.

The souk of Homs was the most animated place in the city, inviting crowds of shoppers, many of them from the surrounding countryside, who converged on the marketplace in their best apparel to admire the gold jewellery and clothing on sale, perhaps looking to purchase finery for a wedding or special occasion. The women of Homs, who were mostly Muslims, would come to the market in groups to visit the gold shops, most of which were run by Christian traders. The shopowners would usher them inside and bring out the jewellery from inside locked display cases, then vacate the shop and go out onto the street while the women tried on earrings, necklaces and bracelets in privacy. Nothing was ever stolen. Trust was absolute.

Just as Muslims did not form a homogeneous grouping across Syria, but were divided between the majority Sunni, who formed roughly 70 per cent of the population, and the minority groupings of 'Alawis, Shi'a, Isma'ilis and Druze, there were of course also many Christian denominations throughout Syria. These, like the Muslim communities, were often at odds with each other, locked into various rivalries and power plays. Most numerous were the Orthodox, who accounted for about 70 per cent of all Christians in Homs, but there were also the Melkite Catholics (about 25 per cent), and the Syriac Christians, known as *Suryani* in Arabic, as well as the Armenians, Chaldeans, Anglicans and others. Homs boasted the second largest Christian community in Syria, after Aleppo. Overall, Christians accounted for around 12 per cent of the country's population.

The Orthodox Christians played an integral part in the social fabric of Homs and were especially influential in the town's principal industries of silk- and cotton-weaving, leather and tanning, and the distribution of these goods to the markets. Homsi handicrafts had traditionally been exported by land to central Anatolia and northern Iraq, and to Izmir and Istanbul by sea from the port at Tripoli, which was connected to Homs by a small rail line. But with the collapse of the Ottoman Empire, Homs was severed from its traditional markets, especially after the French had erected new and hostile customs barriers. Before World War One Homs had boasted nearly 4,000 small workshops, but by 1922 the number had shrunk to 1,000. Trade stagnated even further during the Great Depression, but the Orthodox community in Homs, unlike other religious minorities, was not dependent on links to foreign capital. Like the Muslim community, the Orthodox perceived French rule and European economic penetration of its markets as a direct threat, and took part in strikes during the 1930s after wages in Homs' textile industry were cut three times in three months. The Catholics on the other hand were closely allied to the French, and their missionaries worked very hard to recruit converts from among the Orthodox, often bribing them with economic privileges that were hard to come by any other way, like lucrative agencies for foreign imports. Their efforts were sometimes successful, and a number of Orthodox converted to Catholicism.

In the narrow alleys of the covered souk near the mosque entrance was the textile shop of Abu Chaker's father, next door to shops owned by Christian traders, all of whom were family friends. Nearby were the gold merchants, the spice merchants and the sweet sellers. The shop beside Abu Chaker's father's shop was owned by an Orthodox Christian, while the neighbour opposite was an Armenian, known as Abu Arshak. Abu Chaker's sons recall spending hours in Abu Arshak's shop, which sold furnishing fabric, while their father's shop sold menswear fabric. The two neighbours would leave a set of keys with each other, so that they could always cover for each other in the event of an emergency. If Abu Arshak's sales dipped, Abu Chaker would lend him money to tide him over till things improved. Abu Arshak's family later emigrated to Venezuela, where there is today quite a large community of Syrian Christians, as in Argentina and other parts of South America.

One of the most memorable stories about inter-communal relations which Abu Chaker's sons recall being told by their father concerned the villagers of a Syrian Orthodox village called Kafr Ram in Wadi al-Nasara (The Valley of the Christians) west of Homs. It is the highest of the Wadi al-Nasara villages, from which on a clear day the coast at Tartous can be seen to the east, along with Homs to the west and Tripoli to the south. For a few minutes every day, the rising moon in the east and setting sun in the west can be seen at the same time. Kafr Ram is famous for its fine-quality 'araq, a grape-based aniseed-flavoured spirit, made from the vineyards that surround the village. The community's proud residents were distraught when, in the late 1940s, Anglican missionaries started building a new stone church in their village, with money coming in on the back of the British army after World War Two. This Anglican church was much finer than the local Orthodox one, causing upset in the community. It provoked such extreme jealousy that when a young man from the Homsi Orthodox Elias family fell in love with a girl from Kafr Ram, her father told the hopeful suitor that he could only win his daughter's hand if he proved the strength of his commitment by blowing up the Anglican chuch—the young man duly did as instructed, and then married the girl, after first spending a few months in Safita prison.

In Homs the Chamsi-Pashas, like the other local urban notables, were keen to find ways of securing their position under their new French masters after the collapse of the Ottoman Empire at the end of World War One. Their primary concern was to maintain their wealth and protect their property and business interests, and so they developed considerable skills as mediators between regions, classes and ethnic alliances. They resented the presence of the French authorities as foreign rulers, but always avoided confrontation. If there were disturbances in the streets, the family would shut up the doors and wait for the unrest to subside, both at home and at the souk.

Christian school ran from Mondays to Fridays, and on Saturdays Abu Chaker was sent to a traditional Muslim religious school, a *kuttab*, where the local imam taught pupils the Qur'an by rote, as is customary in the tutelage of many Muslim children. When he first attended school, one of his older sisters would always accompany him—a curious reversal of the *mahram* or male guardian role. Abu Chaker's sister acted as his protector to see to it that no harm befell her little brother, though it would be she who would require a *mahram* once she reached puberty. The whole family wanted to ensure that, as the only son, Abu Chaker was always protected.

It was ironic, therefore, that despite their best efforts, Abu Chaker's family were ultimately powerless to protect him from tragedy. Without warning or previous illness, his father died suddenly of a presumed heart attack at the age of forty-five, and the young Abu Chaker woke up one morning beside his corpse. Aged ten, his comfortable life was turned upside down. Childhood ended and the small boy was abruptly catapulted into adulthood. As the only male, with a mother and seven unmarried sisters to support, Abu Chaker could no longer indulge in the unnecessary luxury of education; his uncle—his father's brother—put him to work in his father's now unmanned textile shop in the Homs souk, selling rolls of *joukh*, or broadcloth woven from fine wool, from which men's suits were made. The young boy had to toughen up fast. From having been a cosseted only son, Abu Chaker was now compelled to hold his own amongst the traders of the souk, and through the course of his teenage years he struggled to build what was to be the foundation of his future career as a textile merchant. These were the years that were to test and shape his character.

Though still only semi-literate, Abu Chaker was competent with numbers and was able to keep accounts and record sales and transactions. Luckily for him, all men at the time wore suits or full-length robes, *jalabias*, and so woven cloth was an essential commodity, not a luxury. Before the advent of jeans, light tweeds and flannels were tailored into garments worn by all men. When jeans arrived on the market, Abu Chaker's hatred of them was instant and passionate—this never changed, and all his future children and grandchildren were forbidden to wear them.

The year of his father's death, 1932, coincided with the worst drought Syria had suffered since World War One. It led to many catastrophic social consequences, including banditry in the countryside. People tried desperately to make ends meet as poor agricultural harvests forced the prices of basic foodstuffs up. Quite apart from natural disasters, the commercial climate under the French Mandate was an exceptionally turbulent one, with wild currency fluctuations. To protect against such unpredictable swings, Abu Chaker honed his skills in bartering and trading all sorts of commodities, prepared to try whatever he could to supplement the family income. He found that many people from the countryside, who needed to buy his fine worsted cloth to make the warm outer garments which would shield them from the harsh, sub-zero temperatures of Syrian winters, often did not have the money to pay him. In a system predicated on honesty and trust, he would allow them to pay for his goods later, in the summer or in the autumn once their harvests had come in.

As a consequence, he would often spend long periods away from the city of Homs at harvest times, collecting dues from farmers who had bought cloth from him on credit earlier in the year. Travelling on horseback he would make extensive tours of the rich agricultural land around Homs. He learnt to recognise the accents of the local villages, even to the point where, decades later, he astonished a Syrian officer at a checkpoint in Lebanon by correctly identifying the man's village from his accent alone, going on to recount the names of the key people in that village. Despite his lack of a formal education, or perhaps because of it, Abu Chaker's oral memory was a powerful tool.

The fertile soil of the Orontes valley guaranteed many crops, notably fruit and nut orchards. Abu Chaker often had to camp out alone, sleeping rough with just his horse for company at a time when wolves, polecats and even bears still roamed the countryside. His only protection was a stick, which he learnt to wield to great effect. Years later as an old man, he would still carry a stick on trips outside urban areas, "for dealing with hyenas," he would explain.

It was during these regular sorties into the countryside that he acquired a deep love and appreciation of the wonders of nature. He enjoyed observing the phases of the moon and the seasonal changes, how in springtime the hillsides would come alive with the pink and white blossom of apricot, cherry and apple trees, or the buds of pistachio, almond and walnut. Delicate wildflowers in yellows, reds and blues carpeted the fields or sprang up from nowhere in the semi-steppeland after rain. The sight was truly enchanting to behold. In her book *The Desert and The Sown* the British traveller Gertrude Bell, who journeyed extensively though Syria in the early 1900s, marvels at "the magic of the Syrian spring."

Abu Chaker retained this interest all his life, nurturing and tending the produce of his farm outside Homs. He never lost his connection to the land and to nature, and liked to sit quietly in his courtyard, inhaling the scent of jasmine, damask rose and citrus and absorbing the garden's tranquil beauty. He had a deep love of animals that was uncommon among Arabs, and kept deer, antelope and even a moose at his farm. "It was like this little zoo in the middle of nowhere in Homs," his eldest granddaughter later mused. Though the appreciation of flowers is a deep-seated Ottoman tradition—visible everywhere in floral-inspired tiles, paintings and the decorative patterns of carpets whose colourful borders recall the efflorescence of gardens—Syrians for the most part, and Arabs in general, do not have a pet-keeping culture. There is little sentimentality towards animals such as cats and dogs, which are primarily kept to meet a practical purpose. Animals are certainly not required to serve as companions, especially since the extended family system ensures that loneliness is never an issue. Caged birds like canaries may be kept in the home for their song, and a man may have a relationship of respect with his horse, his camel or his falcon, but that is usually the extent of it.

Abu Chaker, on the other hand, made a habit of looking after injured creatures, often birds whose wings had been damaged, and would nurse them until they recovered. His empathy for the defenceless, stemming perhaps from memories of his own vulnerability and the early loss of his father, compelled him to take on the responsibility of caring for all those in need. His sons recall the way their father had related the story of the death of a neighbour in the Homs souk. Abu Chaker had watched how his neighbour's young son had to open the family shop on his own, but had been so stirred by painful memories that he hadn't been able to look the boy in the eye. The enduring resonance of Abu Chaker's early experiences of adversity was reflected in his favourite Qur'anic chapter, *Al-Duha* (The Forenoon), which he would often recite:

> We call to witness the growing brightness of the day, and We call to witness the stillness of the night, that thy Lord has not forsaken thee, nor is He displeased with thee. Surely every succeeding hour is better for thee than the preceding one. Thy Lord will keep on bestowing His favours upon thee so that thou wilt be well pleased. Did he not find thee an orphan and give thee shelter? And find thee enamoured of thy

people and in search of guidance for them, and showed thee the right way for them? And find thee having numerous dependants and bestowed plenty on thee? Then oppress not the orphan and chide not him who asks, and keep proclaiming the bounty of thy Lord. (Qur'an 93)

The sudden death of Abu Chaker's father affected him profoundly in many ways, some of them surprising. His sons recall being amazed at the way in which he used to interact with child street vendors. If approached by a young boy eking out a living by selling packs of tissues on the streets, dodging between the cars paused at traffic lights in Beirut, their own inclination might be to overpay, sometimes even telling the boy to keep the product. Their father, in contrast, would only buy the tissues after a proper haggling session. He would chide his sons' behaviour, saying they were not being kind—quite the reverse, they were harming the boy by teaching him to expect easy money. Abu Chaker would also turn beggars away, sometimes quite dismissively, if he sensed that they were simply scrounging. His preference wherever possible was to help by giving people the means to help themselves, by employing them, for example, so they could have the dignity of work rather than become dependent on handouts. But to anyone who he was convinced needed it, he would always give generously.

From his experience of the chaotic French Mandate and wartime markets, Abu Chaker learnt first-hand about the destructive economic cycles of boom and bust. He learnt that at times of great uncertainty and instability it was often easier and better to do nothing, not to trade at all and simply to hold onto goods—rather like refraining from investment in a falling stock market and waiting for prices to rise. "Goods are better than money. Goods hold their value," he would tell his sons. It is a common view in the Islamic world that money in the form of cash can be a force for corrupting the social order. It is better for the community that value is tied to actual commodities, and much of Islamic law concerns itself with the rules for fair exchange, a system which reinforces trust between the parties involved.

War was something he never experienced first-hand as a soldier. Only sons are by Syrian law automatically exempt from military service, in recognition of the fact that they need to be the breadwinners for their families. Others could only escape it if their families paid the *badal* or substitute, a considerable sum of money beyond what most families could afford. There was therefore never any possibility, or indeed inclination on Abu Chaker's part, to get involved in military activity, let alone a military career. His entire upbringing was steeped in trade, not warfare, and the overwhelming instinct of his family was to preserve what they had, not to risk it all through challenging the political powers.

Nonetheless, he was exposed to military personnel because of the Homs Military Academy, which was set up on the outskirts of the city in 1933 by the French. Unlike some of his friends who had sought out useful commercial contacts at the Academy, Abu Chaker did not make a habit of befriending military men, be they French or Syrian, just as he never joined any political party. He did have links with a soldier from Hama, but purely because they had been old school friends. In one of the military coups of the late 1940s during which allegiances could switch overnight, this friend was thrown out of the army and left with no income and no pension. Abu Chaker gave him a salary for two years, until he was able to find work again and regain his independence.

There was one French officer, however, who was a regular client at his shop, and used to joke with him, picking up cloth samples and asking him, "C'est bon?"—"Is this OK?" Unable to speak French but knowing a few basic words, Abu Chaker would reply "Bon, bon," which always made the French officer double up with laughter. Only when the officer was leaving Homs at the end of his course did he tell Abu Chaker what "bonbon" meant in French and explain what had so amused him.

One of Abu Chaker's lifelong friends, with whom he had shared those early years in Homs, was Wasfi Tayara. When I met him in Sidon, Lebanon in late 2014, shortly before his death in 2015, Wasfi was a very frail old man, confined to his chair in his daughter's flat.

Though his body was weary his mind was still totally focused, and at the very mention of Abu Chaker's name his dim eyes lit up as he recalled his friend and the Homs of their childhood.

They had first become acquainted with each other as neighbours in the old cloth souk of Homs. As in all souks the products were grouped together so that all the textile merchants were clustered in the same street. Rather than setting them against each other as rivals, this had the effect of making them club together and look out for each other, so that merchants would even pass on customers to neighbouring shops that hadn't yet had any business that day.

Wasfi was born in 1927, making him five years younger than Abu Chaker. Like Abu Chaker he was educated by nuns of the Syrian Orthodox Church, in mixed schools during his early primary years and later at a single-sex high school, which Abu Chaker never had the chance to attend after the sudden death of his father. Wasfi never met Abu Chaker's mother or his sisters, since women did not play a role in the running of shops in the souk. When the two met, he was studying law at Damascus University, but used to help out at his family's shop during the holidays. Wasfi's family shop sold many types of material while Abu Chaker's shop only sold *joukh*, or broadcloth. As neighbours in the souk they would mind each other's shops when they each went separately to pray at the Al-Nouri Mosque nearby, often taking money for each other's goods if a customer came along and keeping it in a safe place till the other returned. "In Homs everyone went to pray, everyone, it was just normal," Wasfi explained. "But Abu Chaker was religious for himself, not for political reasons. He never took part in any protests or demonstrations, it was *tijara bas* (trade only)."

Wasfi described how Homs at that time was modest and quiet, with no extremely rich people. Muslim and Christian merchants worked happily side by side in the souk. "People were friendly, all the families knew each other." This neighbourhood sense of familiarity started to change in the 1950s with urban immigration, as people from the surrounding countryside moved into the city. Their customers were mainly middle class, though there were also many farmers who needed clothing but frequently lacked the cash. For them, Wasfi explained, Abu Chaker would take payment in kind, extending to them lines of credit until their harvests came in and they could sell their own produce. That was during the 1940s, he recalled, when Homs was still a simple and close-knit agricultural community, before its development into Syria's chief industrial city after Aleppo. "Society changed a lot."

Wasfi explained how difficult it was to run a business under the French Mandate. "Trade in Syria was very weak. Most trade was done through barter, to avoid the extreme currency fluctuations. There was no scope for improvement in such a climate." This lack of opportunity frustrated Abu Chaker, who always had a strong drive to succeed. Wasfi described him as energetic yet always straight in his dealings. "His ambition is what led him to expand into Beirut, where he became a big importer of British broadcloth (*joukh*). People wanted it because it was extremely hardwearing and weatherproof. The wool was so densely woven that it was more like felt, and could be cut without needing to be hemmed. It was beautiful, top quality from Bradford, designed to last."

Wasfi recalled how optimistic Abu Chaker had been, looking forward to the challenge of what lay ahead. "He had faith in the future." Yet in spite of that ambition, he never wanted to cut his links with Homs and with the shop that had been his childhood learning centre. He wanted to hold on to his origins, even though he never did more than make ends meet at the Homs shop. "He wanted it almost as a symbol, a constant reminder of his humble beginnings."

Wasfi's life was to change too, giving him another point of commonality with Abu Chaker. His own father died when he was just twenty years old. There was no university in Homs at that time, so his law studies in Damascus had to be abandoned, and he was obliged to go instead into business to support his family. Yet his life was to run a very different course to that of Abu Chaker—he was to spend all his life in Homs, and eventually became president of the

Homs Chamber of Commerce. One of his sons now lives and works in Birmingham, having first qualified as a doctor in Syria.

Wasfi was Abu Chaker's closest friend for over sixty-five years. Throughout that time, he said that Abu Chaker's character had never changed. Abu Chaker had been a taciturn man with a soft voice, who spoke little but always listened attentively to others and enjoyed laughing at their jokes. He never drank alcohol, and was religiously devout. Despite his ostensible shyness, he enjoyed having guests at the dinner table and was always generous in offering plentiful food. Though he did have a few political friends, he never got involved in politics himself and kept well away from all *ahzab* (political parties). Wasfi described Abu Chaker as *'isami* (noble due to merit, as opposed to *'izami,* noble-born), *sadiq* (genuine) and *karim* (generous, honourable and decent).

There was a sadness in Wasfi's eyes at the end of his reminiscences, born of a knowledge that such shared times would never return. His daughter showed him an Arabic book about Homs, bought in a Beirut bookshop the day before. When he saw its photos of the souk bombed and burnt out, tears began to run down his pallid cheeks. "That was my souk," he said softly, his voice broken.

5

THE FRENCH MANDATE
AND THE GREAT SYRIAN REVOLT

When a ruler is just, everyone wants to be in his army.

(Persian proverb)

As the Ottoman Empire disintegrated, Syrian society was undergoing a period of major transformation. The first of these had been the emergence of the new elite, as the powerful military *aghas* and the old notable families began to intermarry for the first time to their mutual benefit. But much greater changes were to come. The new elite considered a military career beneath their dignity and went to great lengths to secure exemptions from military service for their sons, whom they sent to public administration schools in Istanbul, not to military academies. This disdain towards the military was to be their downfall. Up till that point their position had faced no serious challenge from lower down the social hierarchy, and had seemed insulated from the restless classes below.

Societal changes were then accelerated by the Ottoman government's ill-judged decision to enter World War One on the side of Germany and the Central Powers. The economic and political turmoil brought on by the war interrupted such progress as there was and resulted in misery and suffering for all sides. Christians were suspected by the Ottoman authorities of pro-French sympathies, while Syrian Muslims were suspected of pro-Arab leanings. Both groups were viewed with suspicion as non-Turkish, and their leaders were either exiled or hanged. Contemporary reports estimated that during World War One a quarter of the Syrian population perished through poverty, disease or famine.

Life in the cities of the interior was especially tough. The Ottoman government was in its financial death throes even before the war, with the Thomas Cook Handbook of 1911 advising travellers "not to carry Turkish money, as it is rather difficult to understand and its value varies in different parts of the country." Widows, orphans and pensioners were frequently denied part or even all of their stipends. When they were paid, it was in depreciated Ottoman paper currency which was almost worthless. Flour rationing led to malnutrition which in turn led to epidemics of dysentery, typhus, smallpox, diphtheria, malaria and cholera. The Damascus press reported rising rates of suicide, crime and homelessness. By the middle of the war, gangs of deserters from the Ottoman army were pillaging the villages and destroying local trade, in turn triggering waves of rural refugees seeking safety in the cities. Urban overcrowding then boosted housing prices in the city centres, and exploitative landlords grew rich.

Prices for all basic commodities rose, while certain essentials like coffee, sugar and rice virtually disappeared from the market. The Ottoman Fourth Army which had its headquarters in Damascus impounded all farm animals for its own use. These human-led catastrophes were then followed by a series of natural disasters: a devastating drought and a plague of locusts in 1915, and a heatwave that reduced harvests in 1916. By 1917 the Ottoman paper currency had plunged to 25 per cent of its face value, so farmers in the Hawran region south of Damascus refused to sell their wheat for anything but gold. By 1918 the paper currency had crashed to just 14 per cent of its face value, and merchants, threatened by harsh Ottoman tax penalties, resorted to straightforward barter transactions to avoid losing more money.

The consequences for the poor were calamitous, yet on the notable classes the effects were mixed. Some were caught as speculators, political criminals or deserters and were arrested or sent into exile with their property confiscated. Others managed to grow rich from speculation, smuggling and selling supplies to the Ottoman army, since they were able to pay the right bribes and manipulate contacts within the Ottoman administration.

Throughout their four centuries of rule, the Ottomans had never drawn an actual territorial border for Syria, but since the sixteenth century had administered it in a number of divisions called *vilayets*. Sometimes the area was known simply as "Natural Syria", since it fell within the natural geographical boundaries of the coasts of Aqaba and Sinai to the south, the Taurus Mountains to the north, the Syrian desert to the east and the Mediterranean to the west. Today this same area encompasses modern Syria, Lebanon, Jordan, Palestine, Israel and even parts of southeast Turkey.

The British and French, who would emerge as the Allied victors in the war, were quick to divide the Middle East according to their respective national interests. By 1916 they had negotiatied the secret Sykes-Picot agreement to carve up the Ottoman Empire between them, drawing now infamous "lines in the sand"—thinly disguised colonies masquerading as mandates. Proxy rule through carefully chosen monarchs was the easiest and most expedient option, and securing strategic and economic interests was the primary concern. Britain wanted to safeguard its route to India and ensure access to cheap oil for its empire, insisting that the oil-rich Mosul area be included in its Iraq mandate. France was more interested in Syria and Lebanon because it sought to secure a strategic and economic base in the eastern Mediterranean and to guarantee a cheap supply of cotton and silk. From a political standpoint, France also wanted to prevent Arab nationalism from spreading to its North African colonies, and to retain its long-held connections with Lebanon's Maronite Catholics and Syria's Melkite Catholics.

The United States on the other hand, in its first foray into the region, had somewhat sounder intentions. In June 1919 President Woodrow Wilson sent the Inter-Allied Commission (also known as the King-Crane Commission) to Greater Syria to "elucidate the state of opinion and the soil to be worked on by any mandatory"—in other words, to take soundings of local opinion as to what residents wanted for the future of their country. The Commission visited over thirty-six major cities from Beersheba to Aleppo, met over 2,000 delegations from over 300 villages and accepted over 3,000 petitions from local people. Their conclusions were that the population overwhelmingly rejected the proposed French Mandate, as well as the British Balfour Declaration announcing support for the establishment of a Jewish homeland in Palestine. What locals wanted was a unified Greater Syria with Palestine incorporated. But the results of the Commission, deliberately not published till 1922, were rejected by France and ignored by Britain.

Before World War One Lebanon had been part of Greater Syria, and had always acted as Syria's route to the outside world. It was vital for its port cities—Beirut, Tripoli and Sidon—and while neither Lattakia nor Tartous, Syria's major ports today, had natural harbours, the Lebanese had inherited the seafaring inclinations of their Phoenician ancestors and sought to head out across the Mediterranean and beyond.

Emigration from the region to the Americas was encouraged from the late nineteenth century onwards and by World War One about half a million Syrians, mainly farming peasants, had travelled to North America and over a million to South America. A Brazilian leader had made two trips to the region, in 1877 and 1887, looking for farmers to develop Brazil's huge untapped agricultural potential, and had struck a deal with the Ottoman government under which the Syrian peasants were given free passage to Brazil. There were numerous reasons why rural villagers were willing to leave their homeland, including to escape heavy Ottoman taxes, landlord exploitation and neglect. Sometimes they left because their own crops had fallen victim to plant diseases or been eaten by plagues of locusts, and sometimes it was because of the dissolution of traditional trade routes, such as followed the construction of the Suez Canal in 1860. Those in the textile business were particularly badly hit by the collapse of natural silk production after Japan started making synthetic products that mimicked silk. Life in the Americas, by contrast, held the promise of freedom, citizen equality, full employment, prosperity and the rule of law, though it became harder to emigrate by the 1920s after North America introduced much stricter immigration rules. The first Syrian emigrants formed strong communities in Boston and had an intense loyalty to each other, treating friends as if they were family members. They were poor and usually illiterate, but brought with them their craft skills, music, cuisine, clothes and culture of hospitality. Even though some have now adopted other nationalities, especially US nationality, a great many continue to send remittances back home to help their families and to support philanthropic and educational enterprises. Their educational aspirations were transformed in their new countries, and in this way they often contributed hugely to the modernisation of their homeland, directly accelerating the urge for self-rule under democratic processes.

In March 1920 the predominantly conservative elected Syrian National Congress, the first national parliament in the history of modern Syria, headed by Hashim al-Atassi and including representatives from Lebanon and Palestine, rejected the French overtures and declared the independence of the Arab Kingdom of Syria "in her natural borders", including southern Syria, as Palestine was known. Emir Faisal, a descendant of the Hashemite family of Mecca, was installed in Damascus and proclaimed king of Greater Syria. This was part of the campaign against the Ottoman Empire led by the British, who had first encouraged the Arab Revolt against the Ottomans that ended in 1918. The promised aims of the revolt, which took place under the direction of Faisal and British intelligence officer T.E. Lawrence, were to secure Arab independence, but once the Ottomans had been overthrown, it became clear that France and Britain had other ideas. In April 1920 the Supreme

Inter-Allied Council went ahead with their division of the territory into British and French mandates. The Syrians reacted with violent demonstrations and elected a new government on 9 May. They decided to bring in conscription and form an army to defend themselves against French imperialism. Faisal declared to the King-Crane Commission that "French rule would mean certain death to Syrians as a distinguished people."

In his brief few months as king of Syria, Faisal tried hard to win popular approval. His government restarted the welfare programs the Ottomans had suspended during the war, and resumed payment of pensions to war widows, orphans and former Ottoman civil servants. It attempted to maintain stability of prices and to prevent food shortages by buying grain directly from the merchants in the Hawran area. Local committees were set up to oversee the distribution of foodstuffs, providing seed to impoverished farmers and dispensing grain from captured granaries to the urban poor. In one of the earliest recorded instances of the use of the media for propaganda purposes in this part of the world, Faisal's government made sure that whenever delegations of high-ranking officials would visit quarters of the cities and the countryside handing out gifts, they would be accompanied by journalists and even poets, who had been commissioned to write paeans to Faisal for his largesse.

In Homs a general amnesty was announced for criminals, honours were awarded to local big-wigs, and money was dealt out for the settlement of Syrian soldiers returning home from Anatolia where they had been fighting as part of the Ottoman army. In Hama and Aleppo farmers' debts were forgiven, local charities were given donations, seed was supplied to local villagers and public works were commissioned. Whenever adulterated flour was found after inspection of bakeries, or short weights were exposed, those responsible were publicly arrested. Sometimes Faisal himself would make such tours, always heavily publicised by his media.

Much of the money being distributed came from the subsidy the British were paying the new Arab government, and whilst the British officials did not object to it being used to help the poor in this way, they did object to it being used to buy the loyalty of the wealthy and powerful. Tribal leaders, politicians, religious leaders and journalists were paid off, the exact sums dutifully recorded in the records of the financial adviser: 100 Egyptian pounds to the grand rabbi of Damascus; 25,000 Egyptian pounds for propaganda work in Beirut; 1,500 Egyptian pounds to the Orthodox Church in Damascus. They were listed as "Donations" or "Extraordinary Expenditures", often paid to journalists and newspaper proprietors. Sometimes such payments totalled 10 per cent of the entire government revenue.

The size of these payments reflected the level of mistrust the notables felt towards the new government, which they perceived to be full of upstarts and foreigners. Their local interests often clashed with those of the government as it attempted to impose centralisation policies, and they were jealous of the attention showered on the capital city. Government relations with Aleppo's notables were particularly bad, since the latter had not supported the Arab Revolt and resented what they saw as interference in their foreign policy and trading habits. A group of Aleppan notables had even demanded autonomy for their city and its surrounding countryside when they arrived in Damascus in the spring of 1920 during Faisal's coronation celebrations.

All the Arab government's efforts to win over the population were in vain. Permanently short of funds, they attempted to increase taxes and fees on earnings, on the use of roads, on real estate, sheep and the proceedings of the courts of justice by up to 50 per cent. New taxes were levied on matches, cigarettes and playing cards, and the *badal* fee (paid in lieu of military service) was likewise raised.

But life for the fledging state was unsettled from the start. The turbulent aftermath of World War One had left the young Syrian Arab government facing total insolvency. With trade between Damascus, Aleppo, Homs and their hinterlands virtually at a standstill, commerce collapsed, thanks to a combination of the huge currency fluctuations, an 11 per cent customs duty imposed on all exports to Mesopotamia and Turkey, and, as the final straw, the Bedouin raids conducted against all merchandise on the move.

Such raids had long been a way of life among the nomadic tribes, but the new government could no longer afford to pay them the bribe money which had previously curbed their activities. Gertrude Bell, who was employed as a political officer and spy for the British government, lamented the government's inability to control the Bedouin, even commenting that Nuri, the main Bedouin chief, sometimes seemed to be more in charge than King Faisal himself. "Nuri took toll of all merchandise going out and coming in and even levied tolls on the donkey loads in the streets."

Robbery, kidnapping and extortion were rife and the economic crisis touched Syrians of all classes. Hardest hit were merchants across the range, from large to small-scale retailers. Faisal's government attempted to regulate matters, setting up a Ministry of Supply which strove to fix prices and break the practices of speculators and hoarders. None of their measures proved to be enforceable and the merchants simply resorted to smuggling, underground cartels and other illegal activities to evade the new rules.

Real panic set in among the merchants when rumours spread that the French were planning to impose a new currency, the Syrian pound, *la livre syrienne*, in the coastal areas under their control. This presented the merchants with a crisis, because if the Arab government refused to authorise the use of the Syrian pound within inland Syria, all their trade with the coastal cities would collapse. It also became clear that the new currency would be linked to the notoriously unstable French franc, whose value had been steadily depreciating since the November 1917 armistice.

Government employees suffered as they were obliged to subsist on fixed salaries at a time of high inflation. Salaries were often late or even withheld altogether. Military personnel fared even worse, and soldiers whose pay had been reduced by 75 per cent could be found in the souks selling their equipment and uniform to buy food. Many deserted or mutinied.

The crisis meant that the government in all the cities was no longer even able to provide fresh drinking water, public lighting or basic sanitation. Gertrude Bell recorded that the cities were "many degrees dirtier" than they had been in Turkish times. "The bazaars were littered with vegetable and other refuse and secluded corners were no better than receptacles for filth of all descriptions."

Gun battles between armed gangs and police broke out frequently on the streets of the cities. Most people did not venture out after dark, and if they did, they made sure they went carrying arms. The main cities of Aleppo, Hama, Homs and Damascus were all linked on the railway, but security was so bad on board the trains that people could only travel if heavily armed, with robbery, hijacking, brigandage and extortion all commonplace. The increase in violence was so alarming that Muslim notables in Damascus met with their Christian and Jewish counterparts to raise a petition demanding the construction of police posts in strategic locations. In Aleppo the American consul said that "families absent from their homes but a few hours return to find them pillaged even in the daytime."

The already severe overcrowding in the cities was then exacerbated by an influx of refugees from Anatolia and the Beqaa Valley in Lebanon. The first wave came after the war: 21,000 of them were soldiers demobilised from the Ottoman army, together with Arab war refugees, but many more were Armenians still fleeing the 1915 genocide against them in Turkey. Aleppo took in 70,000 of these displaced Armenians, while Damascus took in approximately 35,000 and Homs and the surrounding villages took in 20,000. Most arrived with little or nothing by way of possessions. In the centre of Homs a British report counted 2,000 destitute Armenian refugees. Many of them depended on charity provided by the British army and Faisal's government. Even while the government was facing insolvency it was spending 45,000 Egyptian pounds on Armenian relief. In Aleppo a British-run soup kitchen fed up to 1,500 people daily and more than 8,000 Armenians in the city received other forms of assistance. A British-run orphanage housed almost 2,000 Armenian children, while more than 4,000 Armenians lived in barracks housing.

The second wave of refugees, mainly Syrian Arabs, began arriving in Syrian cities in 1919. The collapse of rural security had made village life precarious, so most had decamped from the Syrian countryside. Bedouin tribesmen followed age-old patterns, pillaging defenceless villages and settling old feuds, knowing full well that the weakened government authority was powerless to curb them. These opportunistic raiders were a mix of Circassians and men from the 'Anaza, Banu Sakhr, Shammar, Haddaydin and al-Mawali tribes.

Deserters from the Arab army teamed up with local brigands and sent thousands more fleeing to the cities for safety. The Beqaa Valley was disputed between the French and Faisal's government, leading to further inter-communal and inter-village animosities. Villagers who had the misfortune to live in border areas found themselves caught between the French army and Syrian nationalist guerrillas. In response to guerrilla raids, the French bombarded the valley using tanks, artillery and fighter bombers. One such French reprisal raid in 1920 left 20,000 homeless.

The previous Ottoman government had collected all the taxes for the year in advance even before the Anglo-Arab army arrived in Damascus in September 1918, so the population was already utterly impoverished. The British found government accountants to be "very incapable" and "deplorably behind". Many were dismissed for corruption.

In response to the general chaos, the working population tried to protest in the only way they knew how, by going on strike. In Damascus, railroad workers, printers, tram workers, glass and textile workers, electrical employees and other independent artisans demanded higher wages. Bread riots erupted in spring 1920, with rioters in Hama chanting: "You offer grain to France while we starve." They demanded the government reduce the price of flour, ban grain export to the western coast and break up the big monopolies. In Aleppo local rioters attacked the Armenian refugee community, leaving forty-eight dead and up to 200 injured. In spite of Aleppo's reputation for cosmopolitanism, the influx of refugees led to high rates of unemployment and overcrowding, with Aleppans resenting the special treatment given to the refugees. The local population also feared the competition—one refugee camp alone housed 4,000 looms, rivals to their own textile production.

The single most unpopular programme introduced by the short-lived Faisal government was conscription, which began in December 1919 and was further expanded and strengthened in May and June 1920. The draft was met with both individual and collective resistance. Enterprising young men forged their birth documents to prove they were not old enough to be drafted. Others fled their towns, or even the country. So common was draft evasion that Faisal's government banned the emigration of young men of draftable age. Those that were forcibly conscripted simply deserted as soon as they could in droves. Desertion in fact reached such high levels that even Faisal commented that the numbers deserting often outnumbered those enlisting.

By July, after just four months of the new government, the treasury was empty. King Faisal was given an ultimatum by France: submit to French authority, or face military invasion. Faisal was described by a contemporary Western observer as a man "pleasing of manner and countenance, liberal-minded and kindly disposed to all parties. But he is not a strong man and is surrounded by clever, shrewd and unscrupulous politicians, who can easily influence him." Realising his new army had no chance, he and his cabinet decided to cooperate and cede to the French. But Faisal's young and idealistic minister of war, General Yusuf al-'Azma, was staunchly opposed to surrender and instead set off with his troops in honourable defiance, even though he knew his odds were hopeless. He marched out from Damascus at the head of the Syrian army to meet the French forces at Maysaloun, 25 kilometres to the west, where they clashed on 24 July 1920. The French numbered 12,000, mostly Senegalese and Algerian mercenaries backed by tanks and aircraft. They had chosen to capture Khan Maysaloun, an isolated caravanserai on the crest of a pass in the Anti-Lebanon range, because of its abundant water sources and its proximity to the Hijaz Railway.

The Syrian army of regulars, civilian volunteers and Bedouin camel cavalry numbered around 2,500 and was wiped out within hours. The civilian militiamen had been assembled and led by a Damascene merchant and a former imam of the Umayyad Mosque, as well as many other Muslim scholars and preachers. They had no military experience and no proper weaponry. For them it was like a national "jihad" against the infidel invader, a matter of honour. Over 1,500 Syrians were wounded and 150 killed, their leader Yusuf al-'Azma among them, while French casualties were just forty-two killed and 152 wounded. Surviving Syrian fighters were bombed from the air as they attempted to retreat towards Damascus. The French general then marched on into the heart of Damascus, going straight to Saladin's tomb to announce: "Saladin, we have returned." He encountered little resistance.

The day before the Battle of Maysaloun, French forces had taken Aleppo without a fight. Faisal tried to resist by heading south to the Hawran, where he enlisted the allegiance of local tribal leaders, but the French sent an ultimatum to the tribal leaders telling them to expel Faisal or face bombardment of their camps. On 1 August Faisal headed west to Haifa in British-mandated Palestine to avoid further bloodshed, and with his departure came the end of his aim to establish an Arab-ruled Kingdom of Syria. The British, feeling he would make a good ruler because "he had learned the limits of Arab nationalism and of Europe's superior strength," later appointed him king of their mandated territory of Iraq, where he ruled for twelve years until his death in 1933. As for Yusuf al-'Azma, a statue of him stands to this day in the heart of the Damascus commercial district in Yusuf al-'Azma Square, a perennial symbol of the brave defiance of this countryman who died defending Syria's independence. He was of Kurdish ethnicity, as was another famous warrior claimed by the Arabs, Saladin.

"Tell the Pope," the headlines of the local patriotic press had run, "the clericalists, the capitalists, and the politicians who aim at conquest, that young Syria will never submit to old France." Yet in the event young Syria had no choice, and after the occupation of Damascus the French prime minister declared that Syria would be held by France: "The whole of it, and forever." The net effect of this apparently endless succession of crises that had overwhelmed the country was that it was near impossible to govern. Although Faisal's Arab government had declared its independence in March 1920, the Entente powers had refused to recognise it, and two months later at the San Remo Conference they awarded France the mandate for Syria.

The brief experiment in Arab rule was over. France's mandate over Syria had begun, a twenty-six-year period which was one of Syria's darkest hours, putting in place many elements of today's security state. Explaining these developments and their aftermath, contemporary Syrian journalist As'ad Daghir wrote in his memoirs:

> In truth the politics which followed in Syria was strange, inasmuch as the intellectuals, the leaders of public opinion, and the men of government themselves stirred up, by all means possible, the excitement of the people and pushed it to the extreme. Then, all of a sudden, they retreated before the slightest obstacle which blocked their way. They abandoned the people, who were perplexed, not knowing how to explain their position. On the one hand, they pressed for preparations to resist the French, and urged the population to resist by blocking their communications and setting up obstacles in their path. On the other hand, some of them adopted a policy of flattery and flexibility, and promised the French government that they would direct the country on a path which they had incited the country to oppose.
>
> This created a situation of enormous turmoil and squandered the faith which the people had placed in their leaders. It made them openly accuse some of them of treachery so that gradually their trust was dissolved. The leaders to whom the people had entrusted the reins of government were not able to lead after the confidence of the people was torn away from them and they were scoffed at.

The centuries-long relative quiet of the Ottoman provinces in the Middle East had now been shattered by the intervention of Britain and France after World War One, and the creation of their respective mandates. Syria, Lebanon, Iraq and Palestine were about to become some of the most unstable and explosive states in the world. In theory the mandate system was a "provisional arrangement of unspecified length", initially expected to last a mere three years. No one imagined that the mandate would persist for twenty-six years in the case of Syria, twenty-three in Lebanon. In practice, it was no more than a convenient guise for French imperialism, designed and repackaged to look like a form of self-determination. The aims were purportedly to guide the less advanced state towards full independence, to tutor it in the modern methods of self-government, in what was termed a "sacred trust of civilisation."

Once the mandate was in place, the French set about arbitrarily dividing the population, determined to prevent nationalist sentiment from developing and causing trouble. The French language became compulsory in schools, and pupils were required to sing "La Marseillaise". They established a facade of indigenous administration, behind which the French themselves had full control over what they called "la Syrie Intégrale". They partitioned Syria into four regions, each ruled by a local governor supported by a French adviser. The largest was the central state of Syria with the main towns of Damascus, Homs, Hama and Aleppo. Then there was the mountainous Druze area in the south whose capital was Suwayda; the 'Alawi State on the coast and mountainous hinterland with its 80 per cent 'Alawi population and Lattakia as the chief town; and finally the Sanjak of Alexandretta in the northwest, which had a significant Turkish population and its own largely autonomous administration.

Before the imposition of the mandate, Syrian Arabs at all levels of society were largely ignorant of the deals that had been struck thousands of miles away to apportion their land in European interests, establishing a Jewish homeland in Palestine and a French domain in Lebanon. Much of Aleppo's hinterland as far as Gaziantep and Urfa was lost in France's concessions to Turkey, leaving Aleppo constricted in the north and northeast by new international borders. Aleppo felt it would have been better off as part of the new Turkey since it had in many ways enjoyed closer relations with Istanbul than with the rest of Syria. From the Syrian point of view it seemed as if the defeated Turks had actually emerged from the war as victors and been rewarded with extra territory at Syria's expense.

France's mandate was ostensibly granted in recognition of its special relationship with Syria, when in actual fact the French had maintained minimal interests in the region since the Crusades. They came to Syria with hardly any understanding of the complexities of its society, having established links almost exclusively with the Catholic communities, though even in cities like Aleppo, the Muslim population was well over 60 per cent. Such facts were ignored. The French attempted to divide and rule through their maladroit partitioning, failing to see that their own heavy hand and the fact that they so clearly put Arab interests last would ultimately lead to the rise of a Syrian and Arab nationalist sentiment that had barely existed before 1920.

Under the French administration, Catholic missionaries became increasingly active. The Capuchin Order established over a dozen centres between Tyre and Aleppo, the Jesuits set up a series of European-style schools and the American Protestants founded primary and secondary schools for boys and girls in cities like Beirut, Tripoli, Sidon, Zahleh and even in the mountain villages. These schools became permanent features of the social fabric and were increasingly attended by Muslim pupils. By 1950 most rural centres had schools, though they were mostly for boys, not girls.

Very slowly the family structure that had dominated Syrian society for so many centuries, across all religious groups, changed under these new influences. The endogamous framework of marrying within the tribe or family was gradually challenged. Poor living conditions were no longer simply accepted as "the will of God". Marriage between cousins, which had long been practised by both Muslims and Christians as a way of keeping family property under the grandfather's control, became less and less common.

A new class was born in Syrian society, a class made up of modern businessmen, lawyers, doctors, teachers and other professionals, who slowly inched their way into the middle of the social hierarchy between the two traditional groups. At the top there were still the privileged landowners, or officeholders in the government or church; at the bottom were the underprivileged manual labourers and farmers. The new middle class grew, gradually acquiring more economic and social control.

The French authorities also set about controlling the tribal elements in Syrian society. From the 1930s onwards, they began to pay subsidies to tribal leaders in the eastern desert, and allotted grazing and property rights to tribes that pledged allegiance, forcing others to pay taxes. It was the beginning of the end of tribal influence in the country. The Hassana tribe, for example, which was based in central Syria near Homs, had long been revered on account of its genealogy linking it to the Al Saud ruling family of Saudi Arabia. The French granted the Hassana tribe large tracts of territory and registered the land to the head of the tribe, Shaikh Trad al-Milhem. While individual peasants could not afford registration and the extra taxation it would incur, the Hassana shaikh was able to acquire land from the French and ratcheted up over twenty villages in his name. But with no accompanying political authority, he became dependent on the French for the enforcement of these new property rights.

When French troops first entered Syria in 1920 the monetary and fiscal state of affairs in the country was already dire. A variety of coins and paper money was in circulation. Many Syrians continued to use Ottoman and foreign coins, their values based entirely on their metallic content, since the currency itself, backed by the worthless German mark and issued by a government that no longer existed, had become obsolete. The British General Allenby had tried to impose the use of the sterling-backed Egyptian pound as legal tender, but it was in short supply as a guard against inflation, and many Syrians encountered difficulties when trying to convert from one monetary system to another. Relative currency values fluctuated wildly, often in response to decisions taken in London, Paris, Istanbul and even Baghdad. When the British administration in Iraq declared Turkish silver and nickel coinage illegal, it led to an abrupt depreciation when the coins flooded the market in Damascus. The Turkish silver *mejidi* in particular was often used to pay wages, but had now been rendered almost worthless. Small wonder in such times of political turbulence that people learnt to dispense with money wherever possible and rely instead on sensible barter arrangements for the necessities of life. Their very survival was at stake.

There were intermittent revolts against the French all over the country, but by 1925 the resentment of the local Syrians towards their unwanted rulers boiled over into what was at that time the largest, longest and most destructive uprising in the Arab Middle East—the Great Syrian Revolt. The French Mandate authorities had presumed, after five years of their military rule, that their occupation and pacification of Syria was complete, yet their policies of deliberately creating separate "statelets" for different religious and ethnic groups, in a blatant "divide and rule" policy designed to weaken any opposition, completely backfired and instead inadvertently united people from the different regions, awakening a feeling of common "Syrianness" in opposition to the unpopular foreigners in charge. By separating the countryside from the cities of Damascus, Aleppo, Hama and Homs, the French authorities had made the assumption that an opposition power base against them could never form. They were wrong, and what is more, the revolt began where they least expected it, in the remote Jebel al-Druze countryside, from where it spread to Damascus and the cities. Syrians had watched with admiration and amazement as Mustafa Kemal Atatürk, an ex-officer in the Ottoman army, had led Turkish troops and succeeded in expelling the European would-be occupiers in order to become an independent Turkish state. As with that Turkish uprising, the Great Syrian Revolt was a mass movement, but the French never understood the relationships that connected Syria's various regions, classes and sectarian groups. They thought of all rural society in Syria as feudal, with deep class divides. Instead, broad coalitions of Syrians joined together to resist France, their shared colonial enemy.

The leaders of the Great Syrian Revolt were not from the great landowning families, but from the rural shaikhs, demobbed ex-Ottoman military officers, and headmen from both the villages and the city quarters. It was the first spontaneous welling up of Syrian nationalist sentiment, the first breakdown of the previous elite where the notable families had dominated. For over two years a motley collection of farmers, city tradesmen and workers, and junior ex-officers from both the Ottoman and the Arab armies, challenged and often defeated the colonial army of one of the most powerful countries of the world. The traditional notables distanced themselves, focusing instead on ensuring the security of their property. It was the harbinger of much bigger changes in Syrian society to come.

The main trigger for the revolt was the same as it had been throughout the nineteenth century under the Ottomans, namely the exploitation of the agricultural surplus, chiefly of wheat grain, which was used to make bread, an essential staple. The main breadbasket of Syria had since Roman times been in the southern Hawran, its volcanic soil perfectly suited to providing abundant harvests. This area was largely settled by the Druze, migrants from a minority sect who had been based in the mountains of Lebanon. Druze farmers had made contacts with the emerging class of grain merchants from the Damascene suburb of Midan, 10 kilometres south of the city centre. Midan is known today for its Shi'a shrine of Sayyida Zainab, daughter of Fatima and 'Ali and granddaughter of the Prophet Mohammad, built in 1990 by the Iranians, and around which a considerable Shi'a community has since settled.

Grain production in the 1920s was based on contractual agreements made between these Damascene merchants and the village leaders in the south, but the large notable landowning families were mainly excluded from such deals. The Midan merchants were very rarely from landowning families, and neither were the village leaders. A pattern had therefore emerged in that the grain merchants of Midan were often in alliances with the rebellious rural areas. In contrast, the powerful notables tended to be aligned first with the Ottoman state, then the French mandatory authorities, since they shared the mindset of seeking to profit from the agricultural surplus.

A destructive late spring frost coupled with a long summer drought further catalysed the revolt. Instead of reducing taxes, as the

Ottomans before them had done whenever the weather conspired to create poor harvests, the French nearly doubled land taxes to protect the Treasury from the collapse of the French franc. They dispensed with the Ottoman tax farming system which had long favoured the absentee city landlords, who had in any event generally bribed the tax assessors and bought off judges to ensure a smoothing of their finances. The French then conducted a cadastral survey and set up a more equitable taxation system designed to protect smaller landowners, less out of any social conscience than to try to break the power of the urban notables. "All along," as Philip Khoury, a key historian of the French Mandate, explains, "the French played the countryside against the city, by promoting rural notables and village *mukhtars* against city-based landlords." Many landless peasants joined the revolt thinking that the land of the urban notables might be confiscated and redistributed to them. Others joined because, as young unemployed men with nothing to lose, it was a way of expressing their anger and frustration at the socio-economic inequities of the time—the same reason many young men joined the recent Syrian uprising against the Assad regime.

The reward of the rebel upstarts for their impertinence, then as now, was to be violently crushed. The French initiated what they called *opérations de nettoyage* (cleansing operations) in areas like the Ghouta Oasis, east of Damascus, where—like today—many of the rebels came from. They had difficulty dislodging the dissidents as the terrain of orchards of olive, apricot and walnut trees gave the rebels perfect cover for sniper fire against the linear columns of marching French soldiers, who were only accustomed to fighting in open ground. To protect themselves they sealed off central Damascus with a 12-kilometre impenetrable "iron barrier" of barbed wire fences and machine-gun posts, completed by February 1926. The French military governor of Damascus observed that there were thousands of unemployed men in Damascus and that "it was not good to leave them in their indolence when they could be used for works which would 'sanitise' the city for the benefit of the whole population."

The French brought in foreign mercenaries from their colonies to unleash a period of unprecedented brutality on the citizens they were supposed to protect. They used collective punishment of whole towns, demolishing entire villages for harbouring rebels and holding mass executions in public squares, the plundered loot then sold openly in the souks. They flattened houses, drove tanks into urban areas, ordered round-the-clock aerial and artillery bombardment of civilian populations and even enforced wholesale population transfers from region to region. Thousands were killed, and hundreds of the rebel leaders were sent into exile.

While this kind of state violence has since become the norm in the Middle East, it was the government of Syria's French Mandate in the 1920s that paved the way by first using such tactics. Never before had such methods of repression, mechanised warfare and aerial bombardment been unleashed on civilians to this extent, let alone by a government whose duty under the terms of the Mandate was supposed to be to advance the interests, development and welfare of the mandated population. But altruism was never the motivation behind the French Mandate. The French made little attempt to train local officials, fearing that any cohesion of the Syrian state might be a threat and a dangerous influence on their French North African colonies. They courted potentially Francophile minorities like the Christians at the expense of the majority Muslim population.

Reporting their damming verdict on the behaviour of the French in Syria, even the League of Nations stated in 1926:

> The Commission thinks it beyond doubt that these oscillations in matters so calculated to encourage the controversies inspired by the rivalries of races, clans and religions, which are so keen in this country, to arouse all kinds of ambitions and to jeopardize serious moral and material interests, have maintained a condition of instability and unrest in the mandated territory.

But the brutality had worked and the revolt was crushed into submission. In its aftermath a huge internal security apparatus was established that would become an enduring feature for the rest of the mandate and beyond, into the post-independence government.

Syria today still lives with the consequences of that French legacy. The French authorities and the Syrian elites recognised their common interests, namely the preservation of the civil order and social system inherited from Ottoman times. They joined forces to ensure the system was not destabilised again and that their interests could never be re-threatened in such a way by a popular revolt.

Rebels who survived the Great Syrian Revolt gradually returned to their devastated homes, their hopes crushed. For decades only the French version of events was circulated, but more recent research by Arab scholars has unearthed many contemporary accounts from the Arab press. Despite censorship and frequent closures, it emerged that Damascus and other cities enjoyed a far livelier press back in 1925 than today's Syria. The largest Syrian daily *Al-Muqtabas* was so stridently nationalist that the French authorities shut it down and jailed its editor twice. Some of the newspapers were completely subsidised by the French Mandate High Commission, but even those were sometimes closed. The French also encouraged anti-British editorials in both the Syrian and Lebanese press, just as the British encouraged anti-French editorials in the Egyptian, Palestinian and Transjordanian press. Over a hundred years ago, the propaganda wars familiar to our age of "fake news" were alive and thriving.

One of the leaders of the revolt, Fawzi al-Qawuqji, a former Ottoman army officer born in modest circumstances in Lebanon's Tripoli, later wrote about the failure of the Great Syrian Revolt, blaming the vanities of the rebel chiefs:

> The best among us were the ordinary class of people. All our calamities and defeats were due to the ambitions and rivalries of our leaders, who were concerned only with showing off and with their love of display. I saw that the true revolt against the imperialists should be based only on the ordinary and honest classes of the people.

The stage was set for the future history of Syria—struggles for dominance between the new classes of modest origin and the old landed elites, who not only colluded with the political masters of the day but also took part in government.

6

MARRIAGE, DIVORCE AND REMARRIAGE

Man is a river; woman is a lake.

(Kurdish proverb)

After his father's sudden death, Abu Chaker had worked incessantly, trying to maximise the income from the family textile shop in Homs to support his mother and sisters. For twenty years, until he was thirty years old, he struggled to grow the business and steer it through the economic upheavals of the unstable political climate. His prospects looked bleak.

His paternal uncle had mentored him from a distance throughout, travelling up periodically from his Damascus shop to see how his nephew was getting on, but life was very different now. Abu Chaker's father had been a naturally generous, even extravagant man. He had tripled the family wealth during his short lifetime, and enjoyed distributing largesse widely. He had been well loved, combining his charity with a good sense of humour. His grandsons recalled being told a story about how, on passing a pair of men digging the grave of an unpopular Homsi resident who had just died, his father had quipped to the gravediggers, "Dig it deeper to make sure he doesn't come up again!" Even the deceased's own relatives had burst into laughter.

Abu Chaker's uncle on the other hand, though a very wealthy man, was much more careful with money, an entirely different personality to his brother. The privilege Abu Chaker had grown up with as a child and taken for granted had disappeared overnight on his father's death. In his own family he had been the only son among many daughters and in the heavily patriarchal society of the time had been spoilt accordingly. His uncle already had several sons to care for, so Abu Chaker's position as the favoured child was lost, leaving him as one among many.

Apart from his ongoing battle to keep the business afloat, Abu Chaker was also reaching the age where, in the traditional Homsi environment, he was expected to marry, and one of the natural duties which fell to his uncle, as the senior male in the family, was to arrange his nephew's marriage. Throughout Syria—and indeed most of the Arab world—first cousin marriage was extremely common, mainly in order to keep money and land within the extended family. Even today it is still a somewhat widespread practice in the region. So it was that the young Abu Chaker, aged thirty, under heavy family pressure, married his first cousin, Fattat, his uncle's daughter and therefore also a Chamsi-Pasha, in autumn 1952. He described it as "like marrying my sister", something he was simply expected to do for inheritance reasons and to comply with local custom.

It didn't work. The marriage was consummated on the wedding night, and Fattat conceived a child, but Abu Chaker divorced her before the child, a daughter called Buthaina, was born in July 1953. Fattat returned to her father's home in Homs, which was customary after the failure of a marriage.

Divorce was not common in 1950s Syria. Indeed, even as late as 1984, statistics show that only 7 per cent of marriages in Syria ended in divorce. Of these most took place in the cities, and in rural areas the figure was as low as 2 per cent. In today's Syria, reflecting the chaos of the war-ravaged society at large, there has been a 25 per cent increase in divorce rates since conflict broke out in 2011. With the arrival of Syrian independence in 1946 the Syrian constitution stipulated that secular courts should administer civil and criminal cases, but matters of personal status like marriage, divorce, custodianship and inheritance were dealt with by religious courts, following the Shari'a as laid down in the Qur'an. For Muslim men divorce, or *talaq,* was relatively simple: a husband only had to go to the court and pronounce "I divorce you" three times, whereupon the court would make the divorce legal, as long as the man was not found to be intoxicated or under duress. If a woman wanted a divorce, the process was far more difficult and drawn out, and she woud have to prove that her husband had either abused her or been impotent. In Christian families divorce was even rarer, and it was unusual for a divorced woman to be able to remarry—the social stigma was considerable.

In traditional Islamic households children from a first marriage always reverted to the father's family at puberty, not least because a woman's new husband would not wish to take on another man's children. According to this system, a second wife instead had no choice but to take on responsibility for children from her husband's previous marriage. This patriarchal tradition might seem harsh by modern Western standards, but this was the established practice of centuries and was not questioned, especially not by women.

Abu Chaker's divorce from his first cousin Fattat was acrimonious, perceived as an insult to her family. It destabilised family relations and led to a severe rift between Abu Chaker and his uncle and even to a separation of their businesses. Abu Chaker, as the younger partner in the business, came off worse in the arrangement. His uncle kept the shop in Damascus, which was more profitable and had more reliable payers, while Abu Chaker was left with only his father's shop in Homs and a load of debtors. He had no cash and no family apart from his dependant mother and one sister, the other sisters having by now married and moved out to join to their husbands' families. Any prospects he might have had of expanding the business and bringing success to his family were over. He was on his own. It appeared he was doomed to lead life on a treadmill, his ambitions for betterment thwarted.

As Abu Chaker sat outside his shop one day in the months after the split, gloomily pondering his fate, his father's close friend, the biggest sheep trader in Homs province, happened to pass by. As soon as he saw Abu Chaker's sullen face the sheep trader understood what was plaguing him, as he had already heard news of the divorce and business split. He told Abu Chaker to close up his shop or get someone to mind it, took him by the arm and led him to his own office, not far from the souk. There he opened his safe to reveal a huge stash of banknotes in the French-imposed currency, *la livre syrienne*. The French franc formed the base of the economy, but currency management was in the hands of French bankers, concerned with the interests of French, rather than Syrian, shareholders—many of whom made fortunes from currency deals. "Take what you need," the man instructed Abu Chaker. "I don't need any of it now till next season."

To a Western way of thinking, such a break may seem to be an astonishing stroke of luck. But in the context of the times, offers of this kind were built into the normal codes of social behaviour within a cohesive society. When people within the community fell on hard times, the instinctive response from others was to help them. It was no different when Abu Chaker offered farmers his cloth and trusted them to pay him back when their harvest came in. The kindly sheep trader had just sold all his sheep and fleeces, so had a surfeit of cash that he didn't need. The cycle of the seasons led to natural peaks and troughs in people's incomes, so it was regarded as normal for these to be smoothed out. No one within the community was left to go bankrupt under such a scenario, unlike under Western capitalism where bankruptcy is an acceptable way of erasing past debts in order to start all over again. In this sense Islam offers what some have called a "moral economy", in which a system of Islamic finance avoids debt and payment of interest.

According to his sons, Abu Chaker, at the sheep trader's insistence, helped himself to a sizeble wad of cash. It was not counted out, and nothing was put in writing. When Abu Chaker tried to draw up a receipt for the sum, the sheep trader stopped him, saying, "Don't you dare." With this money stored in his own safe, Abu Chaker felt a surge of new confidence, secure in the knowledge that if he needed it, he had a fallback.

The system of buying in Beirut was that merchants would ship goods to Homs that had to be paid by return or through IOUs. Abu Chaker still had access to some of the credit lines that were available to the Chamsi-Pasha business, but with certain suppliers these now had to be split between him and his uncle. Abu Chaker travelled immediately to Beirut, where he purchased bulk quantities of cloth from Lebanese wholesalers at a heavy discount, buying up virtually all their stock of British broadcloth. As it happened, he was able to sell the goods remarkably quickly with low profit margins, which gave both him and his suppliers the confidence to increase the turnover exponentially. After a short time he was able to open a second shop in the Homs market, piling it high with rolls of cloth, and even acquired a large warehouse behind the shops so he could store the remainder of the stock. His business was soon well off the ground—and remarkably, he had never even needed to touch the cash in the safe. He returned the full amount to the sheep trader within a few months, his fortunes transformed thanks to the good reputation of his father, whose friend had wished to honour his memory with an act of generosity of the kind that he knew Abu Chaker's father would have approved of himself.

On hearing of the sudden change in fortunes of his nephew, his uncle was furious. He travelled up from Damascus to the Homs souk and stood, shouting abuse and hurling insults at Abu Chaker, calling him a thief and accusing him of having stolen the stock. Abu Chaker kept his silence. His uncle even went so far as to buy a second shop for himself in Homs, hoping to derail Abu Chaker's quickly expanding business.

The bold and resourceful way in which Abu Chaker used this cash injection to kick-start his stagnant business was a turning point for him. He became a semi-wholesaler himself in Syria, thanks to all the Beiruti stock he had been able to buy, and was now in a position to sell on the British-made cloth to traders in Aleppo, Hama and Damascus, supplying their shops in the markets, increasing his business and his profits enormously. As his business expanded, Abu Chaker came to the attention of one of the biggest textile traders, a Christian called Shukeir who took him under his wing, telling him he had a good future ahead of him. Shukeir allowed Abu Chaker to choose and buy more than his competitors, and was impressed with how quickly he seemed able to sell the textiles on without trading down too much. Abu Chaker took a smaller profit margin in order to increase business and grow, undercutting his competitors thanks to his newfound purchasing power.

One of the key lessons Abu Chaker taught his own sons, based on the experience he gained during this period of growing his business, was: "Always make your profit from your suppliers, never from your customers." By sticking to his word, dealing sharp but fair, he built up his reputation and good name. Nothing was more important, he told his sons, than having a good name.

After the disastrous failure of his first marriage, Abu Chaker was in no hurry to marry again, and besides, he was now fully occupied and very busy building up the new wholesale business beyond his simple Homsi shop. The push that spurred him to consider another wife came from an unlikely source—his Christian colleagues in the souk.

These Christian souk neighbours knew Abu Chaker well, and had a clear idea of the sort of woman who might be a good match for him. They mixed with liberally inclined Sunni Muslims, and recognised that Abu Chaker, as a forward-looking and ambitious personality, might be more likely to find a suitable wife not among conservative families of Homs like his own, where his first wife had come from, but rather from a more open-minded family—like the Atassis. Abu Chaker and his father and grandfather belonged to the smallest and strictest school of Sunnis, the Hanbalis, as did Fattat, his first wife. The Atassis belonged to the more tolerant and numerous Hanafi school.

The woman that Abu Chaker's neighbours had in mind was Rihab Atassi. She was eleven years his junior, a common age gap between husband and wife, then as now in Syria. She had left school after completing her diploma or *Brevet* at fourteen, the usual age for girls at that time, so had acquired basic literacy and numeracy in Arabic, with a little French.

Rihab was a strong and unusual woman, though she described herself in those days of her youth as very shy. She had already had two previous engagements, but had broken both off. In Syrian society of the 1950s—and still today—becoming engaged was not seen as binding or decisive as it is in Western societies. After a family-approved engagement, a couple was allowed to meet and go to cafés together, so being engaged was like an exploratory process, an experiment, a socially acceptable way to find out about another person. It was therefore quite normal and understood that one might get engaged a number of times. Two or three times was quite common; even up to six or seven was fine.

Rihab's first engagement had been to a doctor when she was sixteen years old and had lasted three or four months. She had instinctively not liked him, and had told her mother that she didn't want to marry him. Her parents were understanding and accepted her decision. She explained the way her father would listen to and respect his children's wishes: "My father was very nice and said to me: 'Do as you want.' I have three sisters and just one brother, Abdullah, and my father told him not to go to school. 'Why do you need to go to school?' he said, 'You have thirty farms, you do not need to go to school.' But we, the sisters, said to our father: 'Let him go to school if he wants.' So he did, he went to school till the Baccalaureate."

Her second fiancé, when she was aged eighteen, was also an Atassi—not a close relation, but a man from the extended Atassi family. He was an engineer, another highly educated man who was thought to be a suitable match. But Rihab decided against him as well, feeling no particular connection with him.

In Rihab's own account of her courtship with Abu Chaker, she described how on their first meeting, arranged by her parents, she knew immediately that he was different. From his calm presence and arresting blue eyes she sensed that he would be more difficult to pin down, a challenge that she relished.

"I could see he was very intelligent," she said, even though he did not have the formal education her previous suitors had enjoyed. She was not already acquainted with him, though she confessed to going to the souk with a girlfriend to take a look at him before agreeing to meet him for the first time. It was her father and her brother who had both known him by reputation and had vouched for him.

A preliminary meeting was arranged through Rihab's father and brother, in which Abu Chaker and his mother came to call on them at their house in Homs. This was the standard procedure in society: the prospective suitor's family would contact the family of the prospective bride, and ask for an initial meeting. Sometimes, even that initial meeting was turned down, if the bride's family felt the suitor was not up to scratch in some way.

The two mothers had chatted and got on very well together, but Abu Chaker had been largely silent and had refused to eat, Rihab laughingly recalled. "I don't know why he didn't want to eat our food! He just said, 'No, I don't want to,' so we said, 'As you like.'" It was 1954, when women from liberal families like the Atassis were not headscarved; Rihab would have been dressed in quite a Western style in a knee-length skirt and blouse, her hair uncovered. Only in traditional conservative or rural peasant families would women have worn head coverings at that time, and indeed on into the 1960s and 1970s, and later. Rather Rihab herself had insisted that Abu Chaker stop wearing the fez after their marriage, which he duly did.

From many perspectives Abu Chaker was an unusual choice for her. The Atassi family has always been one of the major "notable" families of Syria—from the "Top Ten", as her sons said—and owned much land in the Homs area. At election times, Rihab said, there were 2,000 Atassis who could vote. She felt a real sense of pride in her family name, well aware of how prestigious they were. On one occasion, sitting in her London flat, well into her eighties, Rihab had been looking at an Arabic map of the province of Homs with her sons. Suddenly she pointed to a village called Aabel, a few kilometres south of Homs. "This was my father's village. We used to go there for picnics," she said excitedly. Her sons laughed and explained that what she meant was that her father had owned that village. In Syria's feudal system of landowners and agricultural labourers, prominent families like the Atassis owned entire villages and tracts of land, exacting taxes and rent from those who lived there—not unlike British aristocratic families, such as the Grosvenors or Cadogans, who still own land granted to them centuries ago by monarchs in gratitude for loyal service; or like rich merchant families in the Gulf, who are to this day gifted land by their rulers. A little later in the conversation Rihab pointed out another village called Al-Mubaraki near Aabel. "This is my sister's village," she said. "No, that was your sister's husband's village," her sons corrected her, laughing again.

As an Atassi she could have married, as her sisters did, another Atassi, with apparently better prospects. But this was not the real issue. "It was very difficult, you know," Rihab explained, "for an Atassi to marry someone like this who had already been married and who already had a child." Abu Chaker's divorce from his first cousin, she suggested, was almost scandalous for the times.

Her friends had asked her if she was out of her mind. "A divorced man, with a child, who is not fully educated?" But Rihab was a risk-taker. Moreover, her father was in favour of the match, and assured Rihab that Abu Chaker was a good man. So, aged twenty-three, she made her choice, relying on her father's judgement. Under Islamic law marriage was not regarded as a status, but a contract, in which the woman's consent was essential, even when she was represented by a male relation. Rihab and Abu Chaker's marriage contract was dated 16 January 1955, and was stamped by the Religious Court in Homs, Ministry of Justice.

They signed their marriage contract together at the Shari'a Court in Bab Houd, close to the Homs souk and Abu Chaker's house, in the presence of the two witnesses on Rihab's side—her brother

Abdullah al-Atassi and Hicham al-Atassi, who was married to her elder sister. Abu Chaker represented himself, with no witness. The magistrate signed and sealed the contract, affirming that it had been accepted by both husband and wife, and that the *mahr* or bride's compensation had been paid in accordance with the Shari'a and legal procedure. The sums mentioned in the contract as dowry or bride's compensation would have been agreed between Abu Chaker and Rihab's father. In pre-Islamic times these sums would have been paid by the groom as a bride-price to his wife's father or male guardian; in an Islamic marriage contract it must be paid to the bride herself as part of her personal property, a kind of safety cushion which remains hers to keep in the event of future divorce. In this respect Islamic legislation represented enormous progress in a patriarchal society that had previously restricted all inheritance to male relatives. The *mahr* was also a way of passing money on to daughters, since under Islamic inheritance law the proportion of an estate that can be passed on to one's children is fixed as two thirds to sons and only one third to daughters. Women were additionally allowed to administer the wealth they brought to the family or which they had earned from their own work.

Another aspect of Rihab's marriage to Abu Chaker was that by entering into this contract with him, she was moving into a household with other women already in place. Abu Chaker's mother Fatima, who was a strong-minded woman, was still alive, and one of Abu Chaker's sisters was not yet married, so all were living under the same roof. Although such an arrangement was the norm, the potential for things to go wrong was still considerable. Rihab saw immediately that if the marriage was going to work, she would have to negotiate with Abu Chaker's mother as to what their respective responsibilities would be within the household, so that they could coexist harmoniously. It would have been so easy for frictions to develop over who ruled the roost, to argue about who did what for whom.

They agreed on a "division of duties". Abu Chaker's mother was a keen cook and had always been in charge of the food and the kitchen. She did not want any interference from her daughter-in-law in this realm, and Rihab therefore, right from the outset, made it clear that she would never get involved in the kitchen, but would leave all such domestic matters to her mother-in-law, unless expressly summoned. Only occasionally, Fatima would call out: "Come into the kitchen, Rihab. I am making pastry and I need your warm hands to help me!" Laughing, she would go into the usually forbidden domain and do as she was told. As for the cleaning arrangements, her mother-in-law supervised the two maids, and generally ran the household on a day-to-day basis. Abu Chaker had always wanted two maids, Rihab said, to ensure that the household was a peaceful place, so that when he returned home tired from work, he knew he could relax without stress.

Abu Chaker's unmarried sister who still lived at home used to help her brother get dressed every morning. This too Rihab allowed to continue, without jealousy. As a result, her own duties were limited to looking after her husband in all other ways. The thinking behind this scrupulous division of duties, both by Abu Chaker's mother and by Rihab herself, was that neither of them wanted him to divorce again, so they both did their utmost to ensure a harmonious household. Very early on Fatima explained to her daughter-in-law how to handle Abu Chaker. She warned her that he had a fiery temper which could erupt suddenly, but because she was in situ, she was able to defuse potentially difficult situations before he exploded. As Abu Chaker's sons later explained, Fatima saw Rihab as an ally, a breath of fresh air, someone from a different milieu. Her son's first wife, Fattat, had been from the same family, and therefore Fattat's own mother, from the Zihrawi family, had taken charge, especially after Abu Chaker's father had died, leaving her "in power" as the head female. Fatima was determined not to inflict such a situation on her own daughter-in-law. She was keen not to repeat the power struggles she herself had been forced to endure.

"That cemented their relationship," her sons explained, "and they reached some sort of understanding very early on. Fatima said to Rihab, 'You look after your husband and your children. I'll look after the food and the household.' Father was not a big eater, but what he did eat he enjoyed very much—that was a very big part of his life, very important to him. We used to joke that he lived from meal to meal. 'What are we having today?' he would say before he set off in the morning. 'Are we going to have this? No, I want that.'

"Food was a huge passion in his life," they recalled, "home-cooked food, not restaurant food. These days we are much more detached from our food sources, just going to the supermarket and picking up strawberries flown in from America or mangoes flown in from Pakistan without a second thought. He would never have dreamt of eating food that was not seasonal or local. He was very, very particular, very exacting in his demands of what he ate. That carried on throughout his life. It all came from his mother, from his closeness to the countryside and to nature. His own mother had provided him with that, so my mother—coming from a more refined environment whereby she didn't need to cook herself, she didn't have to go into the kitchen—she found the arrangement perfect."

So Rihab let her mother-in-law and her sister-in-law carry on doing what they had always done. She made no attempt to try to break the patterns of the household into which she had married. Each woman respected the others' realm and none of them attempted to trespass. It was a series of alliances based on mutual benefit.

Not too long after, Abu Chaker's sister got married and moved out into her new husband's house, and things became simpler. Free from household chores, Rihab was always available to be Abu Chaker's mainstay, at his disposal in all ways, on hand to aid and support him. She would continue to meet her relatives from the Atassi family, though she never used them to help find opportunities to expand his business dealings. She was not a "networker" in that sense, but rather a shy and socially retiring girl by nature.

Through her marriage to Abu Chaker, Rihab gradually gained confidence and learnt from him. She was his protégée. As an only son, he had no brothers to help him and on whom he could depend, and needed her all the more. Little by little, he involved his wife in his business, which was unusual in those times, trusting her with more and more as time went on. He helped develop her skills and taught her how to drive a hard bargain. Step by step, Rihab acquired enough knowledge and experience to be able to advise her husband and become his loyal confidante, a true asset to his business. As one of their granddaughters remarked years later, "It was almost as if he didn't want just a wife. He wanted a business partner as well."

When she had married him, all Abu Chaker owned by way of land was an orchard and a farm. The ceremony itself was a modest affair, unlike the large and fancy parties which are the custom these days in the upper echelons of Syrian society. For their honeymoon the pair spent three or four days in Stoura in Lebanon's Beqa'a Valley, then flew to Cairo.

A few months after the newly-wed couple returned to Homs in 1955, their first son, Chaker, named after his grandfather, was born. Now Abu Chaker had a son of his own, and thanks to the strength and cooperation between his mother and his new wife and their joint determination to keep his domestic environment calm and stable, the young family was able to thrive in a way that might have been impossible had he married someone different, someone of a more timid or conservative mindset. Professionally Abu Chaker had already established a reputation as a trustworthy and honest merchant, someone who, once his word was given, never went back on it.

And yet he had, Rihab explained, a kind of "*tawattur dakhili*", an inner stress or tension, which he usually "swallowed", but which every now and then would break out if things got too much for him. She put this inner tension down to his huge sense of responsibility for having had to support his family financially after his father's death, and for being forced at such a young age to shoulder adult burdens. Understanding this, she resolved to "swallow" her own inner tension—most of the time—and to bite her tongue rather than risk being divorced. Their sons recall that, later in life, their parents did have their arguments—sometimes Abu Chaker would go into a sulk and not speak to his wife for a day—but the next day everything would have returned to normal. When he was at home, they explained, he wanted her to be there, and didn't like her going out to socialise with her own friends. There was a palpable sense that Rihab's role as his wife was to be there for her husband and for him alone. The old patriarchal attitudes of Abu Chaker's childhood were deeply embedded.

An unexpected drama in the life of the newly-weds was the arrival of Buthaina, the daughter from Abu Chaker's first marriage. Buthaina's mother, Fattat, was getting married again, and in accordance with Islamic law, her new husband was not expected to accept the child of another man into his household. It was equally unacceptable to Abu Chaker that a child of his should be brought up by another man, so Buthaina had to be returned to him. In other words, neither the mother's nor the child's wishes counted for anything. It must have been extremely difficult for Fattat to give up her child, who though four years old would have been old enough to know what was going on—but for the society of the time such considerations were not relevant.

Under the Syrian law of personal status the same would have applied had they been Christian. Regardless of religious affiliation, Syrian family courts were united in their shared cultural understanding of the patriarchal model, the role of women, family relations, and social norms of behaviour. In practice the situation would have seldom arisen since less than 1 per cent of Christian marriages ended in divorce. Even if Fattat had not remarried, as a divorced mother she would in any case by law have lost custody of any male child once he reached the age of nine (raised to thirteen in 2006) and of any female child once she reached age of eleven (or fifteen since 2006). As it was, the move had to take place at an earlier age, which might arguably have been considered easier. Only in 1953 did the Syrian state introduce its own Personal Status laws. Before that the Ottoman Law of Family Rights governed all matters of personal status such as divorce, polygamy, dowry, maintenance, nursing costs and guardianship. Both the Ottoman and the Syrian laws stipulated that rulings from the Hanafi school of law should be taken as the most authoritative source.

The International Religious Freedom Report of 2006 still states that custody in Syria can be taken away from a woman prior to her children reaching the designated ages should she "remarry, work outside the home, or move outside of the city or country". The paternal side of the family always retains guardianship of children even today after children have reached the designated ages, unless of course the families agree otherwise without going to court. Fattat and her second husband continued to live in Homs, where they went on to have five children of their own. Though such laws seem alien nowadays to those in many Western societies, it is a credit to all concerned and a testament to the strength of Islamic family values that today these children from Fattat's second marriage, and indeed Buthaina herself, are still in regular touch with Abu Chaker's children and that relations remain very cordial.

And so Buthaina joined her father's household and together Rihab and Abu Chaker's mother Fatima looked after her. Rihab and Abu Chaker's own sons were born soon after in quick succession. Buthaina was like their elder sister, and according to the sons, their relationship was always good, with no frictions or jealousies. "She was already there, and we didn't realise she was the child from Father's earlier marriage till much later," they recalled. Rihab remembered how she had put Buthaina in school with the nuns in Homs when she was four years old. She felt responsible for her, and Buthaina used to call her "Mama". Buthaina herself then left home when she in turn married.

Abu Chaker's attitude to women was mixed and complicated. On the one hand, he wanted his wife to be at home with him at all times, always at his beck and call. On the other hand he wanted someone with whom he could share his business aspirations, who could be almost like a business partner for him. When he married he never attempted to change or control the way his wife dressed, in a skirt and blouse, her hair loose and uncovered. Rihab had been the first woman in Homs to wear trousers and to drive a car. She would go to the cinema in Homs with friends, and had insisted on the right to continue with such freedoms after their marriage. Abu Chaker had agreed.

All four of Rihab and Abu Chaker's sons felt that growing up with two parents from such contrasting backgrounds gave them two different perspectives, enhancing their understanding of both from an early age. They also felt they benefited from mixing with different societies, Muslim and Christian, not only in Syria, but also in their later childhood in Lebanon, and later on in the UK.

"We were lucky," they acknowledged, "we had the best of all worlds."

7

SYRIAN INDEPENDENCE AND THE RISE OF THE BA'ATH PARTY

A man who takes up politics is like a man trying to climb into the garbage.

(Lebanese proverb)

When it finally achieved independence in 1946 Syria had shrunk from the "Natural Syria" of the Ottomans, an area of over 300,000 square kilometres, to just 185,000 square kilometres. Most of this territorial loss was due to the French creation of the state of Lebanon, but the French had also handed over the whole of the province of Alexandretta to Turkey in 1939 in return for the promise of Turkish neutrality in World War Two, a bribe that was rationalised as being necessary for the preservation of the European alliance. France was willing to sacrifice Syria's territorial integrity for the sake of its own larger international interests. Two years later, in 1948, Palestine was also lost. Every Syrian schoolchild after independence was brought up to hate the Sykes-Picot Agreement of 1916 and the Balfour Declaration which led to the creation of Israel, the two foreign edicts responsible for carving up Greater Syria. The cities of Jerusalem and Jaffa (both now in Israel), Tyre, Sidon, Beirut and Tripoli (all now in Lebanon), Damascus, Homs, Hama, Lattakia and Aleppo (all in today's Syria) and Alexandretta (in today's Turkey) were all counted as Syrian, with Damascus seen as the central and most important city in the wider nation. Syria had suffered the shock of amputation.

The legacy of the French was to leave Syria with no experience or institutions of self-government. France had failed to prepare its mandated territory for independence—quite the reverse, it had done its utmost to prevent the emergence of proper self-governing institutions. In theory Syria should have benefited from achievements such as the maintenance of law and order, improved communications networks, extensions to the areas under agricultural cultivation, better educational facilities with new schools and the setting up of a new framework for modern government and a Syrian parliament. In practice the French stranglehold on Syria stifled any democratic advancement, and the simmering resentment continued until the last French troops were expelled, nearly three years after Lebanon had itself succeeded in breaking free of French rule and proclaimed itself a republic in 1943. The French had discouraged the use of Arabic, failed to recognise the rising Syrian national spirit and depreciated the Syrian currency by tying it to the French franc. They had openly favoured the Christian leaders in Lebanon, devising a power-sharing system that was advantageous to their Christian allies. Corpses of uncooperative or disobedient Syrians—mainly Muslims—had been strung up in Marja Square in central Damascus, while others who dared to oppose colonial rule were imprisoned or exiled.

In such unequal and divided circumstances, it was no accident that Ba'athism, an ideology based on socialism and nationalism that has dominated politics in modern Syria, was founded in 1947, by sons of Damascus grain merchants and Druze shaikhs from the agricultural Hawran region. Neither was it happenstance that the post-independence rulers were displaced by another generation of young men of rural origin—the 'Alawis—who had received their fully subsidised military education from the Homs Military Academy, founded in 1933 by the French.

It is one of many historical ironies in Syria that the French raised the status of the 'Alawis by recruiting them as "*troupes spéciales*" into the French army, along with other minorities including Christians. They were even given their own 'Alawi statelet from 1923 to 1936, an area that roughly corresponded with today's Lattakia and Tartous provinces. Located on the northwest edge of the city, the Homs Academy was the country's main training establishment for the armed forces, initially just for infantry officers. It remained the only Syrian military training centre till 1967, producing many of Syria's future leaders and ministers. The officers from the academy made their presence felt in Homs, and were often seen walking around the city centre and in the souk.

Under both Ottoman and French rule the deal had been that the political notables would enjoy qualified access to political power and tremendous economic power, in return for minimising the political aspirations of the masses of the subject population. Local power was based on control of the land and its agricultural surpluses. The notables claimed a "natural" leadership based on their ability to dispense patronage among the subordinate classes, be they peasants or inhabitants of an urban quarter dominated by a notable family. Single extended families controlled scores or even hundreds of villages consisting of thousands of individuals.

Damascus' landed elite generally sent their sons for higher education if not to Istanbul, then to Maktab 'Anbar, the civil Ottoman secondary school set in a series of courtyard palaces in the heart of the Old City. They came back as lawyers, engineers and scholars, and shared a distaste for the army. It was the rural shaikhs, village elders and middling urban merchants who sent their sons to the state-subsidised Damascus Ottoman military academies, as that was all they could afford. Many leaders of the Great Revolt of 1925 had been educated there and were bound by solidarity because of their humbler origins. They likewise shared a desire to expel the French, agitate against the Christians whom the French had both protected and given special status, and to advocate popular Islam and class warfare against the urban landlords and notables. The French colonial functionaries believed—as many scholars did—that commercial and social relations separated rural people from one another and from urban populations. They did not understand that commerce would in fact bond people from different parts of the countryside with each other and with the cities, serving to bring them together. It was the grain–trade alliance.

The struggles of Syrians against foreign rule, by the French and previously the Ottoman state, were now over, leaving veteran nationalists in charge of their own country at last. The structural conditions that had once required a certain kind of political expertise, where the notables had acted as brokers between the ruling authority and the populace it presided over, ceased to be relevant, and yet that same ruling elite which had governed before continued to control the country after independence, and in just the same way, as though nothing had changed.

In such circumstances it was inevitable that sooner or later a new type of social hierarchy would arise, one which these notables, as the urban absentee landowning class, could no longer control. Restless forces lower down the social scale were beginning to mobilise and challenge the status quo, but changes did not take place overnight. In fact, despite the turbulence, the notables managed to hold on to power for nearly twenty years after independence, far longer than their counterparts in Egypt and Iraq, for a number of complex reasons tied to the nature of Syrian society.

Syria had for centuries been a rural semi-sedentary subsistence economy with most people employed in agriculture, but after independence this balance began to shift. In the laissez-faire period of the late 1940s and 1950s, the merchants of Aleppo and other urban centres brought their money and new machinery to the Jezira province in the country's northeast and the Euphrates Valley. The resulting rapid mechanisation of cereal agriculture in the Jezira and cotton along the banks of the Euphrates generated a great deal of money, and with it a new social dynamic, encouraging the Bedouin desert nomads to form settled groups. Much economic activity in the western, more urbanised parts of Syria had long depended on the exploitation of resources in the rural northern, eastern and southern provinces. Aleppo, for example, lost its connection to its natural Turkish neighbourhood with the end of the Ottoman Empire in 1920, when Mustafa Kemal Atatürk founded modern Turkey within its new borders. Aleppo's merchants responded by building themselves a new hinterland, with local entrepreneurs investing in crops like cotton in the Euphrates Valley in order to establish strong Aleppo-based textile factories.

By the 1950s, the landowning tribal chiefs had emerged as a new social class and were nicknamed "the cotton shaikhs", leaders of an entrepreneurial capitalist style of agriculture quite different to the simple subsistence economy of the past. At first they employed their fellow tribesmen to work the land, but as their agrarian enterprise expanded, they found themselves needing to seek additional labour from outside their kinship groups, something that had never before been necessary. The result was to weaken the links between the tribal cotton shaikhs and their kinsmen. As new capitalists, the shaikhs were now more interested in their connections with the city merchants who would buy their produce. As they grew increasingly wealthy, driving Cadillacs and employing slaves to be their domestic servants, they grew ever more distant from their roots, and in the process lost much of the authority they had once held over their communities. Tribal solidarity was the casualty of greed. On top of that the tribal land ownership rights upheld by the French fell away after independence in 1946, leaving the tribal leaders unsure of their status. The Syrian government then went on to cancel the Law of the Tribes in 1956, which had granted tribal shaikhs independent legal status and the right to carry weapons.

The social system that prevailed in Syria after independence therefore continued to be one of gross inequality. Some 3,000 elite families (now including the cotton shaikhs) who represented just 2 per cent of the population owned half the land in the country and took half the revenue from the country's agricultural produce for themselves. The middle classes, consisting of merchants and landlords with small- to medium-sized holdings, formed 18 per cent of the population and pocketed another quarter of the agricultural revenue. Over 65 per cent of peasants owned no land at all, and had to work in poorly paid manual labour jobs on the land of the richer classes—and yet these peasants comprised 80 per cent of the country's population.

It was the same feudal system that had prevailed throughout the French Mandate period, based on well-established landowner–peasant class differences. Such social antagonism would inevitably lead to the landowners' downfall. Indeed, these were the inequalities that the Ba'athist land reforms sought to address in the late 1950s, through the redistribution of the vast landholdings of the old notable classes to the benefit of the peasant class.

For the most part the trajectory of people's lives and the choices open to them were already dictated at birth in such an inequitable society. While Abu Chaker, as part of the establishment of minor notables in the inland city of Homs, was working to build up his family textile trading business, another young man living over the mountains was growing up with a very different set of experiences. The young Hafez al-Assad, future president of Syria, was born as the fourth child of a second marriage on 6 October 1930, in a simple two-roomed stone house giving onto an earth yard. His 'Alawi village of Qardaha looked out across the coastal plain towards the Mediterranean and the local metropolis port of Lattakia, which was reachable only by donkey.

Despite their difference in wealth, Hafez and Abu Chaker were raised in settings that were otherwise very alike, in environments that were highly patriarchal. Hafez's father, born in 1875 and already aged fifty-five at the time of Hafez's birth, enjoyed the love, respect and obedience of his children. His sons would kiss his hand in the morning, waited for him to take a seat before sitting down themselves, and never dared, even as adults, to smoke in front of him. Hafez's four brothers and sisters from his father's first marriage seemed to him more like uncles and aunts. The family house had a few fruit trees and a mud extension for the animals, and olives were used for cooking oil, lighting and soap-making.

Hafez's grandfather was a formidable figure and was known as al-Wahhish, meaning "wild man", because of his physical strength and courage—a nickname that was later adapted to al-Assad, meaning "lion". Wielding old sabres and muskets, he used to fight off the Ottoman Turkish governor's soldiers who came to the village to collect taxes and to recruit soldiers for the army before World War One. Many 'Alawi notables had found it in their interests during the seventeenth and eighteenth centuries to dominate local society on behalf of the Ottoman state through tax-farming, to raise revenue both for themselves and for the state. But by the nineteenth century, most of their local subjects had enough of the ever-increasing tax demands and would regularly come down from the mountains to raid coastal villages, burn gardens and steal horses in disputes that all boiled down to squabbles over taxes and occasional political rivalries.

From this point onwards, Ottoman court records begin to show that the 'Alawis were increasingly viewed as a threat—representing a troublesome social (rather than religious) problem—and their treatment deteriorated accordingly. Many of the challenges of the nineteenth century were not unique to Syria but affected much of the world: increasing industrialisation, tighter government controls, growing inequalities between the haves and have-nots, greater public mobilisation, migration and struggles for emancipation, all against the backdrop of the increasing economic, cultural and political hegemony of Europe and America. Before World War One the various Sunni and Shi'a Muslim populations of the Ottoman Empire were not subject to sectarian differentiation. There was no institutional church-like authority that existed to impose standardised religious teachings and rites, in the way that the rival Catholic and Protestant confessions did in Europe at around the same time. Specific to Syria (and Lebanon), however, was France's unparalleled commercial and diplomatic offensive against the waning Ottoman state.

Around Lattakia, a separate 'Alawi statelet had been carved out by the French, consisting of about 300,000 people. They had not taken part in the 1925 Great Syrian Revolt and the French considered them to be "reliable minorities" like the Circassians and the Armenians, whom they sought to recruit into the army. Before the Great Syrian Revolt the 'Alawis had, however, fought against the French occupying forces from 1918 to 1921, not as a rejection of French authority, but in a coordinated effort to link up with Turkish Kemalist forces as part of the "southern front" in the Turkish War of Liberation. The Kemalists encouraged them, hoping to reconstruct the 'Alawis as "Hittite Turks", much as they attempted to reconstruct the identity of the Kurds as "mountain Turks".

From the mid-nineteenth century onwards the 'Alawis were treated as "outlaws in their own country", in the words of Assad's biographer, Patrick Seale. It was the French who unwittingly began to change this by using local conscript labour to build dirt tracks up into the mountains and by bringing education to remote villages for the first time. Illiteracy had been almost universal in the mountains. The Ottoman Turks had discouraged literacy, even sending soldiers to give village prayer leaders a beating if they heard boys were being taught how to read. Education, emigration, new communication networks and city contacts gradually began to change the traditional socio-economic structures in the villages, but kinship and leadership structures stayed the same. Before 1950 the villages had been self-contained and self-sustaining, in a simple subsistence economy based on the land where everyone, including the women, worked hard in the fields.

Like Abu Chaker, Hafez al-Assad grew up under the unpopular French Mandate in a Syria that had been shaped by four centuries of Ottoman governance, and like so many of his fellow countrymen, he too inherited the mindset that the state provided no justice and no services, but only oppressive tax collection or forced recruitment into the army. Hafez's father and Abu Chaker's father both enjoyed reputations as fair-minded, independent men. Their services were regularly called upon to arbitrate in the many disputes that arose between neighbours about things like boundaries, water rights, stray animals and alleged slander, and they often succeeded in resolving these quarrels and effecting reconciliations. Hafez's father, 'Ali Sulayman, also had a reputation for protecting the weak, and in the 1920s had helped destitute refugees who had fled south towards Lattakia when France gave parts of the former Aleppo province to Turkey.

When the first primary school was opened in Qardaha by the French, 'Ali Sulayman al-Assad, who was a minor notable and one of the few literate 'Alawis, made sure his son got a place. He was the only man in the village to subscribe to a newspaper, which used to arrive a few days late from Lattakia. From reading the paper Hafez's father even monitored the ups and downs of World War Two, and would mark out key battlegrounds on a wall map in his house.

Aged nine, Hafez was sent to school in Lattakia, where he was lonely and homesick, and had his first taste of what it felt like to be a member of a minority community. While the local population was predominantly 'Alawi, they were almost entirely spread across rural areas rather than concentrated in the cities. Lattakia at that time was 75 per cent Sunni Muslim and only 25 per cent Christian and other minorities, very few of whom were 'Alawis. The city had however always been dependent on the 'Alawi hinterland for its supply of export tobacco and most of its foodstuffs. The American tobacco leaf had originally been imported through Lattakia and was duly taxed as early as 1690 in line with its popularity. Lattakia's pungent signature tobacco, Abu Riha (Father of the Aroma), was very popular with upper- and middle-class society throughout Syria, and its production employed large numbers of 'Alawi peasants. As Lattakia's key export it was traditionally traded by foreign merchants. It could only be sold a full year after planting, an exercise which required great investment and coordination by a new class of rural entrepreneurs.

At school Hafez saw that rich boys—sons of landowners, merchants, financiers and religious dignitaries—were often bullies and, in his own words, "didn't bother to work, simply giving themselves whatever marks they wanted at the end of the year," while the teachers were too afraid to stand up to them, well aware that their jobs were at stake. His own school reports, not doctored like those of his brother Rif'at and later his son Bashar, show that he came top of the class from 1944 to 1946. He was determined to work hard, since even getting into the school had been such a struggle; only one secondary school served the whole coastal region, and entry for boys from his background was by means of a fiercely competitive exam. Hafez learnt that jobs in Lattakia were bestowed by the wealthy notables, who sold them to the highest bidder, and that routes to the top were blocked for 'Alawis, with one exception— the army.

Arab historian Hanna Batatu describes the social process that soon evolved, changing Syria forever:

> Rural people, driven by economic distress or lack of security, move into the cities, settle in the outlying districts, enter before long into relations or forge common links with elements of the urban poor, who are themselves often earlier migrants from the countryside, and together they challenge the old established classes. But in sharp contrast to the outcome of urban-rural conflicts of past centuries, the country people clinched a more enduring, if unstable, victory by virtue of their deep penetration of the Syrian army.

With Syrian independence came conscription, as military service helped to build the armed forces of the new state. The forces of the countryside were stirring and once they realised they could rise unhindered through the ranks of the army, they found themselves able to use the apparatus of state as a method of coercion to achieve their own ends. The wealthy notables, who had shunned the army as a career for their own sons, had only themselves to blame. Their disdain of the military for their own offspring left the way clear for the talented sons of the rural poor. Some were Sunni, but disproportionate numbers were 'Alawi, like Hafez al-Assad and others who have formed the ruling clan of Syria since 1970.

'Alawis have historically clustered in the mountains above Lattakia and the coastal plain. Figures are notoriously unreliable but most estimates put them at about 12 per cent of the population before 2010. Their religious practices differ greatly from mainstream Sunni Muslims in that they do not fast in Ramadan, pray five times a day or attend mosques. They believe in reincarnation and the transmigration of souls, revere the fourth caliph 'Ali as the incarnation of the deity, drink wine, and observe Christmas and Easter. 'Alawi homes often display pictures of Christ and the Virgin Mary. Western travellers and missionaries of the nineteenth century became obsessed with decoding the 'Alawi religion, attributing to them a succession of esoteric beliefs—that infidels will be reborn as animals, for instance, while 'Alawis themselves will be reborn as stars after seven successful lives on earth. Such misinterpretations of the 'Alawi creed—as with similar confusions over the symbolism used in the Druze and Yazidi faiths, with the result that Yazidis have been reviled by mainstream Muslims as "devil-worshippers"—have led many even to misconstrue their other name, "Nusayris". The name is taken from their tenth-century founder Ibn Nusayr, but some have persisted in asserting that the word is the Arabic diminutive of *Nasara* (Christians) and that the 'Alawis must therefore be a long-lost Christian sect. Adding to the group's air of mystery, Western scholars have also focused heavily on the supposed practice of *taqiyya* (dissimulation) whereby 'Alawis, allegedly to avoid persecution, concealed their beliefs and pretended to be mainstream Muslims.

Canadian academic Stefan Winter debunks such myths in his 2016 *A History of the 'Alawis*, pointing out that in earlier centuries 'Alawis would have been more clearly distinguishable by their dress and dialect than they are today, and therefore could not possibly have concealed their identity: "*Taqiyya* was, historically speaking, simply never a factor in their interaction with the state or with members of other communities." His detailed studies of the relevant Ottoman archives have also proved that, far from persecuting and oppressing the 'Alawis for their beliefs, Ottoman authorities were in fact much more interested in them as taxable subjects. Special taxes were imposed on their fruit trees, on their acreage, on their falcons, bees, buffalos and wage labour, and on their silk and flour mills. As non-Muslims Christians had to pay the *jizya* poll tax as well as church charges, while Turkmen and Arab nomads had to pay wintering dues. Sect was not relevant, and the court records show murder and embezzlement trials between various chieftains, some 'Alawi, some Kurdish, centring round various feuds in which rival groups vied for economic dominance, cutting down each other's mulberry trees—in one case felling 124,000 trees—and burning each other's tobacco crops on farms outside Lattakia.

Winter's researches into the Ottoman court records also show that in earlier centuries 'Alawis had their own landed gentry or notables; rich families worked with the state as tax farmers whose wealth rested primarily on the development of commercial tobacco farming, an activity 'Alawis continue to dominate to this day. The common depiction of 'Alawis as a persecuted underclass is thus a gross oversimplification, since there have always been rich and poor 'Alawis, just as there have always been rich and poor Sunnis, and indeed rich and poor Christians.

By the end of World War Two poverty in Syria was widespread across all sects. A British officer wrote in 1944: "For a small country that had been under European mandate for twenty-two years the conditions everywhere were unbelievably bad." The women from the poorer villages formed over 40 per cent of the workforce in local tobacco factories, engaged in sorting the leaves into different sizes and qualities. Women from poor backgrounds would also often work as domestic maids in the households of wealthy notables, a practice that had been ongoing under the Ottomans in earlier centuries and even under the ten-year Egyptian occupation of Syria, when Mohammad 'Ali ordered the execution of one of his own officers for setting up a trade in 'Alawi girls. The practice accelerated in the 1920s under the French who imposed heavy collective fines on rebellious villages. To cope with the resultant penury, peasants felt coerced into selling their sheep, their land and their daughters, usually for ten years, but sometimes for life. Many comfortably-off families in the city, usually Sunni, because of their natural majority, had their maids from the countryside, often 'Alawi, and Abu Chaker's household was no exception. Even into the 1950s at least 10,000 daughters of Syria's peasantry, some as young as six or seven, were working as domestic servants in Damascus, sold by their fathers. 'Alawi men who had joined the army and gained an education in the Homs Military Academy were now however for the first time developing political aspirations. To the Sunni majority, the very idea that an 'Alawi could become leader of Syria was deeply shocking, in the words of American author and political commentator Robert Kaplan, "as shocking as a Jew becoming tsar of Russia or an untouchable becoming maharajah of India." The rise of these new forces sounded the death knell for the old way of politics in Syria.

Within Syrian society the biggest divide historically was never between religious groups, but rather between the city and the countryside. Across the centuries Syrian cities have been regarded by the rural poor as alien places, often established by foreigners— Seljuks, Mongols, Mamluks, Turks—and in any event dominated by them. The relationship between these cities and their rural hinterlands had always been an exploitative one, with the city taking much and returning little. Even worse, the city was generally equated directly with the state, its rulers and its government, in whom there could be no trust because they always put their own interests first.

It was against the backdrop of these social tensions that the Ba'ath Party was set up in Syria in 1947 based on a blend of nationalism and socialism. The years from 1941 to 1948 marked a period of remarkably free speech in Syria, probably freer than at any time since. The choice of the word *ba'ath*, or "renaissance", reflected a conscious decision to revive pride in the great Arab history and heritage before the Ottomans, to shed the shackles of backwardness and foreign control.

Rooted firmly in the secular ideology that religion must be separate from the state, the Ba'ath Party was founded by an Orthodox Christian school teacher, Michel Aflaq, and a Sunni school teacher Salah al-Din al-Bitar. Aflaq, as an Arab Christian, understood that Islam had to be reconciled with Ba'athism, not least in order to counter Muslim Brotherhood preaching and to placate dangerous rivals, and so he developed the theory that "Islam was the most sublime expression of Arabism: the one had grown out of the other and there could be no contradiction between them." His argument was that Islam as a culture rather than a faith should be valued highly, especially for its achievements in the field of philosophy and for its legal and social systems. Both Aflaq and Bitar were sons of grain merchants in Midan, the southern suburb of Damascus that had been so instrumental in organising the 1925 Great Revolt against the French. The two men had met in Paris in the early 1930s while studying at the Sorbonne (courtesy of their French rulers) and their power base began as a grouping of middle-class professionals and intellectuals, inspired by "enlightened Europe". Their backgrounds could hardly have been further removed from those of both Abu Chaker and Hafez al-Assad.

The young Hafez al-Assad decided to join the Ba'ath Party in 1946, aged sixteen, the same year that the French left Syria. He recalled how in school he and his fellow pupils threw away all their French books that day and lit celebratory bonfires. "*Shou deenak?*" or "What is your religion?" was a common question he remembered being asked as a teenager by his peers at school in Lattakia. But the question was not really about religion, and actually meant something like "Where do you stand?" According to Patrick Seale, the answer was expected to be one of three: communist, Ba'athist or nationalist. Inspired by the leader of the local Ba'ath recruitment office in Lattakia, Hafez stood out from the start as keen and capable, organising local anti-government protests, daubing Ba'athist graffiti on walls and gathering signatures on petitions.

His mother had some sympathy with his views, but his father, more naturally suspicious of ideological parties like most of the older generation, feared he was wasting his precious education. Hafez's fellow Ba'athist activists were far from exclusively 'Alawi, and he actively made considerable efforts to look for allies among poorer, non-landowning Sunnis who were equally opposed to the ruling establishment. The early Ba'athists were bound together by their shared sense of grievance against the elites, not by any sectarian ties. It was during these early years as a schoolboy activist that Hafez al-Assad made some lifelong friends: one went on to become his foreign minister, another his longest serving prime minister. Both were Sunnis.

Just two years after gaining independence the young Syria was dealt a massive, destabilising blow when the state of Israel was created in 1948. The resulting Arab–Israeli War forcibly displaced hundreds of thousands of Palestinians. As Jewish militias started razing villages to seize Palestinian land for their new state, waves of Palestinian refugees, half a million in one year, were taken in by Syria. The young Syrian government established a number of refugee camps, three on the outskirts of Damascus alone. Among them was Yarmouk in the southern suburbs, where decades later thousands of Palestinians were caught up in the 2011 Syrian war and subjected to a "starve or surrender" siege by the Assad government.

The establishment of the state of Israel generated immense problems in the region, including for the many Jewish families still living in Syria at the time—about 30,000 people, all of them Arabic-speaking. Synagogues in Damascus and Aleppo were attacked by angry mobs in retaliation for Israeli war crimes against the dispossessed Palestinians. Some Jews left to settle in the new state and some moved to Lebanon, but a few stayed inside Syria.

Hafez al-Assad, who was still at school, was too young to fight in that war, and in any event, on finishing his *baccalauréat* in Lattakia in 1951, he wanted to become a doctor. It was a huge aspiration to step up into the professional middle class for someone from an impoverished 'Alawi background. Hafez tried to get into the medical faculty of the Jesuit University of St Joseph in Beirut, but the application process was difficult and expensive. His parents approved of his plans, but his father was by now seventy-six years old and the family had little cash or income. The only option, therefore, if he wished to enter higher education, was to enrol in the Military Academy in Homs where tuition fees had been abolished since independence in 1946. Cadets were given board and lodging, plus a small salary. As a result, disproportionate numbers of poor but talented young men from the 'Alawi, Druze and eastern Bedouin communities joined. The army was rising in importance nationally, and a two-year military service had been introduced in 1950. After finishing, privileged young men from urban areas returned to cushier options in the cities, using their family connections to secure jobs in government or business circles.

Whilst at the Homs Military Academy, Hafez al-Assad met another Sunni Ba'athist, Mustafa Tlass, one of the ninety cadets on the same intake. Tlass, like Abu Chaker, was from a notable family in Homs, but his family traded in ammunition rather than textiles. He went on to become Assad's loyal defence minister, serving from 1972 till 2004, a total of thirty-two years, suppressing all opposition and dissent to Assad's one-man rule, irrespective of where it came from. Their friendship was one of many such inter-confessional alliances typical of early Ba'athism.

In 1949 there were no less than three military coups in Syria, testimony to the fragility of the series of early independence governments and their poor relationship with the armed forces. After the first coup *waqfs* were taken out of the hands of private religious bodies and put under government control through the setting up of the Ministry of Awqaf. For the first time in Syrian history the *waqf* administrators were appointed by the government, not voted for, and by 1965 leaders and teachers of mosques were nominated by the prime minister. Half the personnel were secular, the other half religious, with the appointment of the minister of Awqaf (always a Sunni) the prerogative of the president. The ministry administers all *waqf* wealth, which now accounts for much of Syria's state property, but precise figures are never disclosed.

The leader of the third coup in 1949 more than doubled the size of the army, bought new military equipment from the French and sent his officers to France, Britain, the USA, Germany and Italy for training. In the early 1950s he banned all political parties, forcing the Ba'athist founders Aflaq and Bitar to flee to Lebanon. There they came into contact with a Sufi lawyer from Hama called Akram Hawrani. He was of humble origins, the son of a weaver, but was also a more experienced Syrian politician who had built up a considerable following in the surrounding countryside by championing the rights of the poor against the feudal landlords. "The land belongs to him who works it," was his slogan.

Hawrani's home city of Hama had a reputation for conservatism, religious extremism and xenophobia. Just four families—the 'Azems, the Kaylanis, the Barazis and the Tayfurs—owned 91 of the 113 villages in the Hama countryside, so Hawrani had plenty of pent-up resentment and frustration against the rich and their flagrant oppression of the poor. He began organising rallies against the landowners, which started peacefully but became increasingly violent, with crops burnt and shots fired at landowners' houses. In 1951 he organised a massive three-day rally in Aleppo against the feudal landlords, the first revolutionary protest of this scale in the region, in which thousands of angry peasants came together to demand reform. The economic and social order of the Syrian central plains was being challenged in a way it had never been before.

Akram Hawrani also had good contacts in the young Syrian army and is thought to have been instrumental in organising some of the later coups of the 1960s. In 1952 the three men—Aflaq, Bitar and Hawrani—agreed to merge and form the Arab Socialist Ba'ath Party under the slogan "Unity, Freedom, Socialism", seeking to create a modern industrial economy. Like Hafez al-Assad, who was now receiving free training as a pilot in the nascent Syrian Air Force, they were driven by a liberal and democratically-inclined ideology, but even early on their principles were tarnished with clientelism and tribalism, which they used to spread their reach into the countryside. They cited the corrupt electoral process to justify their approval of military coups as a means of taking control, contending that the political system would never allow them to take power democratically. Yet the Ba'athists themselves have since clung on to power using that same corrupt electoral system, in which their party is privileged and the president has historically been guaranteed 99 per cent of the vote.

With Arab nationalism in the ascendant across the region, the key player in the region quickly became Gamal 'Abd al-Nasser, a fairly low-ranking lieutenant colonel who came to power in the 1952 Egyptian Revolution, forcing King Farouk to flee. Inspired by Nasser's example, Syria's leaders drew ever closer to Egypt, culminating in the ill-fated 1958 agreement to unite the two countries as the United Arab Republic (UAR). Hafez al-Assad and Mustafa Tlass, both stationed in Cairo as officers at the time, worked behind the scenes to break up the union, realising how unbalanced in Egypt's favour it was.

Nasser had immediately banned all Syrian political parties, including the Ba'ath Party, and taken charge of Syrian affairs, insisting all Syrian embassies and government ministries be dissolved since Syria would henceforth be ruled from Cairo. Hafez al-Assad was briefly imprisoned in Cairo by Nasser for his anti-unionist activities. The leaders of the Ba'ath Party were horrified as they had initially campaigned for the union with Egypt, gambling that they would be allowed to share power. Nasser proclaimed himself president and appointed Akram Hourani as vice president. From 1958 onwards, the state began to assume a much more dominant role in managing the economy, as the Ba'athists embarked on a massive programme of nationalisation.

Disillusion with the UAR and its dominance over Syria led another group of army officers to take power in Damascus and to dissolve the union in 1961. The total disarray that followed left the Syrian officer corps struggling with mutinies, purges and transfers, and the instability left the government vulnerable. In 1963 a group of Ba'athist and other army officers seized control in a military coup, and Akram Hawrani fled to Lebanon, never to return to Syria. The coup, afterwards referred to as the 8 March Revolution, was considered largely bloodless by regional standards, with just 820 people killed and twenty executed. Friends were appointed to senior positions, enemies were purged and Syria's drastic Emergency Law was introduced, giving the state security apparatus power to arbitrarily detain citizens.

By 1966 the original civilian founders of the Ba'ath Party, Michel Aflaq and Salah al-Din Bitar, were arrested and exiled to Lebanon, leaving Ba'athist military officers—Hafez al-Assad among them—to take control of Syria. Aflaq went to Iraq where he was instrumental in the rise of the Iraqi Ba'ath party, later led by Saddam Hussein. The Military Academy in Homs was put under Ba'athist control and several hundred Ba'athists, including Hafez al-Assad's brother Rif'at al-Assad, were given a crash course in military training. Hafez himself was made head of the Syrian Air Force while only in his thirties, and was then promoted to minister of defence in 1966. The following year Israel seized the Golan Heights in the Six Day War, destroying most of the Syrian Air Force and triggering the exodus of thousands of refugees, who flooded into Damascus and southern Syria. Far from being weakened by the heavy Syrian losses in the Golan, Hafez al-Assad deflected the blame and deftly consolidated his position. He took power in 1970.

Throughout this period of political instability and successive changes in government, official figures for Syria's national income were not reliable. In the industrial sector in the 1960s there appeared to be modest growth in a limited range of consumer goods, mainly in textiles, which employed some 70 per cent of the industrial workforce in 1964–65. Subsequent Ba'athist regimes then tried to engineer a more rapid expansion based on their belief that new industry was the key to modern economic development. The capacity of the newly nationalised industries was increased, especially in textiles and cement, while new lines were added in metallurgy, chemical fertilisers and the iron and steel complex at Hama. Yet on the whole, most analysts saw the performance of Syria's public sector industry as poor, with bad management, old machinery and problems with irregular supplies of electricity and raw materials.

For all their failings, one area where the Ba'athist regimes did succeed was in the redistribution of income from 1958 onwards. This was most obvious in the rural sector, where land reform reduced the area held in properties over 100 hectares from roughly 50 per cent in the 1950s to less than 20 per cent by 1970. The proportion of rural families without land fell to around 15 per cent. Villagers started being able to sell their own agricultural produce, though the prices and market conditions continued to be fixed by the urban elites. Urban-based merchants and moneylenders also gradually acquired much land for themselves, exploiting the villagers' historic fear of taxation, all of which undermined what was generally held out as a peasants' revolution.

The military Ba'athists had succeeded in their 8 March Revolution thanks to their support from a radicalised lower middle class, minorities like the 'Alawis, the Druze and the Isma'ilis, and rural poor who were determined to overthrow the old oligarchs. Not only had these oligarchs exploited them but they had also failed to defend the country against Israeli aggression. The chaotic governance of the pre–Hafez al-Assad Ba'athists had led to the loss of the Golan Heights. After becoming president, Hafez al-Assad embarked on a tour of the villages to listen to local grievances and earned great popularity countrywide by slashing the price of basic foodstuffs by 15 per cent. One of his first acts was to visit the Druze leader in Suwayda and honour him for his role in the 1925 Great Syrian Revolt. The 'Alawis had not taken part in that particular uprising—though they had revolted against the French a few years earlier in sympathy with the Kemalist Turks—and so on one level the gesture was hypocritical. But unlike previous rulers, Hafez understood very clearly how important the countryside was to his power base. As the first ruler of Syria to come from a minority, he knew his position would depend not just on the support of Syria's minorities, but on the support of the country's historically exploited rural poor.

8

EARLY BUSINESS VENTURES AND POLITICS

The man who has scalded his lips on milk will blow on his ice-cream.

(Turkish proverb)

Abu Chaker, now in the prime of his life, saw clearly the way things were heading. Land reforms stripped the large landowners of their estates, redistributing them in small chunks to landless farmers and improving conditions for agricultural workers. The process had begun in 1958 during Syria's union with Egypt, when Nasser's socialist policies were put into law, fixing the limit of land ownership at 80 hectares of irrigated land and 300 hectares of unirrigated land per family (with extra allowances for up to four additional family members). Some compensation was given, but it was not considered adequate and landowners were aggrieved. In 1963 the Ba'athists drastically reduced the limit even further to just 15 hectares of irrigated land and 55 hectares of unirrigated land. In the same year commercial banking and insurance companies were nationalised, and by 1965 most large businesses and industrial establishments, which produced such commodities as textiles, cement, sugar, dyes, chemicals and soap, had also been appropriated by the state. One of the unforeseen consequences of the land reforms was for inheritance—the ever-smaller divisions of land that could be passed down led to an increased shift in movement towards the cities, where land became proportionately more expensive.

By 1966, the state had taken control of natural resources, electricity and water supplies, together with international commerce and domestic wholesale trade. It also took charge of the bulk of investments and the flow of credit, and fixed the prices of many commodities, services and even wages.

Under the French Mandate Abu Chaker had been constrained by unstable economic conditions, and had only been able to sell to markets in nearby Hama, Aleppo and Damascus. Upon Syrian independence, he along with his fellow countrymen had hoped that Syria would finally be in charge of its own destiny, free of the yoke of foreign dominance. He was determined to do what he could to build his business, well aware that the breakdown in the established social order would almost certainly make it harder for him. Yet by straddling the divide between urban merchant and rural farmer, he in some ways enjoyed the benefits of a foot in each camp, enabling him to make the most of opportunities in both fields.

In Homs, Abu Chaker watched as the Ba'athists conducted careful social engineering under the guise of expansion and renovation, introducing special segregated zones for different sectarian groupings. New suburbs were built for 'Alawi newcomers from the surrounding villages, breaking down the sense of coexistence that had previously characterised the city. These 'Alawi areas—Zahra and Nuzha (Nazheen), whose names mean "flower" and "park" respectively, carrying overtones of prosperity and unblemishedness—ringed the city in the southeast, where the main road from Damascus entered Homs, marked by a huge statue of Hafez al-Assad. 'Alawi newcomers used the expression "*tawwaqnaha*", or "we surrounded it [the city]", a phrase which could also mean "we put a collar round its neck"—a sentiment consistent with the new attitude of superiority they felt towards the majority Sunni residents. Most of the city's Christian population lived in the more central areas like Hamadieh, Bustan al-Diwan and

Bab Sba'a, mixed in among the Sunni Muslims who had been their neighbours for centuries.

"Everyone lost," said Abu Chaker's sons, "but people did not lose everything. They did not take small farms, and with the big farms, they took about 60 per cent and let people keep 40 per cent of their land. Mother lost a lot of her agricultural land, but Father's pieces of land were mostly too small to be taken. His plots were within the city limits, so they became very valuable as the city grew. Today the area is called Al-Qusour, on the road north towards Hama, and that is where the Chamsi Pasha Mosque was built, with an entire neighbourhood growing up around it. Iranians and Iraqi Shi'a have now been settled there and it has been taken over by the municipality."

For those with commercial acumen like Abu Chaker there were always ways to get around the land reforms. He lost some shares he owned in listed companies, and his sons said that the land inherited from his father's family would have been sold off at times of difficulty. At no stage did he acquire land from his wife, Rihab—in accordance with Shari'a law, a wife retains her property and does not pass it to her husband. As to exactly how much land Abu Chaker owned—or indeed lost under the Ba'ath regime—his sons were never completely sure. Abu Chaker had been a very discreet man, so private that when his sons had been told by one of his friends that their father was a millionaire, they had assumed the friend was talking about someone else.

Today the region of Homs, Syria's third largest city, is thought of as a predominantly industrial city, where the country's oil refineries and many factories are concentrated. But before industrialisation, Homs had been a rich agricultural land, watered by the Orontes river which ran about 1 kilometre to the west of the city centre, flowing northwards till it reached the Mediterranean at Antakya, ancient Antioch. This unusual direction of flow earned the Orontes, the only river in the region to follow this course, the Arabic name Al-'Aasi, the Rebellious One. Modern-day images of the Orontes, derived from romantic scenes of the waterwheels at Hama, are highly misleading in the case of Homs. The Romans had first built a dam on the river to reduce the risk of flooding if it burst its banks. The French later built another, creating the Homs Lake to the south of the city, and constructed an irrigation canal closer to the city's centre, just 200 metres from where Abu Chaker's house stands today. There were extensive swamps, which the French brought under drainage schemes, ostensibly to improve public health and get rid of malaria. Most historians agree that their real concern was to improve agricultural yields through better rural irrigation.

Ultimately the goal of the French was to improve the productivity of the territories under their control, to manage and shape the life of the population for the optimal benefit of France. Their other main interest was in the country's antiquities and its archaeological sites, which they diligently mapped, recorded and photographed, dislodging local people who were living among the ruins, such as in Palmyra's Temple of Bel, so that they could begin excavating and cataloguing Syria's many cultural heritage treasures.

A significant industrial innovation post-independence was the country's first oil refinery, built in Homs in 1959 to process oil for domestic consumption. The oil itself was transported from Kirkuk in a 1930s-built pipeline, which followed the ancient caravan route from Palmyra to the Mediterranean, Homs having always been a point of exchange between the city and the desert. The refinery was bombed by the Israelis in the 1973 Yom Kippur War.

Homs is the largest governorate in the country. One of the reasons for the city's high agricultural productivity is its location in the Homs Gap, where it benefits from more rainfall and gentler temperatures than other inland cities. Under the Ba'athists Homs continued to be both an industrial and an agricultural city, growing wheat, barley, lentils, sugar beet, cotton and vines. Its rural hinterland was known for grapes used to make 'araq, nectar wine and red wine. In 1971 a fertiliser plant was built to process phosphates from the desert mines around Palmyra. Industrial zones were developed to the northwest and south of Homs; a new phosphate and oil refinery was built east of the city, as well as a new sugar beet refinery funded by Brazilian money and an automobile plant built by the Iranian Khodro company. Some 50 kilometres to the south a new industrial city called Hissaya has been constructed, with its own Free Zone processing textiles, food, chemicals and engineering. The Al-Ba'ath University was founded in Homs city in 1979, with the largest faculty in the country for specialist petroleum engineering. About 30 kilometres to the west is the German Syrian University, located in the Christian area of Wadi al-Nasara.

Even before the mandate, French investors had owned most Ottoman railways, and in the early 1900s had built a small track for a two-carriage train which ran through the Homs Gap to the coast, connecting Homs with the port of Tripoli, another predominantly Sunni city. The simple train was known locally as the *Automatrice,* and as a young man, Abu Chaker had travelled on it regularly, carrying bagfuls of silk Homsi scarves to sell in Tripoli. The quality and design of Homsi textiles had a broad appeal, popular with both the lower and upper classes of local, regional and foreign markets. The French, in the early years of the mandate, had been keen to promote sericulture in the region they designated the 'Alawi state, just west of Homs, and in 1927 2 million mulberry trees were planted around Tartous, Safita, Masyaf and Banias. Silkworm cultivation provided a viable income for 'Alawis, and the ready supply of local silk also helped ensure that the weavers of Homs were kept busy.

But for centuries before the French Mandate, the looms of Homs had already been famous for their silk products, and especially for women's scarves. Often in reds and blacks, and brocaded with gold or silver threads, these were made by both men and women from Muslim and Christian families from their homes in areas like Hamadieh in the centre of the city. They were beautiful organic creations, fashioned with stone weights balanced on either side of the looms so that the tension would be just right, the large scarves made with a dexterity and sensitivity to the product that had been passed down through generations, possibly even over centuries. Scarves like this were once worn by the women of Palmyra, as was evident from the statues and funerary busts found inside the tombs. One famous stone carving, now destroyed, at the entrance to the cella of the Temple of Bel showed a procession of women following behind a camel carrying a statue of the sun god on its back. The women are wearing exotic scarves, the delicate fabric draped to cover their faces, in an image carved four centuries before the advent of Islam to the region. The scene has been described as the world's first example of impressionist art.

Under the new nationalisation programme introduced by the Ba'athists, the 'Alawis were among the first to benefit. The poorest 'Alawis of all lived on the eastern slopes of the Ansariyeh mountains which looked inland to the desert, on poorer soil and with less rainfall than the coastal western slopes that ran down towards Lattakia. Hunger and deprivation had driven them off the mountains over many generations to work on the central plain around Homs and Hama, effectively as serfs in the service of wealthy landowners. Abu Chaker had employed them on his own fields and in his home as domestic servants, but gradually the labour supply dropped off as the 'Alawis increasingly found other opportunities. Tobacco had historically been their chief cash crop and now they were free to take the profits for themselves, becoming involved in tobacco trading and smuggling, or protecting tobacco-smuggling rackets in return for a share of the loot. To this day drug smuggling is still a lucrative activity freely conducted in the 'Alawi heartlands above Lattakia.

One of the enterprises Abu Chaker embarked on around this time—a venture that exemplified the typical Syrian merchant's ability to straddle the rural–urban divide and adapt to changing commercial circumstances—was a business exporting sheep to Beirut from the Badia, Syria's eastern semi-desert steppeland where many Bedouin tribes raised sheep. His business partner was a Syrian sheep merchant from Homs, and a very astute trader.

This sheep exporting business continued for many years. Lebanon had never had enough sheep, while the Syrian Badia always had more than enough, so this kind of trade had been going on for centuries. Abu Chaker's idea, as ever, was to maximise profit by cutting out the middleman. He and his partner would buy the sheep directly from the Bedouin and sell them at the sheep market in Beirut, incurring as few overheads as possible along the way. To avoid transportation costs, the sheep, his sons recalled, were "marched on foot" in large flocks by one or two shepherds, with the help of a few dogs.

Once, Abu Chaker had sent his eldest son, who was still a teenager, out to the Badia to meet up with the chief of the shepherds overseeing all the flocks—to toughen him up, he later realised. "It was very educational," his son laughed. He and the sheep merchant had eventually arrived after dark at the camp in the eastern desert, near the ruins of Qasr al-Hir al-Sharqi, an Umayyad desert palace between Palmyra and Deir ez-Zour. He had been wearing Arab robes, as his father had instructed, and was invited to join the shepherds for a meal around the fire. "This was real," he said, "not just some holiday camping trip." After eating and before bedding down for a night under the stars, he had asked where the toilet was. "Take your pick," the sheep farmer had scoffed.

The trade mainly went on in the spring, when free pasture in the Badia was available after the rains. It was especially profitable before the two big Muslim festivals, Eid al-Adha or "the Feast of the Sacrifice" and, Eid al-Fitr, which celebrated the end of the Ramadan month of fasting—when there was always a high demand from Saudi Arabia and the Gulf for sheep. Syrian sheep were thought of as among the tastiest, and because of the Islamic rules of *halal* slaughter, where an animal must be bled to death on the day of the festival itself, all sheep had to be transported alive. From Lebanon, they would be shipped to the Gulf via the Suez Canal.

The whole affair involved a lot of careful planning, as the price of the sheep was dependant on their condition, so the trick was to herd them, about 500 at a time, maximising the free pasture en route until the steppeland ended. From that point, they were herded from way-station to way-station where they would be well fed. To retain complete control over this process, Abu Chaker had even bought up way-stations in Lebanon. One was a farm in the Beqaa Valley; another was in the mountains near Bhamdoun. Water supplies en route could not be guaranteed, so arrangements were put in place for a water tanker to come and fill special cisterns along the way for the sheep to drink from.

The success of the exercise relied on the perfect combination of several factors: local knowledge of the terrain and the Bedouin environment, an understanding of the animals' requirements, and the right connections at the Lebanese end to sell at maximum profit. Abu Chaker was in his element in such dealings. "The borders were easy in those days," his sons said, "so you could just cross, and if you saw someone, you just gave them some money."

The sheep would finally arrive at a holding pen above Beirut, where they would be rested and fattened up after their "march". From there they would be sent down to the market, five, ten, fifteen at a time, depending on how high the price was on any given day. Flooding the market with too many at once would have meant getting a lower price; striking the best possible deal was always essential. "The market in live sheep was not as *raffiné* as dealing in fabric," the sons admitted, "but we did OK." Sometimes they also bought sheep from Turkey, or even as far afield as Argentina, where many Syrian émigrés, especially Syriac Christians, had settled over the years. The sheep would arrive in Beirut by ship, but after the Lebanese Civil War broke out, security had broken down in the port area. One of the family's ships was fired on by war profiteers demanding payment to allow the ship to dock, and many of the sheep were killed in the process. By the time deals were struck and they were allowed to offload and transport the sheep to the holding pen, many others had died from lack of water. "That was the point at which Father said: 'We are going to stop this,'" his sons remembered.

Abu Chaker was unusual within the Syrian milieu in having a much closer emotional tie to the countryside than other landowners. He was in some ways more like the Western European landed gentry, whose old bourgeois families traced their roots to the countryside, maintained their connection with it and often returned there for economic and cultural sustenance. In his case these ties were drawn back not to an ancestral country seat, but to his teenage years when he had travelled through the countryside to collect dues from the farmers who had bought textiles from him earlier in the season, and the long periods he had spent alone, camping rough and riding from village to village on horseback. It was then that he had learnt how to rear horses and sheep and to cultivate the best orchards and vegetable gardens. He understood the different soil types, how to fight pests and parasites organically, and how to use natural fertilisers and innovative irrigation methods, all of which he put into practice in his own small farm outside Homs. Smaller versions of the famous wooden waterwheels of Hama were common all over the Orontes valley, essential for raising water from the fast-flowing river to the higher fertile ground. In those early years of his life, Abu Chaker developed an instinctive feel for ecological balance and the rhythms of nature that stayed with him all his life, as well as a sense of wonderment, instilled perhaps by the many verses of the Qur'an that refer to natural phenomena, challenging people to ponder their meanings:

> God has set out for you the stars, that you may guide yourselves by them through the darkness of the land and of the sea. We have detailed the signs for people who know. (Qur'an 6:97)

> ... and in the change of the winds, and the clouds that run their appointed courses between sky and earth, there are messages indeed for people who use their reason. (Qur'an 2:164)

Though Abu Chaker never got involved in politics, humanitarian issues were another matter entirely. In Homs a Palestinian refugee camp had been established in 1949 on an area of land beside what is now the Al-Ba'ath University campus. It had a population of about 14,000 Palestinians, most of whom had fled from the villages around Acre, Haifa and Tiberias in what had formerly been northern Palestine. The camp still exists today—though no longer in the form of a camp, in the same way that the Yarmouk camp in

Damascus has largely been incorporated as a suburb of the city—and most of the refugees are daily wage labourers, local civil servants or street vendors. The sewage system is feeble and overloaded, schools are in a dilapidated condition and poor environmental health remains a major concern for UNRWA, the United Nations relief agency devoted to supporting Palestinian refugees. No one had imagined that the camp would be permanent. When Palestinian refugees first came to Syria, the assumption was that it would be for a matter of weeks, months at worst, not seventy years and counting. The same fear afflicts hundreds of thousands of Syrians today, who worry that in the absence of a political settlement to the war, they too could end up living in temporary camps in Jordan, Lebanon and Turkey for decades.

The Palestinians were not allowed to stay outside the camp overnight, but were permitted to leave during the day. On one occasion a young lad of about ten was running through the souk and accidentally knocked over Abu Chaker's *arghile*, or hookah pipe. Bending down to pick it up, the boy looked up at Abu Chaker in trepidation. Rather than being angry, Abu Chaker asked the boy about himself and on hearing that he was from the refugee camp, he invited the boy to work for him.

Years later, when his sons were wondering what had made him do this, Abu Chaker explained that he had seen a lot of intelligence in the boy's anxious blue eyes. It was clear, however, that the real reason was that Abu Chaker, by then in his late twenties, had been reminded of himself at that age, a ten-year-old fallen on hard times. He made the necessary arrangements to sponsor the boy, 'Ali, to come out to work for him. 'Ali worked hard in the shop and earned money to support his parents and siblings in the camp, much as Abu Chaker himself had worked to support his mother and sisters. He became Abu Chaker's trusted employee and protégé, well before his marriage to Rihab and the birth of his sons a few years later. When 'Ali was older, Abu Chaker even helped arrange his marriage, and sent him to Damascus to run the Chamsi-Pasha shop there. After the Damascus shop closed down, 'Ali came back to Homs and ran the shop whenever Abu Chaker was himself away, in Beirut or elsewhere. He continued to work for the family in Homs for many years. Having been taught everything he knew by Abu Chaker, it is unsurprising that he remained very loyal, and continued to follow Abu Chaker's methods of operating until his own retirement.

Like many other Sunni merchants and businessmen, Abu Chaker frequently had commercial partnerships with Jews, Christians and Druze throughout his career. Their faith was never a relevant factor; all that mattered was their character and honesty as a partner and trader. In the 1960s when he started buying textiles in bulk in Beirut, Abu Chaker hired his first accountant, a Jewish man known as Abu Izdi. The two families developed a close friendship, no doubt encouraged by the delights of the marzipan cake Abu Izdi's wife used to bake. Abu Izdi treated Abu Chaker's eldest son to informal Hebrew lessons during family visits to each other's homes, and was pleased to see his pupil's language improve over the months, spurred on by much marzipan pampering. "I have a life-long love of marzipan cakes from those days!" maintains the son.

Like many Jewish families, Abu Izdi's had emigrated to Beirut from Damascus after the 1967 Six Day War, because of rampant anti-Jewish feeling in Syria after the Israeli army first defeated the Egyptian and Jordanian armies, then seized the Golan Heights. By the early 1970s the Jewish communities in Lebanon and Syria had dwindled to just a few thousand. Sectarianism in the region was generally much less pronounced at that time. Both of Abu Chaker's office neighbours in Beirut were Jewish, but both emigrated overseas after the 1967 war. When the first left, Abu Chaker expanded his own office by paying his neighbour for the lease on the office he was leaving behind. Another Jewish employee, Victor Masrieh, known as Abu Ezzi, emigrated around 1976 soon after the outbreak of the Lebanese Civil War, first to Manchester, then to New York. Across history diasporas have formed again and again far from home, driven by political wars.

Back in the 1950s, Abu Chaker's two largest fabric suppliers in Beirut were both Christian, the first from the Shukeir family and the second from the Armenian Minassian family. His bankers in Homs were mostly Christians from the Eneini family, while in Beirut his main banker was Edouard Nasri—the general manager of the Société Géneral de Belgique and a Damascene Christian who had moved to Beirut in the late 1950s after Nasser's revolution in Egypt. In Beirut Rihab had employed a Jewish seamstress called Esther, with whom she often used to discuss how similar Islam and Judaism were—more similar, in their view, than Islam and Christianity. Both religions, they agreed, were straightforwardly monotheistic, uncomplicated by belief in the Trinity and the divinity of Christ. Both were based on divinely revealed laws, the framework that guided all aspects of life, quite unlike the Christian Bible. There was also the fact that Islam and Judaism both rejected the institution of an intermediary between man and God in the form of a hierarchical priesthood. Differences aside, the remarkable thing, as they saw it, was that all three religions had originated in the Middle East.

Contrary to today's perceptions of Islam, now routinely associated in Western mainstream media with extremism and terrorism, across history Islam has been the most tolerant of the three monotheistic revealed religions, respecting the beliefs of other indigenous religions and even accepting Christian missionary activity to a remarkable extent. One story tells of a lady missionary travelling alone in her Land Rover on her way to a medical clinic in a remote village. She ran out of petrol, but found a chamber pot in the back of the vehicle and headed off to collect some petrol from a settlement she remembered passing a little earlier. On her return she found parked beside her Land Rover a Toyota full of curious Bedouin, who then watched her pour the precious liquid into her fuel tank. "Madam," said the chief Bedouin, looking on with astonishment, "we may each be of a different religion but I have to say I admire your faith."

The rise of the overtly secular Ba'ath Party, with its radical land reforms of 1963, was set to transform Syrian society profoundly and permanently. The reaction of the public, not understanding the consequences till it was too late, was general indifference. Abu Chaker on the other hand, understood all too well. He knew that under a Ba'athist government, the old world of the Sunni notables was over, that their land and businesses would be taken from them, nationalised and redistributed. It was time to rescue what he could, and leave.

9

THE LEBANON EFFECT

Ask advice from a thousand men; ignore the advice of a thousand more; then go back to your original decision.

(Lebanese proverb)

Throughout the 1960s and right up to the outbreak of the Lebanese Civil War in 1975, Lebanon was described as "The Switzerland of the Middle East". Those living outside the region imagined this to be an allusion to the tiny nation's snowy mountains and ski resorts. Those in the know understood it to be a reference to the country's banking. Even in Lebanon's "Golden Age" of the 1960s, it had three ski resorts—and thirty-eight banks.

The Lebanese Banking Secrecy Law came into effect in September 1956 and was the major factor in encouraging foreign capital to choose Lebanon as a refuge. It enabled Beirut to become the key financial and monetary centre of the Middle East, perfectly placed to take advantage of the rapidly expanding wealth of the oil-rich Arab Gulf countries. The secrecy law was not a privilege but a duty, which all banks operating in the country, Lebanese or foreign, had to observe, and guaranteed anonymity to clients, along with a code number deposit account and a safe. The secrecy could only be waived if a person was declared bankrupt, or if the judicial authorities requested access because of suspected illegal enrichment. Any bank official who violated banking secrecy could be imprisoned for up to a year.

The financial climate in Lebanon was ideal in every possible way. With its location on the eastern Mediterranean, open to the West and on a natural crossroads between Europe, the Gulf and the Fertile Crescent countries, Lebanon's ports, airports and transport system became the networks of first choice for ambitious bankers, businessmen and merchants. Goods transited via Beirut's port and airport to and from Arab countries and beyond, while Lebanon's entrepreneurial workforce based in the Gulf or elsewhere sent large remittances home.

Lebanon also boasted the region's most highly qualified population, the product of its excellent education system, with its diverse and multilingual universities attracting the best and most forward-looking talent in the Middle East. In 1964–65 the American University of Beirut had 3115 students from sixty-five countries studying medicine, public health, pharmacy, engineering and agriculture. The skilled labour force of quick-witted professionals was often trilingual, switching effortlessly between French, Arabic and English. Half the population was employed in the service sector, with the other half divided between agriculture and the manufacturing industry. Nearly two thirds of all Lebanese exports were sent to the oil-rich Gulf countries.

In a region of mainly autocratic regimes with highly centralised economies, Beirut and its politically liberal democracy shone out like a beacon of dynamism, the natural choice for international companies looking to set up a head office in the Middle East. The country's beautiful coastline, beaches and mountains also drew real estate investment, leading to a surge in luxury-end tourism, especially attractive to Saudis and other Gulf nationals in the summer months, seeking to escape the debilitating heat of the Arabian Peninsula. Casinos, nightclubs and exclusive shopping outlets were also a draw for Arabs looking to spend their newly acquired oil money on activities that were not possible or not permitted at home.

So it was that during the 1960s Lebanon became one of the world's fastest growing economies. But it was not all plain sailing. In 1966 Intra Bank, the country's largest bank and its financial backbone, collapsed abruptly. Its founder Yousef Beidas, a Palestinian Christian known as the "genius of Jerusalem", was a refugee from the 1948 creation of Israel, and had built up an empire that employed 30,000 people (more than the entire Lebanese public sector at the time) and boasted a budget five times greater than the government's. The Lebanese political and financial elite had felt threatened and wanted to cut him down to size, so they spread rumours leading to a run on the bank's assets, then refused him a loan that would almost certainly have enabled him to survive the crisis. The shock to the financial system caused a loss of confidence in Lebanon's banks, further hit by the outbreak of the 1967 Arab–Israeli Six Day War, which in turn led to another influx of Palestinian refugees. The Beidas episode is still widely seen as presaging the Palestinian/Lebanese disputes that ultimately helped trigger the Lebanese Civil War in 1975.

Until its boundaries were carved out under the French Mandate, Lebanon had never been a state in its own right, and since 1517 had, like Syria, been part of the Ottoman Empire. According to the investigation of the US King-Crane Commission in 1919, its inhabitants were deeply divided over their future aspirations. Many Lebanese Muslims had supported King Faisal's regime in Syria, but most Christians, especially the Maronites, saw their salvation in France and were violently hostile to King Faisal, who was a Sunni Muslim. For them, the extension of the frontiers of Mount Lebanon as a French protectorate seemed the only possibility for their security, what the French called *Le Grand Liban*—Greater Lebanon. In 1919, the Maronite Christian Patriarch led a Lebanese delegation to the Paris Peace Conference presenting these demands, and the Maronite dream of Greater Lebanon was finally realised in 1920 as a French mandate, under a new flag that combined the French Tricolour with the iconic cedar tree of Lebanon.

In addition to the largely Christian mountainous region, the newly expanded Lebanese state comprised the predominantly Muslim coastal cities of Tripoli in the north, Sidon and Tyre in the south, together with their administrative hinterlands, and the capital of Beirut. France also removed the largely Shi'a-inhabited Beqaa Valley from Syrian jurisdiction and placed it within Lebanon's borders. The new country's population was roughly evenly mixed between Christians and Muslims. Since the French openly favoured the Maronites and other members of the Eastern Christian churches, the excluded social and religious groups naturally formed an anti-French, anti-Maronite alliance. Most of Lebanon's newly acquired "citizens" did not want to be part of a Maronite-dominated Lebanon and campaigned instead for union with the rest of Syria. Under the imposed borders of the mandate, Syria had been amputated, but Lebanon had nearly doubled in size.

This huge flaw in French policy put in place the explosive ingredients that would foment future sectarian conflict. With the exception of Beirut, the regions that had been added to Mount Lebanon to form the new state had a predominantly Muslim population, whose members objected to being placed within a Christian-dominated polity. The Maronites did not make up the majority of the population, yet they saw Lebanon as their own Christian homeland. Muslims, however, demanded unity with Syria and looked towards the wider Arab world for their source of identity. From the start, therefore, there was no common identity for the population of Greater Lebanon and no instinct to become a nation.

The French began to import their own culture and politics to Lebanon, and so as to facilitate their control and maximise the country's productivity, they invested in infrastructure, improving the roads between the major cities and enlarging Beirut's harbour. They introduced the French penal code, along with a public health system, free education with compulsory French language teaching and improved agricultural practices. Perhaps their most significant legacy was the "confessional" political system, still in use today, under which power was apportioned along religious or sectarian lines, biased in favour of the Maronite population. In 1926 the country became the "Lebanese Republic", as though it were an independent state, though the French continued to hold all the reins of power.

In 1943, after twenty-three years of French Mandate rule, the country's Christian and Muslim leaders came together to declare Lebanon's independence in an agreement known as the National Pact. It was designed to be the start of a unique multi-confessional democracy, in which the president of the republic is always Maronite Christian, the prime minister is Sunni Muslim, the speaker of the parliament Shi'a Muslim, and the deputy prime minister and deputy speaker of the parliament are Greek Orthodox. Muslims renounced their aspirations to unite with neighbouring Syria, while Christians accepted that the country would have an Arab rather than a European affiliation. Under this system Lebanon enjoyed three decades of prosperity, with agriculture, industry, the banking and service sector, tourism and education all flourishing under a free-market economy. Beirut was dubbed "The Paris of the Middle East" for its chic liberal sophistication, and Lebanon was the indisputable democratic high-flyer among the twenty-two Arab League countries. No other Arab country came close to achieving such levels of multiculturalism and diversity.

Nonetheless, Lebanon was powerless to control the seismic destabilising events in the region which followed the creation of the state of Israel. The first wave of around 150,000 Palestinian refugees fled to Lebanese refugee camps after the 1948 Arab-Israeli War. At first they found in Lebanon an atmosphere of political freedom that enabled them to play an active part in Lebanese politics in ways that would not have been possible in other more repressive Arab countries. The next big shock came with the 1967 Six Day War, which resulted in a second Palestinian exodus. As growing numbers of refugees arrived and settled, Lebanon's Christian and Muslim leaders tried to maintain neutrality to keep up the economic and cultural boom that the country was enjoying. But the Palestine

Liberation Organisation (PLO) and Syrian–Palestinian militias were increasing in numbers and had started to control the Palestinian refugee camps, gaining sympathy from other Muslim groups and Arab nationalists. Meanwhile, the other Arab states were making sure to prevent any Palestinian military activity from taking place within their countries.

More waves of Palestinian refugees arrived in Lebanon in 1970 when Jordan's King Hussein expelled the PLO in what was known as Black September. As Lebanon's stability became ever more fragile, its neighbour, communist-aligned Syria, suffered a drop in aid from the Soviet Union, which was then experiencing a time of economic difficulty. Syria had long harboured ambitions to take over Lebanon as part of the original "Greater Syria" and saw a potential lucrative acquisition. On 8 August 1973, Hafez al-Assad made a speech signalling his intentions: "Lebanon and Syria are one country and one people yet are run by two governments." The Lebanese army grew weaker and weaker, increasingly unable to control the various militias that were building up around the political parties.

In the end, it was not politics but an economic injustice that first set off the hostilities that would lead to the outbreak of civil war. In February 1975, the fishermen at Sidon went on strike protesting President Camille Chamoun's bid to monopolise fishing all along Lebanon's coast. The state attempted to suppress the demonstrators, who were supported in their actions by the political left and their allies in the PLO. In the scuffles Maarouf Saad, a popular figure who had represented Sidon in the national parliament and headed the city's fishermen's union, was killed by a sniper. The final trigger for the descent into full-blown civil war came on 13 April 1975, when Palestinian gunmen shot and killed four Lebanese Christians in front of a church in east Beirut. In revenge, Christian militiamen ambushed a bus carrying Palestinians later the same day, killing twenty-seven.

Hafez al-Assad tried to mediate in the civil war, only sending in his army when it looked as if the leftist forces were going to defeat the Maronites. In 1976, the Syrian army invaded from the north, then advanced into the Beqaa Valley. Hafez explained his actions in a characteristically lengthy speech, in which one critical passage stands out:

> Through history, Syria and Lebanon have been one country and one people. The people in Syria and Lebanon have been one throughout history. Genuine joint interests ensued. This matter must be known by everybody. Genuine joint interests. A genuine joint security also ensued. Close kinship between the people in the two countries also ensued. Many thousands of families in Syria have relatives in Lebanon. Many thousands of families in Lebanon have relatives in Syria.

Meanwhile any Lebanese voices that dared to raise criticism of the Syrian presence were silenced by targeted assassinations. Gradually the Syrian army began occupying more and more of the country, including parts of Beirut, while constantly bombing areas not under Syrian occupation.

Smuggling across the mountains from the free market of Lebanon into the closed market of Syria had long been rampant. The two countries shared a long border that was impossible to police, and for decades whole villages on both sides had lived off smuggling, supplying items that were frequently subject to shortages in Syria thanks to the control of foreign trade by the government and its dearth of foreign exchange. When the Syrian army entered Lebanon, the smuggling trade was virtually institutionalised and officers who were posted to Lebanon immediately saw it as an opportunity to earn a fortune. Smuggling worked in both directions, so that products that were heavily subsidised in Syria, like medicines and cigarettes, could be sold for a hefty profit in Lebanon at the government's expense.

More usually, however, goods were smuggled in the other direction, from Lebanon into Syria. An extensive black economy developed and became impossible to curb, because of the sheer numbers of people involved. Smuggling became the only way of getting automobile spare parts into Syria to keep cars on the roads. As Patrick Seale explains, "For a whole range of consumer products from lavatory paper to washing machines the middle class had nowhere else to turn." The Syrian army controlled the port of

Tripoli and most of the Beqaa Valley. Chtoura, the last town in the Beqaa before the Syrian border crossing at Masnaa, became the Mecca of anything and everything Syrians might want to buy. The shops were stacked high with cheaper toiletries, chocolates, shoes and electrical goods. For people who couldn't afford to buy wares, the temptation to get involved in smuggling itself was strong—especially for anyone stuck in a Syrian government office, barely earning a subsistence level wage. Law and order broke down entirely during the fifteen-year war, and no one worried too much about the repercussions. For many involved it was simply a question of survival, a choice between penury and having enough money to feed the family.

At the same time, a second underground activity was developing, one that was explicitly criminal: drug smuggling. Lebanon became one of the world's biggest narcotics producers during the war, with much of the hashish grown in the fertile Beqaa Valley. A few mafia-type families controlled the business, and also smuggled guns and other weaponry.

The war was financed in part by such smuggling activities, as well as by "taxes" extorted at checkpoints by the different militias, Christian and Muslim. Money also came from Iran, which provided a lot of military training and funding to the Shi'a Amal Party and enabled the creation of Hezbollah, a Shi'a militant group whose members were trained by the Iranian Revolutionary Guard. Hezbollah formed in response to the Israeli invasion of Lebanon in 1982, and was the only party to grow in strength during the war. Other foreign powers also had proxies—Iraqi President Saddam Hussein, for example, backed the Maronite General Aoun.

Today Lebanon still boasts eighteen officially recognised sects, most of them Christian, making it the most religiously diverse country in the Middle East. The sects are, in alphabetical order, 'Alawi, Armenian Catholic, Armenian Orthodox, Assyrian Church of the East, Chaldean Catholic, Copts, Druze, Greek Orthodox, Isma'ili, Jewish, Latin Catholic, Maronite Catholic, Melkite Greek Catholic, Protestant, Sunni, Shi'a, Syrian Catholic and Syriac

Orthodox. Each group has the right to handle its own family law in accordance with its own courts and traditions.

The country's last official census was conducted in 1932 by the French, and though many have called for more up-to-date data, the government fears the sectarian tensions a new census might unleash. In the absence of accurate figures, each sect and denomination has a vested interest in inflating its numbers, so that the sum of current claims reaches over 150 per cent of the total population. The arrival of the Palestinians and later around a million Syrian refugees since 2011 has further clouded the picture. But even without exact demographic data, everyone agrees that Lebanon has the largest proportion of Christians of any Middle Eastern country and that Sunnis, Shi'a, Maronites and Greek Orthodox form the four largest groupings, the reasoning behind the distribution of political offices according to the conditions laid out in the National Pact.

The Christian population ceased to be the majority in Lebanon in the early 1960s or perhaps earlier still, but Christian leaders in government have refused to relinquish any of their powers. As Muslims demanded increased representation in parliament to reflect the changed demographic, sectarian tensions mounted, spilling over into regular violent clashes—a state of affairs that continues today. Most observers estimate that Christians today account for no more than 40 per cent of the country's population, yet the political power balance remains skewed in their favour, with the Lebanese Parliament divided 50:50 between sixty-four Christians (of whom thirty-four are Maronite) and sixty-four Muslims (twenty-seven Sunni, twenty-seven Shi'a). Politics in Lebanon are entirely driven by group interests, and Lebanese invariably vote to support their sect.

The civil war in Lebanon raged from 1975 to 1990 and devastated the state's economy. The previous climate of political tolerance and stability had dissolved, prompting a massive human and capital flight from the country—a million people emigrated, over 40 per cent of the country's population. The intensity and longevity of the war had led to the destruction of a huge amount of public infrastructure, buildings and communications networks. Moreover, the country suffered a ruinous loss of confidence in its stability, an essential prerequisite for investment and prosperity. As a result Lebanon missed out on lucrative opportunities from the oil boom of the mid-1970s and early 1980s. Most foreign companies moved to Dubai, the direct beneficiary of Beirut's demise as the regional business capital.

The fluctuations in the economy's performance over the fifteen-year period of war mirrored the political developments on the ground. While output plummeted by 65 per cent in the war's first two years, half of that loss was recovered when the situation appeared to stabilise in 1977. The Lebanese pound depreciated slightly when war broke out but held its value surprisingly well for a few years, and inflation was stable at around 20 per cent. Output then grew steadily, until it was completely derailed by the Israeli invasion in 1982. The Israeli army inflicted huge destruction on southern Lebanon and on Beirut, which led directly to the phenomenal crash in the value of the Lebanese pound through the remaining years of the war.

Regaining confidence after such a prolonged conflict has proved to be extremely difficult. Economic rehabilitation was the first priority of Rafiq al-Hariri's government after the 1990 Taif Accord put an end to the war. Everyone recognised the need to achieve political and financial stability to rebuild Lebanon's credibility, which would be essential to the repatriation of capital and skilled labour.

The restoration of public infrastructure—roads, communications and utilities—was one of the post-war government's first tasks, together with strengthening public administration and institutions, to try to win back foreign financing and investment and recreate Beirut as a modern commercial and financial centre. In 1991 the government commissioned various consultancies to prepare a $3 billion national emergency reconstruction plan to be implemented over a three-year period. The plan proved to be unrealistic, and the next government produced a more ambitious ten-year plan called Horizon 2000, which would require $13 billion of investments and debt charges. That plan in turn was too ambitious, and was scaled down.

The good news was the gradual recovery in the value of the Lebanese pound against the US dollar from its lowest level in 1992, when inflation had spiralled up to 125 per cent. The pound managed to survive the crisis of the Israeli attack in southern Lebanon in April 1996 with surprising resilience, and that year the Beirut Stock Exchange reopened. The World Bank and the International Monetary Fund insisted on tighter monetary controls over Lebanon's fiscal deficit as a condition for increased loans. Annual growth rates since 1991 have ranged between 5 and 8 per cent and Lebanon's banking and service sector, agriculture and manufacturing industry have retained more or less the same balances and proportions of the economy and employment as before the war. Virtually all manufacturing industry is privately owned.

Beirut's main port was once the most important serving the Arab world, but during the war it effectively closed down. Today the port and its Free Zone have been reconstructed to their pre-war capacity and are even being expanded. The country has also seen a boom in advertising, with 150 advertising companies appearing in the 1990s, fuelled to some extent by the explosion in new TV stations broadcasting from Beirut. Tourism, which accounted for 20 per cent of GDP before the war, has also picked up again after a long hiatus, and major hotels have reopened in Beirut. The internationally famous Casino du Liban was refurbished and opened again in 1996, luring wealthy Arabs from the Gulf and their thousand-dollar room service bills. The tourism industry also relies heavily on the Lebanese diaspora, who return in huge numbers almost every summer, and even in the winter, since the country's ski resorts have all been improved and upgraded. In 2016 an advertising campaign ran in America with the aim of enticing wealthy Lebanese businessmen: "Lebanon is calling, home is waiting."

Lebanon's history bears many similarities with that of its neighbour, Syria, and its experience of fifteen years of civil war may hold clues to Syria's future. In Lebanon unemployment at the end of the war in 1990 was estimated at 35 per cent, and even for those in work, the value of wages had dropped in real terms. During the boom time before the war, the Lebanese government had taken the view that the trickle-down effect of successful growth would resolve most of the country's social issues of poverty and unemployment— much as the Syrian government had. This proved to be a costly miscalculation, since the clashes which superficially appeared to be fuelled by sectarianism in Lebanon almost always had their real roots in social divisions between the haves and have-nots—just as in Syria.

In April 2017 on the forty-second anniversary of the outbreak of the Lebanese Civil War, the then prime minister of Lebanon, Sa'ad al-Hariri, son of the assassinated Rafiq al-Hariri, sounded a new warning for the country's future. "When the civil war broke out in Lebanon," he said in a video posted on Twitter, "nobody knew it would last for fifteen years, killing tens of thousands, wounding many and displacing the Lebanese people and destroying the economy." It was the duty, he insisted, of every citizen to end all divisive sectarian rhetoric and make sure such a conflict was never repeated. In November 2017 he resigned, citing fears that his life, like his father's, would end in an assassination by Hezbollah, only to "unresign" two weeks later.

But of course, the war had not just been about religious divisions and political differences. Underlying everything were conflicting economic interests, something that was amply demonstrated by the intra-Christian and intra-Muslim fighting and by the constantly changing alliances, in line with financial interests that fluctuated from one month to the next. By the end of the war, nearly every faction had allied with and subsequently betrayed every other faction at least once.

The Lebanese Civil War killed 5 per cent of the country's population and left a further 10 per cent wounded. Twenty-seven years after the war ended, over 17,000 civilians are still missing or unaccounted for. An amnesty law allowed many of the war's chief actors to become leading political figures and to take seats in parliament, and under the terms of the 1990 Taif Accord, none of the militias were obliged to reveal information about prisoners of war, executions or kidnappings. The head of the International Committee of the Red Cross (ICRC) appealed to the Lebanese government to address the issue with urgency, encouraging them to adopt measures like those used in Bosnia to provide answers to grieving families. "Unfortunately, we are running out of time," he said. "Mothers and fathers are dying heartbroken without knowing what happened to their sons and daughters. They have a right to know, and it is the responsibility of the Lebanese authorities to provide some answers."

In 2012, the ICRC finally launched a project to create a database of the missing persons, and in 2016 they began collecting DNA samples from surviving family members to try to match them with human remains found in mass graves. The Lebanese government had acknowledged the existence of mass graves in Beirut in 2000. The extreme slowness of progress speaks volumes of the institutional inertia surrounding the project. The police are resistant to requests for information and political will in the government to move the project forward is absent. The subject is simply not a priority, and international justice for crimes committed over thirty years ago seems less and less relevant to today's problems. The project even risks exacerbating present tensions, by unearthing and reopening old wounds. The last thing the former militia leaders who now sit in parliament want is for a light to be shone on their murky pasts.

1. Mohammad Chaker Chamsi-Pasha
(later Abu Chaker) aged six, c. 1927.

2. Mohammad Chaker Chamsi-Pasha
(later Abu Chaker) aged twelve, c. 1933.

3. Abu Chaker in London in the
1990s, as a wealthy man in his
seventies.

4. A portrait of Abu Chaker aged sixty,
taken in 1981 after his acquisition of
the Bradford-based Yorkshire textile
manufacturers, Hield Brothers.

6. An eighteenth-century astrolabe, disassembled.

5. A second-century altar dedicated to the haloed Roman sun god Sol.

7. Palmyra, the merchant trading city that grew up beside Syria's largest natural oasis in the desert, halfway between Homs (ancient Emessa) and the Euphrates river.

8. An original drawing of the castellated Homs citadel as it looked in the eighteenth century.

N° 58/12. DÉPART DU PÉLÉRINAGE POUR LA MECQUE.
ÉDIT. G. F. DEPARTURE OF PELGRIMS TO MECCA.

9. Annual departure from Damascus of the Hajj pilgrims to Mecca, guarded by uniformed soldiers, while the women watch from the rooftops, c. 1900.

10. Aerial view of the Şemsi Pasha Mosque on the Asian shore of the Bosphorus, Istanbul.

11. Church of Umm al-Zinnar (the Virgin Mary's Belt) in the centre of Old Homs.

13. Fabric dye house in the quarter of Shaghour, Old Damascus, 1935.

12. Syrian textiler at his loom, c. 1890.

14. Damascene weaver, 1891.

15. The rectangular interior of the twelfth-century Al-Nouri Mosque.

16. Homs souk under reconstruction, following extensive damage during aerial bombardment by the Syrian government air force in 2012–14.

17. Abu Chaker and Umm Chaker (Rihab al-Atassi) on the terrace of their home in Homs.

18. Abu Chaker checking the accounts at his old shop in the Homs souk in 2006, aged eighty-five.

19. Homs souk in 2017, partially reconstructed, with the new roof still unfinished and a few shops open.

20. Homs Souk al-Harir (Silk Market) in 2009 before the war.

21. Briggella Mills, Little Horton Lane, Bradford, West Yorkshire.

22. Tree-planting ceremony at Briggella Mills in 1981.

10

EXPANSION INTO LEBANON

Life is borrowing and paying back.

(Lebanese proverb)

"Go west"—that was one of Abu Chaker's oft-repeated adages to his sons. When he made the decision in 1959 to move his family and his business from Syria to Lebanon, he put his own advice into practice. The stresses and strains of life in Syria had started to become very difficult for families like the Chamsi-Pashas in the late '50s and early '60s. Nasser's socialism and the decision of Syria to unite with Egypt to form the United Arab Republic had many consequences for the landed elites, and Abu Chaker realised that if his business was going to survive and have any chance of thriving, he would have to move to the much more economically progressive milieu of Lebanon.

During the French Mandate there had been complete economic unity between Syria and Lebanon, with joint customs, a unified currency and tax system, free movement of capital and people and unrestricted freedom of work in both countries. After independence, the two governments had then signed the Chtoura Agreement to form one customs area. But as their economic policies diverged ever further from each other in style—with the Lebanese as transit brokers favouring an outward-looking "open door" policy with no state interference, and the Syrians insisting on military-backed state interventionism and protectionism for their new industries and agricultural enterprises—it became clear the customs union was no longer sustainable.

Homs had historically developed business links less with Aleppo and Damascus than with its nearest port cities, Tripoli and Beirut, with which it had closer geographical ties. The new port of Lattakia that the Syrian government developed after independence was much further north, closer to Aleppo. As his textile import and wholesale business was growing, Abu Chaker did not want his ambitions to be thwarted by the new climate in Syria, its military interference in politics and its economic nationalism, through which it sought to control the movement of goods, people and capital. Given he was not one to align himself politically with those who might have helped him expand his business or promote it, he knew his aspirations could only be fulfilled by leaving the country. He had to prepare how best to enact his decision.

Before his big move to Beirut, Abu Chaker felt compelled to sell his fine black 1957 Chevrolet Bel Air. It was important to avoid drawing attention to himself, and as one of only two in the whole of Homs, the car was too conspicuous. The other was owned by an Atassi, a cousin of Rihab's, who was a civil engineer. When the *mukhabarat* (intelligence authorities) visited him, intending to impound the Chevrolet, Abu Chaker was able to tell them, truthfully, that he had sold it the week before.

Not wanting to cut his losses permanently, however, Abu Chaker decided to keep the flat where he and his family had lived since his marriage to Rihab, and to keep the shop open in the souk in Homs. He would expand into Beirut for his major operations, without flagging the fact up to the Syrian authorities. From the authorities' point of view, he remained Homs-based, a textile merchant trading from the souk in the usual way, who simply made regular trips to Lebanon to buy his stock. His devoted Palestinian protégé 'Ali stayed behind and manned the shop, but Abu Chaker would return in person every week to check on everything.

Many who stayed in Syria suffered the nationalisation of their factories. Some left discreetly, like Abu Chaker, who was far from the only one. Others, determined to keep their wealth away from the new government, even walked to the Lebanese border, bags stuffed with cash, where they were met by friends or relations and whisked off to Beirut. "Everyone lost," said his sons, "but again, Father made success out of misery, and since he was already trading out in Lebanon before the Ba'athist nationalisation policies, he could afford to lose in a way that other people couldn't." Rihab's father and brother, being wealthy Atassis, suffered heavy loses, especially since their assets were in the form of swathes of rural and agricultural land, as opposed to smaller plots in the city suburbs where the price of land was high.

Having made his decision, Abu Chaker drove one day in 1959 to Beirut and rented a flat, without telling his wife or anyone else in the family. The move was carefully planned, despite its apparent suddenness. Abu Chaker had spent time deliberating over the right location for his family to live in Beirut and had chosen Al-Haazimieh, a suburb on the hill above the port and city centre. The area was on the old road to Damascus, so he would be able to come and go between his new home and Syria without getting caught up in the terrible traffic jams that even then were a feature of life in Beirut. The flat was owned by a Shi'i and was in the middle of a very Christian area. "Church bells were always ringing out," Abu Chaker's sons remembered, "we were surrounded by crosses, two churches within a 100-metre radius from our house, and there were lots of Sunday weddings. We lived in a multicultural society, just like in Homs, where our neighbours in the souk were Christian, so we were used to interaction with Christians as normal. In Homs Father used to walk through the Christian quarter from his house to get to the souk and then back again every day. Throughout our own upbringing, we were living in a multi-religious environment."

Homs had been special for its level of closeness between the religious groups, and in Beirut Abu Chaker found a similar openness. In Damascus and Aleppo it was not the same, his sons explained, because the Christian communities were much more aloof, living "in their own kingdoms," not interacting with outsiders. "They made us feel like the newcomers, the interlopers, that they were the educated elite. But in Homs there was much more fusion, you shared bread with your neighbour, whoever he was. All that mattered was: 'Are you honest or not? Are you a good person or not? Are you trustworthy? Is this a good project?' Societies were much more integrated, more bonded, than we give them credit for, based on a common history, a shared sense of culture. In Homs in the 1970s we started a poultry farming business and the other two partners in the business were both Christian."

When Abu Chaker returned to Homs after renting the flat in Al-Haazimieh, he informed Rihab of his decision and she accepted it, as was her duty. Over the course of the next few weeks, the family moved into the flat, making several journeys. The relocation had to happen in stages, as unobtrusively as possible so as not to attract the attention of the authorities.

Social life in Beirut in the Swinging Sixties was very different to the conservative environment of Homs, but Abu Chaker was adaptable. Before making the move, when pondering how much it might cost, he had asked one of his Beirut suppliers, "What do I need to set up business here?" He had meant how much money, but the supplier had replied, "Nothing, just your good name."

Abu Chaker understood that this freer, more liberal and mixed environment would provide the right climate for him to expand for the first time beyond the shores of the Middle East. Before his transfer to Beirut he had been restricted to selling his cloth to markets in Aleppo, Hama, Idlib and Damascus. After the move he was able to trade and sell outside Syria for the first time, into other Arab countries and beyond, expanding his markets and his horizons. He was in his prime, and between 1960 and 1975, from the age of thirty-eight to fifty-three, he developed his business into a worldwide trading network, using the Beirut Free Zone to the fullest advantage.

He worked a seven-day week, never taking holiday. Beirut businesses would close on Saturday afternoons and Sundays, and so every weekend he would set off for Homs. In Syria the souks would be open, as Friday was the only weekly holiday. He would spend Saturday night semi-camping in the Homs flat and return to Beirut on Sunday night, in time for the start of the Lebanese working week on Monday morning. Sometimes he would make a round trip in one day, leaving Beirut at dawn on Sunday to arrive in Homs three hours later at 7:00 a.m., in time for the shop to open at 8:00 a.m. At first, having no car of his own, he would often travel by shared "*service*" taxi, paying for both front seats next to the driver. His first car in Beirut was a brand new Volkswagen, and after a while he saved enough to buy a white new Chevrolet Impala Sedan. Then he often drove to Homs himself, and brought back as much fresh produce as the car boot would hold, bought from stalls set up at the roadside. Syria's fresh fruit and vegetables were always better and cheaper than Lebanon's.

Time was of the essence for Abu Chaker, and he often spoke of the need to use one's time efficiently. The five daily prayers, offered at fixed times in the day, instilled in him an excellent sense of discipline. The strict routine of prayer drummed in the importance of punctuality, getting up on time and arriving on time, and helped him appreciate that time had a value. "Cheques, payments," one of his sons said, "everything had to be done, and the quicker the better. 'Never leave anything till tomorrow,' he would say, 'do it today. If you can do it now, do it now.'" Having the day naturally divided into chunks by prayer times might even have helped him to set deadlines for completing tasks. Without them the whole day might stretch endlessly ahead, making it tempting to procrastinate and be less efficient.

The reason for returning to Homs so regularly was that at that time in the early 1960s, when the Ba'ath Party was in the ascendant and busy nationalising companies and businesses, it was a hanging offence to take money out of the country. Strict laws were in force to make sure as much wealth as possible stayed inside Syria for the benefit of the new government. Abu Chaker would travel a route up the Beqaa Valley, where he had connections with local Shi'a in Baalbek who were well-known drug smugglers. In winter it was icy cold, and heavy snowfall sometimes closed the road, forcing him to stay overnight with them. His sons, who accompanied him on these journeys once they were old enough, remember these tough nights and their struggle to fall asleep on hard mattresses. "They were very hardy people, they didn't seem to notice the cold, and there was never any heating in their houses, but we shivered. Their bedding was so stiff there was a big gap between us and the covers where the cold air always found its way in."

On arrival in Homs, Abu Chaker would go straight to the souk. Over time he expanded his business to own three shops—two shops beside each other and one opposite—and the boys were told to sweep the area in front of them. Some shops in those days were starting to get glass shop fronts to keep the heat in, but Abu Chaker felt that these created a barrier between shopkeeper and customer and might deter people from buying. And so in winter, he used to bring a small portable heater into the shop where he would sit with his staff, while his sons were made to stay out in the cold, freezing. "I don't know what they thought of us, the other shopkeepers, I mean," his sons laughed, "these trilingually educated brats from Lebanon, but Father was determined to treat us just the same as staff. It was good for us. Thanks to that, we've never had a problem doing anything, however menial. Father also taught us the importance of patience, as in retail you have to be prepared to sit for long periods without a customer. You have to be able to handle that."

The family lived in the first Beirut apartment for two or three years until they were able to move to a larger apartment. When he could afford it, Abu Chaker then bought the land next door to build his own apartment block as their new home. Rihab supervised its construction, and like all such developments in the region the block of flats was built very quickly, in under a year, and was funded entirely by cash, as and when money came in. Abu Chaker never used credit for any such personal projects. His maxim was: "If you don't have it, don't spend it, always live within your means."

For Rihab, this was her first experience of such an undertaking. As the person in charge of the building project, she was the one who negotiated everything with the builders, including the price of cement and all the materials. She supervised the architects and the labourers, and generally oversaw every detail, with Abu Chaker's encouragement. "He didn't talk too much," she explained, "just two words, and you had to understand from these two words!" She enjoyed the responsibility and rose to the challenge, gaining a real sense of achievement as the building took shape.

Abu Chaker's routine in Beirut, she recalled, was to rise early, around 5:00 a.m. He would listen to two early morning programmes on the BBC World Service in Arabic—the first, at 5:45 a.m., was a politics programme where listeners would phone in and ask the panel of experts for their views on certain issues; the second was a more general news programme. "Then he would leave for the office at seven," she remembered. "Before he left and before the boys went to school, he always insisted they have a glass of fresh juice every morning: oranges or pomegranate or whatever was in season, or if there was nothing in season, then it had to be a can of Libby's fruit juice." His office would open at 8:00 a.m. but he was always there by 7:30.

He had rented an office near the central mosque in downtown Beirut, on the way to the Free Zone in the port, and had an Iraqi junior partner who ran it when he was travelling. He loved walking, and when he finished at the office he would call Rihab and say, "Meet me halfway." He walked partly to avoid getting caught up in the downtown traffic jams, so that by the time she met him in the car he would be clear of the congestion of the city centre. Rihab had learnt to drive in Beirut, and at this point still dressed in Western-style skirts and blouses, with no headscarf. His sons recalled how their father used to be a very fast walker, and how it was a running joke between them that he would never slow down for them, but

183

used to make them run to catch up. When in later life he slowed down, his sons were suddenly able to overtake him and take their revenge, calling, "Come on, Dad, keep up!"

The sons used to enjoy going into the port's Free Zone, the duty-free area where Abu Chaker's warehouses were. "Father never went, he would stay in his office, receiving Afghan and Iranian visitors in the 1960s, then later, after the '67 War, it was Saudis, and by the '70s it was mainly Saudis, Libyans and Kuwaitis." They remembered one occasion when, packed in amongst the cases of cloth from Bradford, they had discovered some Rolos, chocolates from England. "We ate Rolos for weeks!" they laughed.

For long periods, Abu Chaker would be away trading in Afghanistan, leaving Rihab alone, almost like a single parent, especially with the children out at school all day. Sometimes, if he had been delayed there longer than expected, he would send cash back from Afghanistan with a total stranger, so that she could continue the building project. He would also send her back cigarettes—it was in Beirut that she started smoking, though she always insisted that she never inhaled. Rihab's father had smoked a water-pipe and her mother had also smoked cigarettes.

Although he was a man of few words, Abu Chaker discussed everything with his wife. He wanted her to understand his work and his business and often asked her to accompany him to his office or to business meetings. It was something she missed a lot while he was away. Flights to Afghanistan from Beirut at that time were only once a week and in those pre-internet and pre-mobile days, he had no way of telling her which flight he would return on. Each week she would go to Beirut International Airport when the flight from Afghanistan came in, just in case he was onboard, returning despondent when he was not. Sometimes he was gone for weeks at a time. Again his attitude to his wife's role in society was curiously ambivalent: on the one hand, he didn't want her to socialise with Beirutis in his absence, even though the children were out at school all day, so she was often at a loose end, but on the other hand, he asked her to go to his office every day to keep an eye on the business.

Despite its lonely moments, Rihab remembered this time spent in Beirut as the happiest time in her life, when she enjoyed her own responsibility outside the home. In her eighties, after Abu Chaker's death, she even conceived a plan to return and refurbish the apartment block, and to live there again.

While private spending, like building the block of flats, had to be done with cash, when it came to business enterprises, Abu Chaker would go to the Beirut banks to get lines of credit extended. One of his policies was to use money he had borrowed from the banks to buy in quantity from the manufacturers. As a result he grew to have the largest textile warehouses in the Middle East, holding more stock than anyone else, so that when customers needed cloth, they could always count on him to have it.

Outwardly, during this time in Beirut, he maintained the myth that his business was based in Syria. He never sold his textile shops in the souk in Old Homs, but kept them ticking over, in the care of his loyal employee 'Ali, now joined by Ziad Sbeit, his second-longest-serving employee. Ziad had been drafted into military service after starting at the shop, and Abu Chaker held his job for him until his return two years later. Between them, Ziad and 'Ali opened at the usual times as if everything were normal. Abu Chaker even bought two more shops in Damascus, as his business in Beirut grew. Sometimes Rihab would accompany him to Syria and they would drive back from Homs via the Beqaa Valley, or sometimes via Tripoli, which she said always felt much more like a Syrian town than a Lebanese one, thanks to its Sunni majority.

In Beirut Abu Chaker's lifestyle was always modest. His sons recall that in their first apartment block, a wealthy Saudi playboy prince lived on the top floor above them, whose swanky cars and opulent lifestyle represented the exact opposite of everything Abu Chaker stood for. The prince would pay for the services of Swedish prostitutes, who used to come to his flat at all hours of the day and night. Beirut itself was full of nightclubs and casinos for those who could afford them. There was also a rich Christian family living upstairs; they too owned plush family cars, and the two daughters were always extravagantly dressed. At their young age, growing up in Beirut, the sons remember feeling envious of such luxuries, wishing they too had an expensive car instead of the modest Volkswagen Beetle their father started out with.

Once Abu Chaker had decided to buy something, he did not stint on the cost, believing that quality always paid. "You pay more to get something better," he told his sons as his business income began to grow. He followed his instincts on how to spend money. According to his sons, in 1973 he spent hundreds of dollars on an office calculator with a simple LED display—despite his conservative background, he always wanted to be at the forefront of new developments and embraced modern technological advances. The same applied with cars. In 1974, he bought an American Oldsmobile Ninety-Eight, which had electric windows and seats. When giving a lift to an old friend, he had fun playing with the car's windows, teasingly making them roll up and down randomly to startle his passenger.

When it came to education for his sons, no expense was spared—a decision that had Rihab's total support. Once the children were old enough, they were sent to one of Beirut's top schools: Pinewood College, a grand white palace with the fees to match. The school was co-educational, and pupils were taught in Arabic, French and English. Here Abu Chaker's sons mixed with the rich Christian elite of the city, as well as other royal or wealthy elites from countries like Iraq, Yemen, Saudi Arabia, Kuwait and Qatar. For the Chamsi-Pasha boys this was a somewhat schizophrenic experience, as it meant they mixed with others whose customs were totally different from their own and yet whose lifestyles they felt drawn to. They recalled a school skiing weekend they spent high in the mountains, enjoying the company of jet-setting friends, and the acute embarrassment they had felt when their mother appeared at the foot of the ski slopes of Faraya, telling them it was time to come home, or that she had brought them a picnic lunch in her basket.

The sons share many other memories of those childhood days in Beirut, such as when their father entrusted them with carrying large sums of cash to the bank for deposit. Aged less than ten, each had been appointed to walk all alone through the streets of Beirut from the office to the bank and told not to stop anywhere along the way. It was a test of courage and responsibility. They had all taken this duty very seriously, and had done their best to live up to their father's expectations. On arrival at the bank they could scarcely reach the counter to hand over the money. Only much later did the sons learn that their father had not in fact taken any chances, but had delegated an employee from his office to follow them at a distance and make sure they reached their destination safely. The bank officials had also been given warning to expect them, so that the boys were not overly questioned when handing over the cash.

Another trick they learnt from their father as boys was how to make sure they were paid the money owed by customers, often through post-dated cheques. Abu Chaker used to ask his sons to take these cheques to the bank, and had taught them how, on arrival, to ask the bank manager whether the customers had enough money in their account to honour the cheque. If the account was found to be short by a small amount, they would return with the cheque to their father and report back their findings. He would then give them the missing amount in cash to pay into the customer's account, so that the cheque could be honoured. It was better, he told them, to get most of the money you are owed rather than none at all, which is what would have happened if the cheque had bounced due to insufficient funds. A pragmatic approach like this would be out of the question in today's world, but breaching client confidentiality in those days was evidently not an issue that crossed the minds of bank managers, despite the banking secrecy laws. Abu Chaker understood the banking system in Lebanon very well and knew, for example, how to set up letters of credit, so that others would even come to him for help using them.

Sometimes, however, even he was puzzled by banking mysteries. A large sum of money once appeared out of the blue in Abu Chaker's account. He told the bank it must be a mistake, but they said the account deposit details were definitely correct. Three or four years later, a merchant he barely knew popped up and asked him if he could have his money back. Abu Chaker returned the amount with no questions asked. The merchant had known that Abu Chaker would never steal money that was not his, so the money would be safe there. Why the money needed to be there was not Abu Chaker's concern. Such matters were private and none of his business.

Like many others, Abu Chaker lost almost everything at the outbreak of the Lebanese Civil War, after all his stock was looted from his warehouses in the port's Free Zone. One of the reasons he was able to return to trading so quickly was his good relationship with the banks; he was lent money on the strength of his reputation for reliability and prudence. Nothing was insured, not that insurance companies would have paid out anyway in cases of civil unrest and war.

When the war began and his stock was stolen, Abu Chaker's first act was to gather all his cash and pay off his debts to the banks. "You are the only one paying off your debts!" they exclaimed. But he knew what he was doing and realised that maintaining his excellent credit rating during a war situation would stand him in good stead in the future. Thanks to that wise move, he had lines of credit extended from the banks soon after, based on nothing more than goodwill and trust, so he could trade against future money. When he was stopped at London's Heathrow Airport by immigration officials in 1975, he was asked how much money he had. "Enough," he replied. When the immigration officer became insistent, he produced the bank drafts, and was promptly waved through.

In 1976, after the outbreak of the Lebanese Civil War, Abu Chaker had seen that the souks in Mecca and Medina were empty. There was nothing there, no textiles, as all the Beirut suppliers had lost their stock. Thus, he decided to go the UK to see his main suppliers in Bradford—Hield and Selka—and told them he would buy large quantities of textiles from them, as long as they prioritised his deliveries so that he could meet the supply deadlines required by the Meccan merchants. While his competitors struggled to recover, Abu Chaker quickly took the initiative and stole a march on them, buying up all remaining stock with the money he was advanced by the banks, a move which enabled him to fulfil orders to Saudi Arabia, his chief client market at that point. He travelled constantly, shuttling between Saudi Arabia and Afghanistan to build his business.

Fortunately for him, two shipments of textiles from the UK were diverted to Cyprus when the war broke out, and had therefore never reached Beirut. Abu Chaker was able to retrieve that stock, which he had already paid for, and with his remaining cash he bought his first flat in London's West End, in 1976, when prices were a tiny fraction of what they are today.

His sons put it all in context: "In Lebanon, when the war started, he lost everything he had there. Millions and millions in the warehouses, he lost, so he went to the UK and started again. He developed a catastrophe into a success. All the customers from the Middle East used to go to Beirut to buy their goods, but suddenly it was all gone and nobody could supply. So he set up in the UK and he could deliver straight away. That gave him the edge and [showed] foresight on his behalf."

His warehouses in the Free Zone of Beirut had held one of the biggest textile stocks in the Middle East, so big that they could have supplied customers for ten years, but now they were no more than an empty shell. Later, the looters in Beirut who had stolen the goods had the cheek to offer them for sale back to him, at a lower price, but he was so disgusted he wouldn't touch any of it. "He refused to buy back his own goods," said his sons. "These thieves were from a village called Deir al-Ahmar in Lebanon, on the eastern side of the mountain, near Baalbek, a Christian village. The port was under Christian control, so it made its way to that village. His strength was in having goods ready at any time."

In Afghanistan, his sons recalled, where he had been selling a lot of cloth, the authorities suddenly decided no one was allowed to send money out anymore. "He turned that into an opportunity by starting to buy pistachios locally and exporting them. So when something went wrong in one area, he had an instinct about how to turn it into an opportunity in another. He'd always turn a loss into a profit. Because by doing so, he was earning money selling goods coming in, then earning money selling pistachios out. You could still get money out, but you had to go through the money exchanges, and they'd charge you a fee. He'd save on the fee." Barter deals such as this have always been used when standard economic norms fail. Human ingenuity comes to the fore, and Abu Chaker had plenty of practice from his earlier experience under the French Mandate with wildly fluctuating currencies. The official system was best ignored in such cases.

His sons described how their father flew on business so often with Ariana Airlines, the Afghan national carrier, that they often got free plane tickets. "Father was doing so much exporting from there, that we could travel to Afghanistan from Beirut for free. Once, we missed the last call because of security searches, but luckily the manager of Ariana Airlines was the ex-manager of the Beirut office and he knew us and Father, so he delayed the plane, because there was just one plane a week to Europe. That day we flew from Kabul to Tehran, Tehran to Istanbul, Istanbul to Rome, Rome to Amsterdam, Amsterdam to Paris, Paris to London—it was all one trip, exhausting."

Abu Chaker knew all the Afghan merchants and built up good relationships with them, to maximise his connections and with that, his profit. "He always knew how to cut to the essential of any deal," his sons explained. In Guatemala, for instance, Abu Chaker had started dealing in cardamom. "He even bought a fumigation station there so that he could control that stage after buying the crop straight from the farmers," his sons said. "He would give the farmers money on account so that they had money all year round, instead of just once in a while. This made it cheaper, and he could control the quality, be responsible for the packaging in jute bags, and then sell it to Saudi Arabia at a high price."

They recalled how their father was always exchanging ideas and teaching them new things, like how to keep track of their costs, and even double-entry bookkeeping. "He taught us how to show samples," they remembered, "the art of whether to show the most expensive one first or last. It was always a question of judgement, of being able to judge whether this particular customer would be more likely to buy if he saw it first or last. He always knew his customers, and had different techniques for all of them, according to his reading of them as individuals. In Saudi Arabia, in Mecca on the *Hajj*, he would perform the rituals and then spend hours in the souks, looking at the prices, getting to know who did what and who wanted what. Often the Saudis were not buying for themselves, they were buying for Iranians, Iraqis or Libyans. His skill was in knowing the right approach for each buyer. It was an instinct."

After Beirut collapsed as a sales centre, Abu Chaker realised the solution was to keep the stock warehoused in mills in the UK, and supply textiles directly from there. When he bought the stock, this became part of the deal, so that the mills allowed him to hold the stock at their premises till such time as it was shipped to clients in the Middle East and North Africa.

With Beirut too unstable for business, Abu Chaker decided to base himself and his family in London. The UK was his main source for textiles, though he was also buying from Japan and Czechoslovakia. Most of his customers at that time were in the Gulf, so he could have settled there instead. "But Father decided the UK was the safest, the most civilised, and he wasn't keen on living in the Gulf," said his sons. "It was all new to us, completely different to anything Father had done before. To guarantee our supplies reached the customer we even chartered flights of our own to transport the cloth into Jeddah airport and then got trucks to take it to Mecca and Medina and even to Dammam. We got back into the game and became the biggest dealers in the Middle East. After that, Saudi Arabia took off for us."

Within the Syrian mercantile community much business was done in a spirit of trust and compassion. A young trader of limited means, 'Abd al-'Aziz al-'Abbasi, was starting out in the textile world in Saudi Arabia. He was sent to Abu Chaker's office in Beirut with an introduction from a loyal customer, Hajj Yassin al-Zaytouni, who was based in Ta'if. After being shown a number of sample sets, 'Abd al-'Aziz picked out just one, since that was as far as his £1,000 would go. Abu Chaker replied that since he came with Hajj Yassin's recommendation, 'Abd al-'Aziz was welcome to take as much as he wanted and pay the balance six months later. The young trader could hardly believe his luck and proceeded to buy £15,000 worth of goods, which were duly shipped to Ta'if. Within two months he managed to sell enough to pay back the £15,000, and promptly wired the money back to Beirut. As soon as Abu Chaker received it, he rang 'Abd al-'Aziz to ask why he had sent the money back so soon when he still had another four months to pay. 'Abd al-'Aziz replied that since he had already collected his profits, he wanted to settle his debts immediately. It was the same cycle of helping younger generations that Abu Chaker had benefited from in his own youth in Homs, from the sheep merchant friend of his father.

"Father could always judge who the good people were," explained his sons, "the ones who could be trusted. Sometimes, to keep someone going, or to help them get started, he would write them a large cheque, with no receipt, nothing in writing. He wasn't interested in the actual return. If he knew their family and trusted them, he might also advance them some goods to get them started, and of course that made them loyal customers. We never lost money this way. Sometimes people repaid late, but we were never betrayed, never had to write off any debts. He always knew people's limits, and didn't allow them to overreach themselves—he might give one person £50,000, and another £100,000, according to his judgement of their honesty. We were the kings in the market, because we were trusted."

11

THE COMMERCIAL CLIMATE UNDER
HAFEZ AL-ASSAD

Better to have a thousand employees who steal,
than one partner with whom you have to settle accounts.

(Arab proverb)

Over the course of Hafez al-Assad's thirty-year rule from 1970 to 2000, there were almost no changes in the power structure of Syria. The same key military figures who had been loyal to Hafez in the years before his takeover and in the early stages of his presidency were still there twenty-five years later. The president saw no need to change them. After living through the turbulent years following defeat in the 1967 Six Day War against Israel, which had left the army and government in disarray, Hafez wanted continuity at any cost. That might mean turning a blind eye to the dubious business practices of certain key figures, but it was a price he was prepared to pay in return for their loyalty. He himself lived frugally, never amassing a personal fortune, and there were never any indications that he abused his privilege as leader for his own financial gain.

By the mid-1990s many of his loyal côterie were well into their sixties, but rather than replace them with younger men whose loyalty might be less certain, he kept them on. Occasionally he did retire one or two, only to re-summon them shortly after, preferring their familiar presence to the risk of change. He had found the perfect inner circle, and experimentation might be dangerous. "I have always been a man of institutions," he told biographer Patrick Seale.

Hafez's younger brother Rif'at, on the other hand, was well known to be a corrupt individual, abusing the power that came with his command of 55,000 heavily armed fighters in the Defence Companies. These fighters often acted independently of the army, like a law unto themselves. When Hafez suffered a heart attack in 1983, prompting rumours that he was about to die, Rif'at proved himself to be disloyal and plotted to take over the presidency. Rif'at's eventual exile was the only major break in the continuity of Hafez's thirty-year rule. Before that, in one of his deft political manoeuvres, Hafez had "promoted" Rif'at to the post of vice-president, along with two others, without actually giving him any responsibilities. Another younger brother, Jamil al-Assad, was entangled in smuggling activities in the Lattakia and Tartous regions, along with his son Fawwaz, and became an embarrassment to the Ba'ath Party's reputation and authority. Attempts were made, only partially successful, to rein them both in. Hafez tolerated corruption on his top table, but never treason. He instructed his intelligence chiefs to keep clandestine files on the proclivities of high Ba'ath officials, to collect evidence that could be used against them if necessary.

Across every level of society, both within the party and among ordinary Syrian people—the widespread corruption in government was well known. The Ba'ath's own organisational report of 1985 talks of:

> opportunists infiltrating the party ranks and constituting a dangerous phenomenon... Their main concern is to attain leading and responsible positions, in order to realise moral and material gains and to reap the fruit at the cost of the party's reputation. They believe that the existence of the party is temporary and that it will eventually vanish. Hence, they seize opportunities to make illegitimate profits by purchasing houses, precious objects and agricultural lands, speculating in real estate, acting

as stockbrokers, smuggling and exploiting the party and state mechanisms for their own personal purposes.

Hafez judged this to be a price worth paying and found ways of restraining the public response. Education, "the pride of the Ba'athist state," as Patrick Seale called it, had been nationalised by the state in the 1960s so the curriculum could be properly controlled by the Ba'ath Party, to produce generations of compliant children who would grow up with the party ideology deeply embedded in their way of thinking.

Article 21 of Syria's constitution from 1973 defines the purpose of the educational system as: "Creating a socialist nationalist Arab generation which is scientifically minded and attached to its history and land, proud of its heritage, and filled with the spirit of struggle to achieve its nation's objectives of unity, freedom, and socialism, and to serve humanity and its progress." Until 2012, article 8 in the constitution also stipulated that: "The leading party in the society and the state is the Socialist Arab Ba'ath Party. It leads a patriotic and progressive front seeking to unify the resources of the people's masses and place them at the service of the Arab nation's goals."

School texts were liberally scattered with references to the Assad family and its wisdom and benevolence. Students even had to memorise the leader's sayings, biography, and his role in and details of party conferences. The Ba'ath flag and pictures of the president appeared on educational documents from textbook covers to official records, in classrooms, lecture halls and playgrounds. Under Hafez's guidance the Ba'ath Party offices managed all aspects of national education, from education policy to filling leading educational positions. Appointment to these roles was always subject to approval by both the security apparatus and the presidency.

The National Union of Syrian Students, founded in 1963, predated Hafez's presidency, as did the Revolutionary Youth Union, which was founded in 1968 as a political educational organisation for students aged twelve to eighteen. But following a trip to North Korea, Hafez was so impressed by the ranks of uniformed primary school children that he established the Ba'ath Vanguards

Organization in 1974 for children under twelve. The Ba'athists established a Syrian embassy in Pyongyang in 1970 and the two countries, as client states of the Soviet Union, went on to develop close military ties. The Assad regime has kept up good relations with North Korea's Kim dynasty, and in 2015, to mark the seventieth anniversary of the Workers' Party of Korea, a new park was inaugurated in Damascus named after Kim Il-sung, North Korea's founding father and a great friend of Hafez.

From 1983 co-education for all age groups became the norm in Syria's cities and gradually spread into the countryside too. Beyond the official school day, a wide variety of extra-curricular activities were on offer: conferences, workshops, competitions, festivals, cultural weeks, student exchanges and volunteer work. Attendance at these events was not compulsory, but non-attendance was noticed. Over more than four decades, these institutions helped implant an entire system of values and behaviours in Syrian educational institutions: devotion to the party; adulation of the leader; dogmatism; political and cultural isolation; and belief in repression as a means of resolving differences and conflicts. The standard of patriotism became loyalty to the party and the state, as well as pride in and obedience to the laws and awareness of one's duties.

Not unlike the Workers' Party of Korea, the Ba'ath Party's aim was to form a collective consciousness that would unite all citizens in one cultural melting pot, minimising sectarian differences for the sake of the regime's stability. Inevitably the system was corrupted, and at university level, offers and scholarships were granted to the children of Ba'ath Party officials irrespective of merit. As a young boy Hafez had observed sons of well-connected Sunnis being given inflated grades. Now it was the turn of others, including 'Alawis, to shine, especially if they were well-connected Ba'athists.

Many 'Alawis, of course, were genuinely talented, and entered education after the 1963 revolution with great enthusiasm. They eagerly worked their way up into the professions and senior positions within the state apparatus, unseating their former Sunni and Christian rivals. Others, who were less academic but nevertheless tough and resourceful, instead found jobs as guards or security personnel, often recruited into the Presidential Guard, the Special Forces or the Defence Companies. This marked the start of a demographic change in the capital, as 'Alawi families came in from the countryside and settled in the outlying Damascene suburbs of Mezzeh, Qaboun and Harasta.

There were other ways, too, of binding people to the central state authority. Hafez, from his own modest yet well-connected 'Alawi background, understood the way the fabric of Syrian society was stitched together according to *mahallas* or localities. A *mahalla* could be either an urban area or a rural village in which the residents are linked by a common sense of identity independently of sect or religion. The boundaries of each *mahalla* are invisible to outsiders, but their residents can often trace their family histories back hundreds of years. The Western concept of "neighbourhood" comes nowhere near conveying the strength of the *mahalla*. Hafez knew that if he could tie these *mahallas* into a relationship with the central authority of the state, his longevity was assured.

Hafez's success in this respect is the reason that the Syrian state has not unravelled to this day, even after years of civil war. The Ottoman Tanzimât at the end of the nineteenth century had given administrative control of the *mahallas* to the traditional landowners and notable class, a system that was retained under the French Mandate. The challenge for Hafez and the Ba'ath Party was to replace this traditional class of local leaders with a new local leadership that would be loyal instead to the centralised power structure in Damascus. They began in the 1960s by setting up organisations like peasant unions staffed by young, educated, ambitious loyalists, but these unions were not enough to dislodge the powerful family structures.

In 1985 historian Hanna Batatu observed that the same landowning families held sway in the village of Ibbin Samaan west of Aleppo as in the pre-Ba'ath period, still collecting a percentage, albeit small, of the local farmers' earnings, completely independent of any central tax collection by the state. To break down the frictions between the old and the new leaders, both sets of elites were offered administrative posts in the local government hierarchy, as heads of districts, heads of provincial councils or even as governors, thereby tying them to the regime without giving them any real decision-making power. To bring them further into line, a Law of Local Administration was issued in 1983, the year after the Muslim Brotherhood uprising in Hama.

Hafez started a leadership cult around himself, commissioning large public portraits and statues and styling himself "Commander for Eternity" (*Qaiduna ila al-Abad*). Dissent was never tolerated, and Hafez's response to the Hama uprising was unequivocal: "Death a thousand times to the hired Muslim Brothers, a thousand times to the Muslim Brothers, the Criminal Brothers, the Corrupt Brothers." In 1980, the day after the Muslim Brotherhood assassination attempt on his life, he had ordered the dawn massacre of a thousand prisoners at Tadmur Prison in Palmyra and ten days later introduced Law No. 49 to make membership of the Muslim Brotherhood a capital offence.

Decisions were taken in Damascus by the loyal Ba'athists, a posse that had been expanded by Hafez to bring in many diverse social groups, but the responsibility for implementing these decisions lay with the regime's direct agents—usually the security and intelligence agencies or *mukhabarat*—rather than the local administration, which remained largely powerless. In this way the regime's networks and the local intermediaries became intertwined. Personal benefit gradually took precedence over personal reputation.

Hafez al-Assad's overriding foreign policy goal was to regain the Golan Heights, a focus that drove him to retain relations with the oil-rich Gulf monarchies while also keeping links with the Soviet Union. He had not let go of the territorial losses imposed on Greater Syria when it had been partitioned by foreign powers, and in an address to PLO chairman Yasser Arafat, he declared:

> You do not represent Palestine as much as we do. Never forget this one point: There is no such thing as a Palestinian people, there is no Palestinian entity, there is only Syria. You are an integral part of the

Syrian people, Palestine is an integral part of Syria. Therefore it is we, the Syrian authorities, who are the true representatives of the Palestinian people.

Opposition to Israel determined many of his policy decisions, and was the state's justification for keeping in place the 1963 Emergency Law on the grounds that Syria, as the last of the "resistance" states, was in a continual state of war with Israel. In a memorable speech of 1967, Hafez himself had commanded the troops to: "Strike the enemy's settlements, turn them into dust, pave the Arab roads with the skulls of Jews. Strike them without mercy."

In the 1960s the media was nationalised—Hafez knew all too well that knowledge and information could shape allegiances. Daily papers were authorised and published in the Damascus Free Zone, requiring a daily distribution permit; such permits were only handed to individuals loyal to the regime. Commercial radio stations were allowed to broadcast as long as they aired no political content. Advertising was similarly nationalised, so all content was monitored by the state. Self-censorship was the order of the day, since the consequences of open criticism of the government were arrest and imprisonment.

While education, media and advertising could be kept under tight state controls, the economy presented a much harder challenge. Subject as it was to outside influences and political turbulence beyond Syria's borders, even Hafez could not dictate its course. With the start of the oil boom economic policy in Syria shifted to face the West, then reorientated towards the Soviet Union as Syria became disillusioned with Western policy on Israel, only to turn back to the West after the communist USSR entered its period of *perestroika*. When Hafez became president in 1970 it was the Soviets who reached out to him, selling him hardware to build up his armed forces and arranging military training programmes in Moscow. With Soviet funding and technology, the first ever Syrian dam was completed in 1973, a project that, apart from providing the country's main source of water and hydroelectric power, flooded dozens of Arab villages as the new reservoir, Lake Assad, gradually filled.

Thousands of Arab families from Raqqa province were resettled in the predominantly Kurdish Hasakeh province, where the Kurds still refer to them as *'Arab al-Ghamar* (Arabs of the Flood) and consider them foreign occupants, a thorn in the side of their ambitions for Kurdish autonomy in northern Syria.

Financial aid from the Gulf paid for the expansion of the state sector, along with road, rail and other infrastructure projects. The traditional bourgeoisie was able to thrive on the margins by importing goods and investing in light industries and services. By the late 1970s it became clear that this economic system was unsustainable, because of the inefficiencies of the bloated public sector.

When Hafez al-Assad had first come to power in the 1970s, economic growth was 7–8 per cent per annum. Despite a crash in 1973 after the Yom Kippur War against Israel, Syria achieved full employment briefly in 1974, and even required extra workers from abroad to compensate for the Syrian exodus to the Gulf countries. The country had lost many highly skilled and middle-level managers whom it badly needed—men who left in the late 1950s and early 1960s after the failed union with Egypt—though it also benefited from the remittances they sent home to their families. In 1974 Syria also achieved a peak growth rate of 10.5 per cent, its highest figure ever and higher than any other country in the region, with the Gulf countries peaking at 7.9 per cent. The dramatic rise in world oil prices from 1973 to 1974 led to increased production from domestic refineries, while higher prices for agricultural and oil exports encouraged growth. The financial burden of military involvement in Lebanon from 1976 onwards then pulled growth down again, not offset by the rise in smuggling across the Lebanese border, which sometimes accounted for 10 per cent of GDP. Hafez was shocked at the extent of the corruption among his officials, but all reforms were suspended, as he awaited the conclusion of the interminable peace process with Israel that left him physically and emotionally drained.

Syria's economy did eventually open up—as Egypt did during Sadat's *Infitah* after the 1973 Yom Kippur War—but the process took much longer. By the end of the 1970s, it had shifted from its traditional agrarian base to an economy dominated by the service, industrial, and commercial sectors. Massive expenditures for the development of irrigation, electricity, water, road-building projects, the expansion of health services and education in rural areas all contributed to the country's prosperity. These advances constituted genuine infrastructure improvements that the regime could take credit for. Women's emancipation also moved forward under the Ba'ath Party. Hafez appointed the first woman minister to be minister of culture in 1976, and kindergartens were opened to enable mothers to work.

But the economy remained dependent on foreign aid and grants to finance the growing deficits both in the budget and in trade. As a front-line state in the Arab-Israeli conflict, Syria was also vulnerable to the vagaries of Middle East politics, relying on Arab aid transfers and Soviet assistance to support mounting defence expenditures.

In oil production the country lagged behind its Arab sister-states. Exploration for oil in Syria had first begun during the French Mandate in 1933, but there had been no major finds. The industry did not become significant until 1968, when the Karatchok field began domestic production after the completion of a pipeline connecting it to the Homs refinery.

During the 1970s more foreign oil companies were allowed to operate inside the country, including an American company. US President Nixon even visited Damascus in 1974 to cement the new relationship. Rapprochement with the West grew and private investment from the pro-Western oil-producing Arab countries began to build momentum. In 1976 this alliance was further cemented when the Syrian army was invited by the French and Americans to enter Lebanon on the side of the pro-West Maronite rightists to intervene in the Lebanese Civil War.

But this Western alignment was short-lived. It was first derailed in 1978, when Egypt's President Sadat signed the Camp David Accords making peace with Israel, leaving Hafez feeling deeply betrayed, not least by the USA's massive financial sweetener to Egypt for signing the agreement. The second blow came when he learnt that the West had supported the 1982 Muslim Brotherhood insurgency against him in Hama. That uprising was also supported by a large element of the Syrian merchant class, especially from Aleppo: these were Sunnis who felt discriminated against by the new 'Alawi-dominated power structure, who wanted to take back control of what they felt was rightfully theirs but had been usurped by an inferior class.

Hafez, of course, understood this resentment very well. It was why he went to such lengths to focus on the socio-political dynamics of each locality, rather than on the sectarian grouping of its residents, and why he instituted the ID card system that did not declare the holder's religion or sect. It was in his interest to eradicate sectarian allegiances, so that the 'Alawi minority background would not stand out. If all religious groups could be subsumed within a national identity, the Sunni population would be less able to dominate. "Despite the ethnic diversity within each nation, the social fabric of the region by and large is one," he said.

There is documentation that suggests he may well have truly believed this. A petition signed by Hafez's father, along with eighty-six other 'Alawi notable families, has been found in the French foreign ministry archives, and expresses a very similar sentiment. Dated July 1936 it fiercely denounces the "manipulation" and "capricious dictatorship" of the French governor and argues that:

> religion cannot be the basis of the constitution of a people... 'Alawis are Muslims just as the Orthodox and Protestants are Christians. Are there not, in every city in Syria, a large number of inhabitants of all the religions professed in this country? In a word, in what country in this world do all the inhabitants practice one and the same religion?

Hafez followed the same logic with tribes as he did with sects, continuing a clever process of disempowerment that had begun under the Ottomans in the nineteenth and twentieth centuries and been picked up by the French during their mandate. Before 1970 the Ba'ath had built links with the less affluent tribes, redistributing the vast landholdings of the richer tribal leaders in favour of the smaller tribes and giving them positions of power in the Ba'ath Party. Hafez decided to do things differently. He returned authority to the big tribal leaders by granting them informal control over their own communities, and appointed many to parliament to enhance their status. As a result the tribal leaders increasingly became the state's clients and interlocutors for managing their territories, and the central state authority was able to play leaders off against each other in a contest for its patronage. Raqqa was a typical case, where before 1970 the head of the Peasants' Union Bureau had been the descendant of slaves of the Afadlah tribal leaders, and the head of the Ba'ath Party branch office had been the son of a vegetable seller. Both had been the first in their families to receive a modern education. After Hafez came to power in 1970, both were given seats in parliament. When it came to local crimes, police were instructed by Hafez to allow tribal leaders to deal with cases of rape and murder in their own ways, leading citizens of Raqqa to summarise the regime's policy in a cynical rhyme: "*i'ti wala wa-if'al ma tasha*" (give loyalty and do as you please).

But it wasn't quite as simple as that—in an extra twist, the tribal leaders were made to compete for their role as intermediaries between the state and their local tribal members, leading to internal struggles within the tribe among rivals aspiring to tribal leadership. All contenders were, according to tradition, drawn from one particular family: the shaikhly family, or *bait al-'ashira*. Any male member of this family was eligible for leadership, as agreed by consensus among the leaders of the tribal sub-units. A tribal leader could never be imposed from outside the shaikhly family—not even by the regime. The regime's room for mischief, however, lay in its ability to sow dissension within the shaikhly family itself. Its preferred method was to elevate the position of one member above the other, often giving him connections to the security and intelligence services, linked with financial incentives.

Once again religion was not a factor in such arrangements. When Hafez took power the constitution stated that only a Sunni Muslim was eligible to become president, and that the state religion was Islam. In 1973 he oversaw the introduction of a new constitution, which simply stated that the president must be a Muslim—a move that led to protests at the time. The following year, to ensure no problems could arise from this constitutional requirement, Imam Musa Sadr, leader of the Twelver Shi'a in Lebanon and founder of the Lebanese Amal Party, issued a religious edict or *fatwa* confirming that 'Alawis were Shi'a Muslims. The status of 'Alawis as Muslims was further validated when Ayatollah Khomeini issued a similar *fatwa* after the Iranian Revolution, giving Hafez legitimacy at a time when he was under pressure from the Sunni Muslim Brotherhood. The Iranian government did not condemn Assad's violent repression of the 1982 Hama uprising, in which the Muslim Brotherhood had tried to overthrow the secular Ba'athist regime and its modernist ideology, wanting to replace it with strict Islamic rule and Shari'a law.

Hafez went even further in manoeuvring the boundaries of religious identity, and over his thirty-year rule 'Alawis were in effect outwardly "Sunnified". Sunni-style mosques were built in every 'Alawi village and 'Alawis were encouraged to perform the *Hajj*. In a paper called "Islamic Education in Syria" American academic Joshua Landis writes that 'Alawis, Druze, Isma'ilis and Shi'a are not mentioned in Syrian textbooks but that "Islam was presented as a monolithic religion." This message was reinforced by the chief judge of the Ba'athist state, 'Ali Sulayman al-Ahmad, when he declared: "We are 'Alawi Muslims. Our book is the Qur'an. Our prophet is Mohammad. The Ka'aba is our *qibla* and our religion is Islam."

No amount of manipulation could protect the regime from outside forces, however, like a collapse in world oil prices in the mid-1980s. Syria's economic boom gave way to a period of austerity. Levels of aid from the Gulf states, whose economies had also been hit, plummeted—partly to punish Syria for its support of Iran in the Iran–Iraq War. In 1986 there was an acute foreign exchange crisis. Remittances from Syrians working in the Gulf dropped. On top of that agricultural output was badly hit by a drought.

As Western and pro-Western powers seemed to turn away from Syria, Hafez reorientated the country towards the Soviet Union, signing a Soviet Friendship Agreement in 1980. America had by 1979 designated Syria a "terrorism-supporting" country and the oil-rich Gulf countries reduced their financial support in compliance. The 40,000 Syrian troops stationed in Lebanon switched sides, allying themselves with the Palestinians and against Israel. In 1982 Israel invaded Lebanon, clashing with Syrian troops, and went on to occupy southern Lebanon for eighteen years. Syria was firmly opposed to the Western foreign policy in Israel and Lebanon throughout this period.

From the early 1980s Arab capital began to dry up and the investment climate in Syria became increasingly unattractive. Private job opportunities faded away and unemployment began to re-emerge, reaching crisis levels after 1986 because of the rapid depreciation of the Syrian pound. Inflation reached 15–25 per cent, plunging the living standards of Syrians, most of whom survived on fixed incomes, towards the poverty line. Shortages became common and essentials like cooking oil, tea, sugar and coffee disappeared from the market. The smuggling epidemic across the Lebanese border, which was used by key state officials and large segments of the bourgeoisie to enrich themselves, grew ever bigger. The regime turned a blind eye, allowing Damascus businessmen in particular to conduct lucrative smuggling rackets as a reward for their loyalty in the struggle against the Muslim Brotherhood, while at the same time punishing the Aleppo merchants for having taken the Brotherhood's side.

Communist Eastern Europe and the Soviet Bloc tried in the mid-1980s to revive their private sectors during the period of *perestroika*, and began withdrawing their political support for Syria. This forced the Assad regime to make limited reforms in the direction of private sector promotion and liberalisation. The earlier Ba'athist nationalisation programme had targeted big enterprises, not small and medium-sized companies, many of which had remained active. Agriculture in particular had remained in small holdings except for a few state farms; small manufacturing companies had survived, as had the private artisan sector and domestic trade, where public institutions only played a limited role. New investment in tourism was promoted through tax incentives and import exceptions.

Syria's next chance to realign itself with the West came with the First Gulf War, when it joined the American-led international coalition against Saddam Hussein's Iraq. A year later Syria participated in the Madrid Conference of 1991, a fresh attempt by the George H.W. Bush administration to revive the Israeli-Palestinian peace process. New laws were introduced to liberalise Syria's economy, leading to a wave of investments in the early 1990s, especially in industry and transport. The country was rewarded for its participation in the war with inflows of financial support and easy loans from the USA, Saudi Arabia and the Gulf countries. Syrian entry to labour markets in the Gulf was facilitated. Wealthy Syrian businessmen of the diaspora were invited back by the regime on trade missions, an attempt to woo them to reinvest in their homeland. Some did. The period also coincided with increased oil production from new fields discovered by Royal Dutch Shell and French Elf Aquitaine in the Deir ez-Zour region, which reached a peak in 1996.

More success was achieved in the agricultural sector by providing subsidies to local farmers for products like wheat, barley, cotton, sugar beet, lentil and chickpeas, and providing seeds, fertilisers and medicines at subsidised prices, as well as short term agricultural loans. The result was to transform Syria into a country that was not only self-sufficient in food, but even to become an exporter of wheat. Wheat was the essential staple in the diet of the poor, and bread prices were heavily subsidised in state bakeries with fixed prices.

The problem was that all these measures were not followed up with further steps towards liberalisation, so investment gradually slowed again. The regime also feared that further empowerment of the private sector would lead the bourgeoisie to seek political power again, as it had done in the early 1980s through its support of the Hama insurgency. Syria had looked on with alarm at the instability that had resulted from economic reform in Eastern Europe and in Algeria. Investment slumped again, leading to a negative growth rate by 1999, coinciding with high population growth, unemployment and capital drain. Syria entered another economic crisis and tried to alleviate the situation by improving economic relations with Iraq after years of antagonism. The American invasion of Iraq in 2003 put paid to that, and in fact the closer ties between the two countries meant that over 1.5 million Iraqi refugees flooded into Syria. While this influx of refugees caused a strain on Syria's infrastructure, the country also benefited from the investment of the wealthier Iraqis into the Syrian economy, notably the housing market. But for the ordinary Syrian family, rising house prices pushed properties out of their reach.

Throughout all the political turmoil, the state was firmly held in place by the security and intelligence agencies—all seventeen of them. As Hafez's vice-president and key right-hand man from 1984 to 2005, 'Abd al-Halim Khaddam, explained from exile in Paris years later:

> You have to understand that, at some point, practically half the Syrian population worked for Secret Police one way or another. Remember that we were formed by the Soviets. That's why they were so powerful. The intelligence services soon became the main factor in maintaining the regime. The model was the KGB, or, more to the point, the Stasi. They were everywhere. Thousands of Syrians went to Russia to train and study, learnt Russian, and married Russians. Every student we sent abroad in the West brought back information. And this was left unchanged after the end of the Cold War. That these networks are still in motion is beyond any doubt.

Khaddam was also in charge of Lebanese–Syrian relations during the Lebanese Civil War and recalled how Hezbollah had received weaponry from Iran via Syria, with the blessing of the Syrian regime. Hezbollah was able to amass a larger arsenal than the Lebanese army, making it the most powerful player in Lebanese politics to this day.

"Hezbollah's presence is linked to the presence of the regime in Syria," Khaddam clarified. "And of course, Iran is the sectarian reference for this party, and supplies it with money. However, should the Iranian lifeline get cut off from Syria, then Hezbollah won't be able to stand on its feet. Hezbollah without the Syrian regime is worth nothing."

Hafez al-Assad managed to stay in power for the next thirty years, until his death in 2000, by maintaining a vice-like grip on the security services. He had built them up into networks within networks, interwoven in a tight-knit fabric that incorporated all the powerful players in Syrian society, irrespective of religion or ethnicity. It would not unravel easily, even under duress. Before he died, he told his son Bashar: "I have prepared the country for you for twenty years." It was no idle boast.

12

EMIGRATION TO BRITAIN

Better to tread the pedal of your own loom
than the threshold of a master's house.

(Arab proverb)

In 1975, with the outbreak of civil war in Lebanon, Abu Chaker decided to move the family for the second time. When he had moved for the first time in 1959, he had hoped that Lebanon would provide a safe trading environment from which he could develop and expand his business, away from the politics that had thwarted and penalised him. As fate would have it, instability and war had followed him to Lebanon.

When he had made his very first visit to Bradford in the early 1950s it had been a flourishing centre of the British wool industry, a city at the top of its game. Hield Brothers, a local company well known as a manufacturer of the finest English cloth, announced in its twenty-ninth Annual General Meeting on 30 June 1951 that the company had a "full order book". Its chairman even spoke of the "dangerous level of wool prices".

Other Northern cities also attracted their share of immigrants. Many were even specifically encouraged to come by the British government. In the early 1960s the Foreign Office commissioned a series of four Arabic-language films, "Calling all Muslims" to Manchester, Cardiff, Liverpool and Sheffield. This spearheaded a recruitment drive aimed at attracting Muslims to come and work in Britain's burgeoning industries. In the 1961 film on Manchester, the centre of Britain's cotton industry, an enthusiastic Arab presenter interviews an Islamic scholar, a *halal* butcher and a wealthy businessman in Manchester's cotton trade, before singing the praises of the original Central Mosque in Victoria Park and a library with "the biggest written version of the Holy Qur'an in the world." Ninety per cent of Manchester's five-thousand-strong Syrian community is involved in the textile industry to this day, especially in cotton and yarn.

Abu Chaker had only ever dealt in wool, the top-quality, hard-wearing, weather-resistant *joukh* that was the favourite of his customers, and so he needed no recruitment film to persuade him of the merits of Bradford. For nearly a century Bradford's prosperity had drawn immigrants from poorer countries who were keen to be part of the new industrial boom. Many arrived from Ireland and Germany—indeed so many German merchants, some of them Jewish, came to Bradford in the late 1850s that an area grew up called "Little Germany", featuring grand Victorian buildings and imposing warehouses, showrooms and offices made from finest-quality Yorkshire stone. Today the quarter boasts fifty-five listed buildings, more than any other district in Britain.

Just as Manchester was chosen as a cotton centre because of its wet climate, the reason Bradford was so favoured as a textile hub was the combination of three key advantages it offered over its rivals: locally mined coal, local sandstone for building the mills, and most important of all, uniquely soft water that gave fleeces a special texture. But with its success came other penalties, not least the heavy smoke that poured out of the 200-plus chimneys and made Bradford the most polluted town in England. Life expectancy for the workers was just eighteen, because of the child labour used in the mills.

One leading mill owner and industrialist, Sir Titus Salt, became an enlightened philanthropist, so determined to improve the welfare of his workers that in 1851 he built the model village of Saltaire for them to live in alongside his mill, to help them escape the smoke of central Bradford. Today the village's neat stone houses beside Salts Mills have been designated a UNESCO World Heritage Site, together with their washhouses, bathhouses, hospital, library, concert hall, billiard room, science laboratory and gymnasium—a small self-sufficient community reminiscent of Islam's *waqf* system. The district even had its own school, park and boathouse. Its Italianate Congregational church is Grade I listed. Some of Bradford's German industrialists were like-minded philanthropists, men like Jacob Behrens and Jacob Moser. Behrens helped set up the Bradford Chamber of Commerce in 1851 and Moser founded the City Guild of Help and the Bradford Charity Organisation Society, before going on to become the city's first Jewish mayor in 1910.

Many local sons worked all their life in the wool trade. Former Bradford Lord Mayor Stanley King was taken on aged twenty-one by Stroud Riley Drummond of Lumb Lane Mills just after being "demobbed" from the army in 1953. He stayed with his employer for thirty-two years. "When I started there, trade was phenomenal," he recalled. "The directors sat down on Friday afternoons and would buy several million pounds' worth of combed wool. There was no worry about the bank rate."

Thirty years later, things had changed. For decades Abu Chaker, as he was familiarly known even in Bradford, had been coming to the UK as a customer to buy cloth for his Middle Eastern markets. This time he came as a potential purchaser of his chief supplier, Hield Brothers. Along with many other mills, the British company Hield had hit upon hard times, struggling to survive in a tougher world where traditional textiles were losing out to much cheaper new synthetics.

On 28 May 1980, the headline in Bradford's daily the *Telegraph & Argus* read: "Fall in demand hits Hield". The article talked about the £1 million losses suffered by the worsted cloth manufacturers, who had been forced to slash their share dividend by two thirds. The chairman Arthur Park said that the "serious shortfall in demand affected all production sections" warning that "this year could offer little reward." Plans for the company's reorganistion were in progress, he said, and might take six to nine months to complete. Then, he declared, the company would be "as competitive as any in the industry, and well-equipped to survive and prosper."

His optimism turned out to be ill-founded. While struggling to balance its books, Hield fell victim to a takeover bid from its rival Stroud Riley Drummond of Lumb Lane Mills. For Abu Chaker, this spelt disaster. The business he had so painstakingly built up was already struggling, and now he risked losing his main supplier. Through no fault of his own, he had already lost everything, twice. He could not afford another setback. His business in the Middle East was dependent on the Hield brand.

In Britain the Hield name was not well known, though it supplied famous label retailers like Aquascutum with top-quality cloth for suits. In the Middle East, however, Hield enjoyed high brand recognition. It was synonymous with the highest level of British quality, akin to Harrods in the UK, and was especially favoured by pilgrims in Mecca during the *Hajj* or annual pilgrimage, when they would buy gifts to take back to family and friends. This was one of Abu Chaker's key markets. "Ah, you have some Hield," people would say, "now that is really something!" This huge captive market guaranteed big sales, as long as the product was tailored to the customer.

In hot climates like Saudi Arabia men wanted their full-length robes—*dishdashas* as they were called in the Gulf—to be light and cool. The owner of the company, David Hield, recalled taking a fine light cloth being developed for this market to a customer in Dubai. The customer held the cloth up to the light and immediately dismissed the material as too thin, complaining that it risked leaving the outline of a man's private parts discernible. And so Hield returned with a reinforced fabric, which passed the sunlight test and was deemed a suitable cloth for a *dishdasha*. Hield explained the motive behind the move into this market: "There was a company in Bradford who kind of cornered this *dishdasha* fabric, beautifully soft, and they were getting sales for hundreds of pieces of this cloth. It was really annoying us, and so we thought, we've really got to do our own. It was just white cloth, but then we dyed it all sorts of light colours—sand, beige."

Abu Chaker had been a long-term wholesale customer. Quality English worsted was his bestseller, and Hield was his preferred supplier. This was a relationship that had been cultivated over decades, and the threatened takeover by Stroud Riley Drummond would have brought it to an end. By chance, Abu Chaker happened to be sitting with David Hield in the boardroom at Briggella Mills when the takeover offer came through. Shocked and confused, he asked, "What can we do?" "Well," replied Hield, "you can buy some shares."

Abu Chaker had owned a few shares in Syrian public companies at one stage, but takeover bids were new to him. "So I explained," said Hield. "He decided very fast and bought about a quarter of a million pounds' worth of shares, probably thinking that would be it. But then of course the price went up. We had to explain it might be a battle and take weeks, if not months." The bidding war continued, and Abu Chaker bought more and more shares, until he finally said to Hield: "'This is my last one. Look, are you happy with me? Because I'm happy with you. This is my home. This is my house up in Yorkshire. If you are happy with me, then I will go one more.' So we went one more, and that was it really."

The takeover battle had taken place over a six-month period in 1981, with successively higher offers by Stroud Riley rejected by the Hield board, whose confidence in Abu Chaker and his efforts to continue the reorganisation plans and to secure jobs made him their preferred bidder. David Hield recalled the timing: "I was fishing up at the Spey in May, and they rang me and said, 'Here we go again, David!'"

On 27 May 1981 the *Telegraph & Argus* reported:

Stock market battling for control of Hield Brothers, the Bradford textile manufacturers, has taken a new turn with a former customer, Chamsi Bacha, increasing its original offer of 10½p a share to 13½p a share.

The move comes in reply to a bid by Stroud, Riley Drummond of Lumb Lane Mills, Bradford, who offered shares and cash worth just over 13p a share after Chamsi Bacha's original proposals.

The new offer of 13½p in cash has the backing of the board, which also backed the original Chamsi Bacha bid...

A spokesman for Chamsi Bacha said the firm has been dealing with Hield for 30 years and has great expertise in the Middle East market, where more cloth would go if Chamsi succeeds in taking over the firm.

Stroud Riley came back in early June 1981 with an improved offer that it urged Hield shareholders to accept, but on 17 June 1981 the deal was finally clinched and Stroud Riley conceded defeat. Having bought out all the shareholders, Abu Chaker took Hield Brothers private to ensure his total control of the company and to guarantee its safety from future predators.

"It was these guys—Abu Chaker and family—who saved the day as far as we were concerned," said David Hield. "Abu Chaker said to me: 'We want everything the same. We don't want to change anything.'"

And so began a highly successful partnership: Hield Brothers gained security, kept its employees and was able to expand its business into the Middle East, while Abu Chaker and his sons moved from their traditional trading roots in Syria into a whole new world of manufacturing. "As a merchant buying and selling, you know exactly how much you've made," said Hield sales director Brian Levi, formerly an experienced textile manufacturer from the Stroud Riley rival in Bradford. "But manufacturing is completely different," he explained, "it can take nine to twelve months to make your money, from the start of the manufacturing process, to the shipping overseas and so on. You have a whole new set of responsibilities as a manufacturer, with premises, factories and staff. Abu Chaker had never had to manage people before and he never really understood the business of manufacturing. He left it to others who did, and to his sons who learnt about how it worked. He didn't interfere."

David Hield recalled how times had changed in Bradford. The city's main cricket ground had been nearby, and so spectators used to walk past the mill wearing the same worsted trousers, jackets and shirts. Now, he reflected, globalisation had led to everyone wearing jeans and other cheap products from different parts of the world, undermining the British quality cloth on which Abu Chaker's entire business empire was built. In the boardroom at Briggella Mills, David Hield shared his recollections of Abu Chaker. Looking at the photos of him that lined the panelled walls, he explained: "I first met him in the early '50s. That was when more and more Arabs started coming over to Bradford to buy cloth. Abu Chaker was one of our customers." He remembered Abu Chaker's direct business style, how he would decide on a fair price and stick to it, no argument, no haggling.

Hield recounted his trips to Beirut in an old propeller plane with his father, and their stays at the St George's Hotel. "I remember learning the Arabic numbers there by walking up and down the corridor looking at the numbers on the doors." During one visit, their Lebanese agent had driven them from Beirut to Damascus to meet a customer, "in the old souk, a beautiful place." His father had drawn his attention to the roar of engines outside: "I had just finished my military service, so I recognised the sound of tanks, and sure enough, there were tanks in the streets. That was the day Hafez al-Assad took over as it turned out. We got straight in the car and headed back to Beirut immediately!"

Terry Miller, export manager for Hield, also had many recollections of Abu Chaker, with whom he had worked for decades and for whom he clearly had a great deal of respect. He explained that Abu Chaker liked to have European front men, who dealt with banks and some business clients that he feared might have prejudices against Arabs. "He'd take advice and he'd go round to everybody and say: 'What do you think? Do you think I should do this or that?' Then he'd do his own thing." Occasionally, Terry recalled, Abu

Chaker would shout loudly during business negotiations, but once the deal had been struck, he would relax and even smile, often with a glint in his eye.

If there was anything Abu Chaker couldn't understand, he would get a translation from his sons, so that he was always au fait with what was going on. His sons, Terry explained, would always toe the line and made sure he got the right information, "because if he didn't, they'd be for the high jump. You see he was as tough on them as he was on everybody else."

Miller explained how they had rented a London office in Golden Square, not far from Soho, at the centre of the film industry. At the time London was an essential source of top-end customers. "It was important to have someone on the spot, so we financed a London office." Not only did this decision promote business in the capital, but it also helped with company branding. "If you put 'London office', people knew it was important."

In the end, said Miller, the Middle East provided the answer to what to do in a shrinking market. "You see that fabric over there, that yellow one? It's what they call Venetian." He explained the way the fabric was woven, with three threads on top and one underneath, providing extra strength. "The Arabs liked their Venetian, for their big thick cloaks, the *bisht* as they called it. We had a picture somewhere of Ayatollah Khomeini coming down the stairs somewhere wearing his *bisht* with 'Hield' written down the side."

The *bisht* became popular in America too, as heavy wool but with an unusual lustre. Terry Miller started with one American woman, a fastidious top-end furnisher, who wanted twelve colours to offer her customers. "So she decided on the colours," he said. "What she used was ceramic tiles to guide her, choosing colours from them, and we had to dye the cloth to those colours. The woman was tough, but in the end she got what she wanted." Soon, Hield was ready to take on the bigger American companies. "The Americans were going for a natural product as opposed to a polyester or a synthetic which they knew about. They had plenty of those. So this natural product that was different became very attractive to them. The business started to grow."

At first the Chamsi-Pashas had not been interested in the American venture, but as it grew bigger and became a major source of income, they started to take notice. "The beauty of it was that we were able to command a price," explained Abu Chaker's sons. "The business had usually been to produce a large quantity and negotiate the best deal on the bulk sales, the 'buy one, get one free' approach. The suiting business was cut-throat. But here, we were the only ones offering it, so we were able to charge accordingly. It ended up providing the income that we needed to support the rest of the business." As Miller put it, "The Chamsi-Pashas have survived because they've traded. They don't think manufacturing, they think trading. It all goes back to their background: 'What can I do to get the business?' as Abu Chaker would have thought. In the end they were the salvation of the company."

"There's a booklet we put together for the Americans," Miller explained, "giving a brief history of Hield, going back to 1922. They liked all the stuff about the company twice being awarded the Queen's Award for Export, all that tradition and prestige." The booklet also told the story of Tom and Hugh Hield, uncle and father of David, who had been the two officers in charge of the British army's uniforms. The brothers had commandeered the Victoria Hotel in Bradford to provide military uniforms and blankets, and so Hield Brothers was born. "They started with the army, in fact when I first started they still had one or two army contracts, going back to the old days, making a bit of khaki, or in this case, air force stuff. Alan Hield, who was David's uncle, used to take rolled pieces of 60 metres on the back of his bike from Crosshill to deliver. Such a difference between what they had to do and what their sons had to do!"

In the early 1980s, Abu Chaker's position in Bradford as a buyer was very strong. The market was shrinking, and the mills and textile industries were going downhill, but Abu Chaker was not dependent on local demand. His customers were overseas, above all in Saudi

Arabia, where there was still huge market for quality textiles from England, especially high-quality cloth for making suits and gowns. Since the Hield name was already well known across the Middle East, Abu Chaker decided to keep it. "This is why he bought the company," said his sons, "to keep the name."

Abu Chaker had saved the Hield business. In Bradford today, all the other working mills have fallen silent.

13

BASHAR AL-ASSAD AND THE BEGINNINGS OF ECONOMIC LIBERALISATION

Should my beard catch fire, others will use it to light their pipes.

(Turkish proverb)

In June 2000, Hafez al-Assad died of leukaemia. He had been a diabetic and had a heart attack in his fifties, but was seen as a tough and gritty survivor, and so his death at the age of sixty-nine came as a surprise to many. The strains of ruling Syria for thirty years had taken their toll. In his final two years, he had been almost totally debilitated by ill health, making it impossible for him to carry out his official responsibilities. Syria had gone into a kind of limbo, while the Syrian population itself was primed for the succession of Hafez's son, Bashar. Dutiful comments made by senior Ba'ath Party officials had been regularly published in the national press while Hafez was still alive: "Bashar enjoys great vitality and dynamism. He belongs to the deep-rooted Assad tree... Major Bashar is a guarantee for both stability and [the continuation of] the school of President al-Assad." Bashar al-Assad had been groomed for the Syrian presidency over six years, and when Hafez died, the constitution was hurriedly changed to lower the minimum age of the president from forty to thirty-four, Bashar's age at the time. He took over power smoothly in July 2000, to no public protests.

Vice-President 'Abd al-Halim Khaddam took a different view on Bashar. From exile in Paris years later, he said bluntly, "Bashar is not like his father." Khaddam had known both men well, serving alongside Hafez for sixteen years and alongside Bashar for five. When the moment for accession to the presidency came, the key figures in the Old Guard had already agreed by consensus that Bashar was the best candidate for the sake of continuity. They knew he lacked his father's experience, courage and political astuteness, but, paradoxically, his political weakness was the reason to keep him: they knew how to manage him and get what they wanted. The 'Alawi generals above all did not want to risk another coup that might jeopardise the enormous gains they had made under Hafez. Their overriding concern was to maintain their social status, economic benefits and vice-like grip on the state apparatus. Bashar may be the face of the Assad regime, but he has never been its backbone.

As Hafez's second son Bashar had not started out as the first choice. It had always been clear that Basil, the first-born son, a far more dynamic and popular personality than Bashar, had been his father's intended successor. A fluent francophone, Basil had been introduced to European and Arab leaders, and had befriended Lebanese leaders of all sects. He was known to support his father's policy towards an Arab-Israeli peace in exchange for the return of the Golan Heights, and served as the head of Hafez's personal security force. Put in charge of a highly publicised anti-corruption campaign within the regime, he had set up military road-blocks—"Basil checkpoints" as they were called—near the Syrian border with Lebanon to catch smugglers. Syrians were encouraged to paste dashing photos of Basil in his army uniform in their shops and windscreens. He was a fine equestrian, and the Ba'athist press had dubbed him "the golden knight." But his life was cut short, and in 1994, driving his Mercedes at high speed in thick fog to Damascus International Airport, he crashed and died at the age of thirty-one. It was a fatal error of judgement by someone who was known for his love of speed—fast women, fast horses, fast cars. Just five days earlier Hafez had met US President Bill Clinton in Geneva for a summit that was to have paved the way for a complete Israeli withdrawal from the occupied Golan Heights.

Basil had charisma and was generally admired by most Syrians. Many even started to copy his look, wearing sunglasses and a short shaven beard. Bashar by comparison was gawky and gauche, with an unfortunate lisp and a tendency to giggle. Syrians were unsure what to make of him, but state media went into overdrive to win them over, embarking on a series of campaigns to aggrandise his abilities and his character. After his brother's death, Bashar abruptly ended his postgraduate ophthalmology training in London and was summoned back to Syria. He was sent to the Military Academy at Homs, pushed quickly through the ranks to become colonel by 1999. The press was informed of his excellent progress at regular intervals. He was also the face of tech-savvy Syria, becoming the president of the Syrian Computer Society and advocating modernisation and the virtues of the internet. Posters started appearing all over the country of Hafez flanked by his late son and the heir apparent, Bashar, though his candidature for the presidency was never made explicit.

By studying to become an eye doctor, Bashar had chosen the path Hafez himself had wanted but had been unable to pursue because of socio-economic restraints. "Bashar would have made a good doctor," mused one of his British consultant teachers. But just like his father, Bashar did not get his first choice of profession.

During his studies in London Bashar met his wife-to-be, Asma al-Akhras, a Sunni Muslim of Syrian heritage who had been born and brought up in the UK. He married her just five months after becoming president, in December 2000. His brother Maher had also married a Sunni, a smart move for keeping relations cordial between the sects, though intermarriage between 'Alawis and Sunnis was in any event not unusual.

Bushra al-Assad, Bashar's only sister, was Hafez's first-born child, and by all accounts very like her father. But neither the Syrian people nor the military generals were ready for a female president, no matter what her attributes and qualifications. She had studied pharmacy at Damascus University, where she met her own future husband Assef Shawkat, an 'Alawi from Tartous. Bushra engineered his promotion to head of military intelligence, deputy chief of staff and deputy minister of defence. In 2012 he was killed in a targeted bomb attack, and Bushra fled to Dubai with their children.

Once Bashar became president he was promoted to field marshal, and was appointed secretary general of the Ba'ath Party and commander of the Armed Forces. A well-organised referendum confirmed him as president with 97 per cent of the vote. In his inaugural speech he promised to modernise the economy, fight corruption and lead Syria on a path towards "our own democratic experience." He gave the orders for hundreds of political prisoners to be released. A rash of free and independent newspapers appeared, reading the new environment as a green light to publish uncensored material. Public political meetings were permitted and intellectuals organised critical discussion groups, issuing statements calling for democratic reform. The change in atmosphere was unprecedented, and was optimistically dubbed "the Damascus Spring."

Just months later, in early 2001 the meetings and discussion groups were banned and leading opposition figures were arrested. Some were given five-year prison sentences, while others were held for long periods without arrest warrants under the powers granted by Hafez's draconian Emergency Law in 1963. Press censorship reappeared. Kurdish activists and Islamists were sentenced to lengthy spells in jail.

At first it was generally believed that Bashar had been reined in by his father's Old Guard, whose vested interests would have been threatened by greater freedoms. The regime is so opaque in its decision-making that no one knows the full story. But Bashar gradually began to shed the Old Guard, introducing compulsory retirement for those over sixty, and went on to appoint his own trusted relations instead, notably his brother Maher and his brother-in-law Assef Shawkat. He also appointed technocrats to ministries that he felt required specialist expertise, in what appeared to be a genuine attempt to modernise Syria's economy. He had inherited precarious socio-economic conditions and unresolved social problems. The economy was stagnant, unable to provide jobs for the young, especially educated young people entering the labour market.

Though he began by promising reforms, Bashar never implemented them. His vice-president, 'Abd al-Halim Khaddam, is said to have led the clampdown of the Damascus Spring, expressing fears of the "Algerisation" of Syria. Khaddam felt that changing the Syrian state too quickly would empower and enable the rise of fundamentalist Islamist movements like the Muslim Brotherhood, who had attempted to seize power in 1982 in the Hama uprising. He warned against the risks of economic liberalisation, fomenting a fear of reform among members of the regional command.

Between 2003 and 2004 the French government delegated a number of teams to study the situation inside Syria and to propose judicial and administrative reforms. Committees met and reports were written, trying to work out how to prepare state institutions and society for the changes that were needed. None of the recommendations were implemented, and after the American invasion of Iraq, more caution set in, as fears mounted that Syria might be next in line for a US-style regime change. Moreover, system reforms would threaten the interests of those in power and their ability to enrich themselves. If the private sector became too free it would no longer be controllable, and the state was afraid of a burgeoning capitalist economy that would no longer be beholden or loyal to it.

There was widespread worry about lifting the government subsidy on heating fuel, for fear it would be seen as betraying the poor to serve the rich. This might leave the poor vulnerable to recruitment by Salafi extremists, especially in a country, as Syrian economist Samir Seifan wrote in 2010, "overwhelmed by an undeclared but obvious wave of religiosity." Seifan also points out that Syria lacked (and still lacks) reform leaders or local experts who would be capable of regulating free trade or financial institutions, and that unlike

Eastern European countries which after 1990 received a huge amount of help and guidance from Western countries, Syria was trying to undertake reforms alone, with no international help at all.

On taking power in 2000 Bashar had initially attempted to reorientate the Syrian economy westwards by negotiating the European Union Association Agreement (EUAA). He also put in place the legal foundation for a business-friendly economy, encouraging investment from abroad. The programme of economic liberalisation opened the way for many new companies to be established. But almost all of these firms were based in Damascus or in the other large cities, so that the wealth they generated remained concentrated in urban areas rather than benefiting the wider economy. The urban–rural divide was magnified, as the regime's networks of business insiders took more and more profit for themselves and their own loyal affiliates, becoming a new kleptocratic elite driven by their own greed. Bashar's new business models seemed designed for this new brand of businessmen to pursue personal wealth. They increasingly treated the various *mahallas* (localities) as private enrichment opportunities, and began to buy up land at artificially deflated prices. In suburbs of Damascus like Darayya and al-Moadamiyah, research by Syrian sociologist Mohammed Jamal Barout shows that 70 per cent of available plots had been bought by the new elite. Hafez had been careful to keep the *mahallas* outside the cities engaged, making them feel they had a stake, however small, in the welfare of the state. Bashar forgot his father's lesson. The carefully stitched fabric which Hafez had woven over decades, tying the localities into a social contract with the central state, was beginning to unravel.

In the eastern tribal areas it was a similar story. Bashar issued a decree in 2000 privatising all state farmlands that had been confiscated in the 1960s, so that tribal leaders regained what they had lost in the 1960s' land redistribution. The result was to enhance the status and wealth of tribal leaders, and yet again, the support of the masses was squandered. Under Hafez, these leaders had been able to keep the tribal populations compliant through a mutually beneficial exchange, while under Bashar the shaikhs used their new-found wealth on themselves, losing the respect and control of their tribes.

Clashes developed between Suwayda's Bedouin and its urbanised population in the south, just as there had been clashes throughout the twentieth century and even earlier between the merchant Isma'ilis and the rural 'Alawis, and between the Arabs and the Kurds on the Turkish border. In today's Syria the Sunni tribes of the eastern desert, the Badia, feel excluded and marginalised by the state, and are offered no public sector investment. The illiteracy level here is 30 per cent, double the countrywide average. Unlike Hafez, Bashar never understood the dynamics of the countryside or realised its importance. In Bashar's Syria profits from the agricultural, oil and gas resources of the eastern provinces served more than ever to line the pockets of regime clientele in Damascus and the western provinces.

On top of these social tensions, the geopolitical impact of the 2003 US-led occupation of Iraq destabilised the whole region, especially Syria, which was flooded with waves of Iraqi refugees, most of them Shi'a. At its peak level in 2004, the number of Iraqis hosted in Syria was thought to have been between 1.5 and 2 million. Special legislation was introduced to ban non-Syrians from property ownership, since the influx of Iraqis had sent house prices so high that Syrians found themselves priced out of their own market. The strain on the state infrastructure was considerable, and led to daily power outages and water shortages. Schools also had to adjust to the influx, running classes in two shifts in the morning and afternoon, with teachers severely overstretched.

The invasion of Iraq thwarted Syria's plans to integrate into the international economy. The Iraqi market had been Syria's lifeline, providing an outlet for Syrian products. Syria had imported sanctioned Iraqi oil and resold it, a process which enabled it to accumulate substantial foreign exchange reserves. The loss of the Iraqi market prompted Bashar to accelerate the pace of privatisation. In 2004 private banks were allowed to open inside Syria, the majority of them Lebanese, such as Bank Audi and Banque Bemo. Some economic liberalisation measures were introduced, but once again these enriched the elite at the expense of the poor.

Ordinary Syrians, excluded from the loop of wealth and corruption, watched this happen and were powerless to stop it, knowing that any criticism would be ignored, or worse, punished. The Emergency Law had given the security authorities, the *mukhabarat*, the power to pluck people off the street and have them indefinitely "disappear" into prison and torture cells, sometimes never to return. International advocacy group Human Rights Watch issued a report in 2010 called "A Wasted Decade", detailing a catalogue of abuses of power, from arrests and torture to censorship. Despite Bashar's keenness for the internet, sites like Facebook, YouTube and Blogger, as well as email providers like Hotmail, were regularly blocked in an attempt to suppress dissident voices.

The result was that no meaningful opposition to Bashar al-Assad's regime was ever allowed to develop, despite growing disillusionment among the people, and even among his own elite. Hafez's vice-president and key right-hand man from 1984 to 2005, 'Abd al-Halim Khaddam, resigned publicly after the assassination of former Lebanese Prime Minister Rafiq al-Hariri in Beirut, in protest at what he called "Bashar's blunders" in Lebanon. He fled to France with his family and was sentenced to hard labour in absentia, accused of "slandering the Syrian leadership". His own family had been closely allied with Rafiq al-Hariri, and their respective sons were known to have stakes in many shared business deals in the reconstruction of Lebanon.

Hariri's assassination in February 2005 was laid firmly at Bashar's door. Despite predictable denials of any involvement, Bashar quickly caved in to international pressure to remove Syrian troops from Lebanon, bringing twenty-nine years of military presence to an end. At a stroke, all the lucrative smuggling and bribery rackets that had been controlled by Syrian army checkpoints all over Lebanon, which were channelled into the pocket of one powerful regime figure or another, disappeared, much to the jubilation and relief of most Lebanese. Today the same thing continues at the armed checkpoints in Syria between the Lebanese border and Damascus, run by soldiers on the payroll of either Bashar's cousin Rami Makhlouf or of his brother Maher al-Assad.

The withdrawal from Lebanon and consequent loss of income from the illicit smuggling rackets meant the Syrian economy instead turned east to exploit the post–Iraq invasion oil boom and attract investment from the Gulf. This new era was called the "social market economy". It was marked by the opening of large-scale Gulf-funded projects, like Syria's first shopping malls, the Dubai-style Yaafour Damascus suburb and the construction of grand five-star hotels to encourage tourism. Syria's various economic boom periods can be traced through the history of Damascus' five-star hotels, starting with the Meridien, the very first, built in 1976 under Hafez, and ending with the Four Seasons, completed in 2006, co-owned by the Syrian Tourism Ministry and the Saudi prince Al-Waleed bin Talal. A Kempinski, a Mövenpick, a Holiday Inn and an InterContinental had been on the drawing board before war broke out in 2011. The magnificent but defunct Ottoman 1908 Hijaz railway station was awaiting funds to be developed into a shopping mall and hub of a proposed metro system. It is still waiting.

Summer 2006 saw another wave of refugees flood into Syria, this time from southern Lebanon, after war erupted between Israel and Hezbollah. The war was short-lived and most were able to return within a month or two, after both sides claimed victory. The mainly Shi'a refugees were welcomed and taken in by Sunni families in Damascus. Sectarian affiliations were irrelevant, and were overridden by humanitarian concern.

In spite of regional political turbulence average annual growth rose to 4.7 per cent over the next few years, but the boom came at the expense of social cohesion as the gap between rich and poor widened. Fancy consumer outlets selling luxury accessories began to appear in wealthy Damascus suburbs like Abou Roumaneh and Malki, and even in the heart of the Old City on the biblical "Street Called Straight", where they sat uneasily alongside traditional artisan craft shops. The clumsy juxtaposition summed up the social divide between crony capitalism, fuelled by the consumerist children of Damascus' new elites, and the increasingly excluded rural poor. Further liberalisation measures were unevenly applied, leading to yet more skewing of the market. The public sector continued to employ a huge percentage of the workforce, around 30 per cent, but at subsistence-level salaries. Key commodities like bread, water, electricity, diesel heating fuel (*mazout*) and petrol were still state-subsidised.

Rapprochement with Europe was led in 2008 by French President Nicholas Sarkozy, ending the three-year isolation that followed Hariri's assassination. Bashar welcomed him effusively: "We're very happy to see Europe recuperating its role after an absence of years, and this is the result of French dynamism," he said. Sarkozy replied, "This is how we're going to rebuild our new relations with Syria, by trying to understand each other, by not compromising our principles and by re-establishing trust." The entente was widely seen as a victory for Bashar. The Syrian information minister commented: "There were times when people were betting the regime was living its last days. Now, the regime has proved how strong it is. It is the French who changed their policy, and not Syria." Relations with the European Union continued to improve and by 2010 Syrian crude oil exports were going almost exclusively to Europe, mainly Germany and Italy.

High-end real estate projects sprang up, not just in Damascus and Aleppo, but also in other cities like Homs, where top government posts were dominated by 'Alawis, whose recent arrival in the city did not stop their ID cards miraculously affirming that they had been born there. In 2009 the then mayor of Homs, Iyad Ghazal, authorised evictions and land seizures at less than 10 per cent of real estate value, displacing Sunni and Christian residents from the centre and southwest of the city, in order to build the hyped-up "Homs Dream": a swathe of glass skyscrapers and shopping malls. No 'Alawi areas were affected. Local residents rebranded the development the "Homs Nightmare" and tried their best to resist its implementation, to no avail. In the early days of the

Syrian Revolution, demonstrators in Homs called primarily for the removal of Iyad Ghazal.

The hope had been that economic liberalisation would lead to political liberalisation, that "the pseudo-alliance between 'Alawi-dominated military and bourgeois Sunni civilians," in the words of Dutch diplomat Nikolaos Van Dam, would gradually lead to democracy. In the event, this did not happen. The 'Alawi-majority regime was not prepared to give up its privileged position, fearing that if it loosened its grip even slightly on a system whose repressive institutions kept it in place, it would surely risk takeover by the very same Sunni majority that had mistreated 'Alawis in the previous century. Now that the boot was on the other foot, they feared revenge from the Sunnis they themselves had oppressed, first in Hama in 1982, then in the 2011 Revolution.

In another interesting role reversal, the sons of the top military chiefs like 'Ali Douba and Rif'at al-Assad have not wanted to follow their fathers into the military—just as the sons of the Sunni notables had not entered the military before them. They preferred instead the much easier life of business, commerce or construction, where fortunes could be built up quickly. The *Financial Times* estimated in April 2011 that Bashar's cousin Rami Makhlouf controlled up to 60 per cent of the country's economy through his web of business interests. In the 1990s, Hafez had pushed many of the country's business opportunities towards the Makhloufs, his wife's family, knowing that their loyalty to Bashar was likely to be much stronger than that of other key figures such as Vice-President 'Abd al-Halim Khaddam, whose links were closer to the Hariris in Lebanon.

By the time of Hafez's death Rami Makhlouf was already well established. He owns the daily paper *Al-Watan*, the radio/TV station Ninar and satellite station Al-Dunya, and has a stake in the Chouwayfat schools. He owns Syriatel, the largest mobile phone network in the country, as well as numerous retail, banking and real estate companies. The Makhlouf family also has a monopoly on the import of tobacco into Syria, a continuation of the historic 'Alawi monopoly since Ottoman times. In 2004, Rami allegedly tried to take over the Mercedes concession in Syria by using his influence to ensure a law was passed denying Mercedes the right to import spare parts unless he was made exclusive agent for them. Mercedes did not comply and simply withdrew from Syria altogether till the dispute was resolved. Eventually the dealership reverted to the Sankar family, who had controlled it since the 1960s.

In 2008 Rami was designated by the US Treasury Department a "beneficiary and facilitator of public corruption in Syria." They reported that, "Makhlouf has manipulated the Syrian judicial system and used Syrian intelligence officials to intimidate his business rivals. He employed these techniques when trying to acquire exclusive licenses to represent foreign companies in Syria and to obtain contract awards." Rami's brother Hafez Makhlouf was head of Syria's intelligence agency, the General Intelligence Directorate. In May 2011 he was put under sanctions by the European Union, but continued to use shell companies to avoid the global sanctions placed on Bashar's regime, in order to pay for helicopter fuel for the Syrian Air Force. Helicopters are widely used to drop barrel bombs on opposition areas. His self-aggrandisement is well known by Syrians, and at the start of the revolution in Dera'a demonstrators chanted "Makhlouf, you thief!" Anyone who openly criticised him was put in prison, such as the Syrian dissident Riad Seif, who got a five-year sentence for challenging the way Rami was awarded the Syriatel mobile phone licence in 2001.

Many projects were given the green light because regime protégés were behind them. An outbreak of "modernisation" or "re-development" schemes appeared in cities, often at the expense of the country's cultural heritage. Joint ventures with Iranian funding also started to appear, such as the scheme to clear an ancient residential area in the Old City of Damascus round the Shi'a Mosque of Rouqiyya, granddaughter of 'Ali and daughter of Hussein, in order to turn it into a car park for buses bringing Iranian pilgrims to the shrine. The Damascus mayor Bishr Sabban described the buildings destined to be razed as "garbage", even though one of them was Syria's second oldest mosque. Fortunately the project was abandoned because of the volume of public protest. But other schemes went ahead, like the incongruous concrete Iranian *hawzah* (seminary) on Damascus' biblical "Street Called Straight", marking the gateway to the Shi'a district of Al-Amin.

Some say that Iran is in reality running the show behind the scenes these days. In the same way that the Stasi and the KGB cooperated when the Stasi spied on the East German population, today there is close collaboration between the Assad regime's security branches and Iran's Ministry of Intelligence and Security. But when East Germany collapsed and the Berlin Wall came down, numerous Stasi officials were prosecuted for their crimes. The surveillance files the Stasi had maintained on millions of East Germans were laid open, so that any citizen could inspect their personal file on request. It is hard to imagine anything similar happening in today's Syria, and the fate of its massive security and intelligence apparatus remains a key challenge for the future of the country.

Peaceful resistance of any sort, through civil society activities or public protests, has been historically targeted by the Assad regime, both under Hafez and Bashar, even criminalised. The very term "civil society" was outlawed, with the regime comparing it to Zionism and Masonry. The Association Law of 1958 made civil society initiatives legally subject to supervision, requiring the approval of the security services. When Syrian activist Haytham al-Hamwi decided in 2003 to take part in a public cleaning campaign in Darayya in the southern suburbs of Damascus, he knew it might be a risk. He and dozens of other young men started sweeping the streets and picking up rubbish. They designed posters and put them up in their neighbourhood, warning against bribery. They even opened their own library called "Ways of Peace".

"When I was in prison", al-Hamwi recalled, "the officer asked me during the interrogation period: 'What is your field of study?' I told him: 'Preventive medicine.' The officer said: 'Aha! There you go. I know your group isn't a political party but if we leave you alone, you will become a political party. So, we're going to imprison you from now as a preventive measure.'" Moreover, anyone who worked for an NGO was assumed to be a spy, since anything non-governmental was automatically regarded with suspicion.

Just before March 2011 and the start of what began as the Syrian Revolution, Syria had been increasingly opening up to tourism, and was listed in 2010 as one *The Sunday Times'* top ten holiday destinations. Many Western visitors, mainly from Europe, fell under its spell and Damascus became the favoured place for Western students to spend their year abroad during Arabic language courses at university. Travel agents and tour operators began to proliferate, to cope with the 8.5 million visitors the country received in 2010. Tourism grew to provide 14 per cent of GDP in the same period and brought with it new employment opportunities for tour guides and staff in hotels, restaurants and car hire firms, all of whom learnt English and other foreign languages. Many ordinary Syrians invested their life savings in converting the decaying Ottoman palaces in the historic centres of Damascus and Aleppo into boutique hotels, which would fill up as quickly as they could be restored. Some had just six or seven rooms, lovingly renovated with careful attention paid to every decorative detail. Each hotel was like a mini Paradise, its courtyard fountain brimming, its fragrant jasmine blossoming.

14

A SYRIAN MERCHANT IN LONDON

A guest is a guest, even if he stays all winter and summer.

(Arab proverb)

"I hear your father has a hotel in London!" friends would say to Abu Chaker's sons. The hotel was a myth that had grown up because of the sheer number of people who used to stay regularly at the Chamsi-Pasha flat in London's West End. As the business expanded after the acquisition of Hield, Abu Chaker had been able to buy up further flats in the same building when they came onto the market, eventually owning several in the 1930s purpose-built block, and even one or two in nearby mansion blocks for his sons. He had been keen to keep the family close, to create a community similar to those he had left in Beirut and in Homs. "Home is your insurance policy," he used to say.

Right to the end of his life, he enjoyed having guests and liked to buy food for the home in bulk. He had a lifetime habit of shopping at food markets, and kept this up in London. Even if it was only him and Rihab at home, he would still get his driver, Bob, a loyal employee for thirty-four years, to take him to the Asian market in London's Southall. He would walk around assessing the quality and freshness before buying whole crates of fruit and vegetables. He would then arrange to have the produce delivered to his sons and their families using "the tractor", as their communal minibus was known. Food home delivery services had an early forerunner.

Simple fresh ingredients are treasured across the Middle East, and Abu Chaker's love of food was a reflection of that, deeply tied to his connection with nature and his gratitude for the bounty of the earth. The importance Abu Chaker gave to food was not born of greed or gluttony—far from it. To him food represented a link to his childhood, his identity and his community in Homs, as well as to the Syrian land. What could be better than eating your own produce from your own labour grown in your own soil? It was no surprise that Abu Chaker had no interest in eating out. Why would you want to go out and eat someone else's food, sourced from places round the world with which you had no connection, grown on land you had never visited? His attitude represented the very opposite of our fast-food culture, in which we value choice above all, opting to go to Indian, Chinese, Thai, French or Italian restaurants, depending on our mood. To Abu Chaker such choice was meaningless if one had no connection to the food itself.

To run the London household and cook for the family and guests, Abu Chaker employed two Filipino maids, Eva and Johnette, who worked for him for over thirty years and knew his preferences inside out. Sometimes, they recalled, he would come into the kitchen to taste and check the food, helping a little with the preparation of the fresh vegetables or stirring the soup. "When he said it was good, it was a real compliment," they laughed, "He was difficult to please, everything had to be perfect, but if you got it right, he told you." For breakfast he would have fresh Arabic bread, served with labneh, black olives, honey, cheese, tomato and cucumber. In the morning he would take sugary black tea; at lunch he would drink *ayran* (sour yoghurt; but his favourite drink was fresh lemonade with mint, *laymoun bi-na'na*, made with lots of sugar. Lunch was always the main meal and Abu Chaker decided on the menu, often requesting dishes with aubergine, perhaps stuffed with lamb. In the evening he ate lightly, just a simple meal of bread, labneh, olives and hummus. "He loved his sweet Arabic coffee, and would have one mid-morning and one in the afternoon with his *arghile* around 5:00 p.m.," they recalled. The habits replicated as much as possible his habits in Homs, and both maids would accompany the family on trips back to

Syria, learning enough Arabic to be able to communicate on domestic matters. "He was like a father to us," they said.

An old friend of Abu Chaker's from Homs, Saïd Hafez, who had also left for Beirut, then London, after the Ba'ath Party had nationalised his father's Damascus refrigeration plant in 1965, shared the same work ethic and the same guiding religious principles. He explained their common philosophy: "As a believer in God, you have to be good to others in every aspect, you have to learn to love every creature because God created it." Abu Chaker lived by these guidelines wherever he was. In London he would tend the plants on his balcony and go every day to Regent's Park, not just to visit the mosque, but also to feed the birds at the lakeside. "Today's generation has lost sight of religion," continued his friend, lamenting the ostentation in the way religion is often practised. "God is love. He forgives."

"Abu Chaker conveyed everything by example," he clarified, "He never discussed moral or ethical questions. He lived it. He implied his beliefs, but he was not explicit. He listened more than he talked. When his father died, he had a lot of responsibility. He mixed with an older age group, so it became normal to him to have friendships with older people and to learn from them."

Another man able to shed light on Abu Chaker's way of living in London was Shaikh Saïd, an Egyptian religious scholar whom Abu Chaker had taken in and supported in the 1980s. Shaikh Saïd knew Abu Chaker for thirty years and first met him in 1984 in the Regent's Park mosque during Ramadan. "Lots of people," Shaikh Saïd explained, "are only interested in their work, using their religion as a display, but Abu Chaker was different. He loved work and worship. He would read the Qur'an every afternoon during Ramadan between 2:00 p.m. and 6:00 p.m. in the privacy of his home, with his family, not for show."

He had clear memories of how Abu Chaker used to receive many people, how he would always open his door to anyone who needed support. Abu Chaker had visitors from all backgrounds, ranging from ambassadors to unemployed people. His sons frequently had to give up their bedrooms to guests and share each other's rooms. If they showed any signs of complaint, he would chide them severely. "We used to hate him for it," they laughed, "because we didn't understand what he was doing was in our best interest."

When questioned why, if Abu Chaker didn't care for rank and prestige, ambassadors had been invited to dinner, Shaikh Saïd explained that at that time there were no diplomatic relations between Syria and the UK (just as there are none today). "So Abu Chaker wanted to do something to maintain and develop inter-community relations and [relations] with Syria." He decided to co-found the Syrian Arab Association in the UK (SAAUK). He served as its first president, seeing the organisation as a way of maintaining apolitical relationships with diplomats and political figures. He avoided embassies, preferring to maintain a neutral stance, yet in some ways he gradually took on the role of an alternative ambassador, an impartial figure to whom people could and frequently did come with their troubles. Arab politicians based in London respected his financial acumen, and often sought his advice about how to invest, what to build, or how to run a particular business venture they might be considering.

"The important thing was to be honest and hardworking and to avoid waste, which was *haram* (forbidden)," his sons reflected. "Turning the tap off, turning off the TV, never wasting money, all of it was crucial." They explained that unlike the families of some of their friends in Homs, their father never used to waste food. "He would rather get it right with food quantities, but if there was too much, he would give it to the driver to distribute to people in the poorer area where he lived."

When he gave money to charity, he gave in secret. "His ego was not involved. Often he didn't even know the people he was helping," his sons explained. He did not only help Muslims, Shaikh Saïd recalled, but people of all backgrounds. His outlook was international even in the 1980s. "He was very well-travelled and had experienced a great deal."

Notwithstanding his philanthropy and charitable nature, Abu Chaker enjoyed some of life's finer things. He liked to stay in the best hotels and later in life always travelled first class. He always dressed well and would spend money on items of high quality, like a suit made of good material, which would be more comfortable and would last longer. "You pay more to get something better," he would say. Even when he used to go to the farm in Homs he would wear a good suit, but would choose one that had already served its time on smarter occasions.

Ideologically, he was the personification of the traditional Sunni view that a good Muslim should not interfere in politics or broker revolution but should abide by the laws of their country. He believed in the teachings of Al-Ghazali, an influential eleventh-century Muslim philosopher, whose method of challenging despotic rulers was to call on God to bring relief from suffering. In the '*ajami* rooms of Damascene courtyard houses, wall panels would be inscribed with "poems of relief" epitomising this belief, which would be recited against oppressive rulers. One of the most famous, written by the Tunisian Sufi Shaikh Mohammad ibn Nasir, was chanted across North Africa and was even credited with later inciting non-violent resistance against the French colonial occupation:

> Recite the Qur'an with a heart full of sadness and a voice of sweet melancholy
>
> And the night prayer, and its hours, go through them with understanding and return
>
> And reflect upon it and its meanings; you will arrive at paradise and be relieved...

When Abu Chaker was entertaining at his home in the evening, poetic readings of this sort would follow dinner and continue until midnight.

When it came to cash, Abu Chaker was very strict with his sons. "If we asked for £20, he would give us £10. He would give us travel money, and gave us the best education money could buy, but always warned us not to get materialistic." He used to say to them, "*Anta anta,*" or "you are who you are," not defined by your possessions.

His sons remember that their father had not liked being photographed. "There was no frivolity, no triviality. He was not interested in such things. But if there was a new business opportunity, he paid attention. So if one of us bought a new phone, he couldn't care less," they laughed, "but if we had a new business venture, he would listen." He had wanted to keep up with his sons' news as they grew up: "Every time, as adults, we saw him, he would always say: 'Tell me what has been happening, *min al-awwal*, from the beginning.'"

THE MERCHANT OF SYRIA

Abu Chaker also helped many Syrian students while they were living in London away from home, often acting as a social "godfather", who was always prepared to listen and to help. His door was always open to these students, especially if they were relatives of friends from Homs. He would insist they come and eat at his home as often as possible, and try as they might to refuse, wanting to lead independent lives in London, he would call them repeatedly until they accepted.

On one occasion, a young friend of one of Abu Chaker's sons had asked for his advice on a business-related dilemma. After listening attentively in silence, Abu Chaker related a story that had happened to him many years ago back when he had been a sub-dealer for Hield in Beirut. He explained how a customer who had bought Hield cloth from him a few days earlier had come to him very upset. Holding the cloth, the customer said that he had found exactly the same cloth for sale in the market for a price that was a third less than the price he had already paid Abu Chaker. Abu Chaker was astonished and told him that could not be possible, but the customer insisted it was true. And so he told the customer to leave the matter with him for a few days and that he would get back to him after making some enquiries.

It turned out the customer had seen the cheaper Hield cloth for sale in a shop supplied by a distributor called Khalil Fattal et Fils. The Fattals were Abu Chaker's biggest rivals, and were the main selling agents in Syria and Lebanon for Hield Brothers. They were an Aleppan Christian family who had expanded into Lebanon in the 1930s as general agent representatives of several foreign brands, and who now had the lion's share of the distribution market in Beirut. Khalil Fattal was a powerful magnate, a much bigger fish than Abu Chaker, who at that stage was still a minor merchant trying to grow his business. Abu Chaker had, however, helped the Fattal Group open up in Afghanistan, a market that was notoriously difficult to get started in. As Hield's agents, the Fattal Group earned a commission on all Hield goods sold, including those in Afghanistan.

When he discovered that the Fattal Group had supplied the cheaper cloth, Abu Chaker decided to telephone Khalil Fattal himself and tell him he was terminating his Afghanistan distribution agreement with him. He had been undercut on his price for the Hield cloth, damaging his reputation for fairness with his customers. Two days later Fattal came in person to Abu Chaker's small Beirut office and asked him to reconsider. He apologised for the pricing error and said it would not happen again. Abu Chaker refused to change his position. Fattal was a highly persuasive man, and persisted to beg Abu Chaker to change his mind. He told Abu Chaker he had brought with him a truckload of cloth, furniture and other items as a gift, by way of apology and to show his good faith. In the end Abu Chaker relented and agreed, accepting the goods. Both men resumed business as before and the episode was never again mentioned or repeated.

Over the next few years Abu Chaker's Afghanistan business expanded. When it reached a certain volume Abu Chaker contacted Khalil Fattal again and told him that he now wanted to take 50 per cent of the Fattal Group's commission on the distributed goods, knowing well that if Fattal refused, he had now grown big enough to end their agreement and take his business with him. Fattal, recalling the earlier incident over the pricing of the Hield cloth, knew that Abu Chaker was not bluffing. He knew for certain that Abu Chaker would start up on his own if he did not agree, and that his own distribution group would therefore lose its lucrative Afghan market. It did not take him long to give in.

Abu Chaker had given his sons' young friend clarity, not by telling him what to do directly, but by relaying that the important thing in the world of business was to stick to your principles and maintain your honour. This integrity and self-respect would benefit your reputation in ways that might not be immediately apparent, but that would become clear in the long run. The young man said that this story of Abu Chaker's stayed with him a long time, and he retold it to many people. Abu Chaker was not a talkative man, so on the few instances that he chose to open up, his words were very powerful. The story enabled the man to make his decision about his own business dilemma, which he later confirmed was the right decision, taken for the right reasons.

Abu Chaker's circle of friends and business contacts in London grew even larger after he, Saïd Hafez and Hisham al-Yafi founded the Syrian Community School in the UK. At first they had bankrolled it together, until it expanded beyond all expectations and many families joined in, all keen for their children to attend on Saturdays so they might stay in touch with their Syrian heritage. Through his old friend from the souk in Homs, Wasfi Tayara, in whom he had total trust, Abu Chaker himself continued to maintain business connections and charitable links with Syria from his new home in London. For him business and charity always went hand in hand. It was the traditional conservative mentality of a Syrian merchant firmly rooted in the morality of Islam.

Soon after the 2015 British general election, in which the Conservative Party had won an unexpected outright majority, I enquired of the Chamsi-Pasha sons if their parents had usually voted in the UK at elections. "Always," they had laughed. Both Abu Chaker and Rihab used to vote Conservative since in Arab countries, as his sons explained, "Labour" and "Liberal" had very different connotations. "The Labour Party *(Hizb al-'Ummal)* was always equated with communism, and the Liberals *(al-Ishtirakiyoun)* were socialists. Both were bad for business."

In Syria, on the other hand, Abu Chaker had never voted.

15

THE SYRIAN REVOLUTION
AND THE WAR ECONOMY

If you wish to destroy a country, pray that it has many chiefs.

(Lebanese proverb)

Elections in Syria have been manipulated under the Assads for decades. State employees are bussed from their workplaces en masse to voting booths and the incumbent president is the only candidate on the ballot paper. No one was surprised, therefore, when the 2007 official results showed a 95 per cent electoral turnout with 97.62 per cent voting for Bashar al-Assad to remain president for a second seven-year term. The minister of the interior seized on the opportunity to announce: "This great consensus shows the political maturity of Syria and the brilliance of our democracy." In the elections of 2014, three years into the civil war, a few token opponents were allowed to stand, but voting could not take place in areas held by the regime's opposition, and refugees outside the country were disenfranchised. No surprise again, therefore, when Bashar was re-elected with 88 per cent of the vote, to begin a third seven-year term as president until 2021.

In such a controlled security state as Syria, long known for its prisons and detention centres from which few emerge, it is astonishing that on 15 March 2011 the Syrian Revolution ever began at all. It would never have started had it not been for the wave of protests collectively known as the "Arab Spring". Beginning in Tunisia in December 2010 and sweeping to Egypt in January 2011, then Libya in February 2011, three long-term autocratic rulers were toppled by what appeared at the time to be an unstoppable popular force. Syria shared many of the internal dynamics of these nations: a large population under twenty-five, high youth unemployment, and the dominance of a rich, corrupt elite who exploited a massive poor underclass. Underlying all those factors was another, from which Syria suffered especially—a deep urban–rural divide, the same divide that had triggered the Great Syrian Revolt of 1925 against the French Mandate.

When the peaceful demonstrations calling for reform first began, they were organised by young activists using social media like Facebook and Twitter, the same methods used in Tunisia and Egypt. Sometimes there were spontaneous rallies, in small towns and in the deprived suburbs of a few urban centres, while big cities of over a million residents remained largely unaffected. The flashpoints where the revolution began—Dera'a, Douma and Rif Dimashq (the Damascus countryside)—were afflicted by marginalisation, oppression from the local authorities and arbitrary repression by central government. They were areas of high unemployment and poverty, excluded from the benefits of economic growth. Raqqa, Deir ez-Zour, Hasakeh, rural east Aleppo and rural east Damascus share similar characteristics: a high dropout rate from school, roughly a third of girls married before the age of eighteen, and limited opportunities for migration. Dera'a has the country's second highest population growth rate, putting severe pressure on its surrounding land.

As the regime lost control of the oil resources in the Deir ez-Zour province, tribal leaders got caught up in power struggles with Islamist extremists, squabbling to take charge of the wellheads.

In the ensuing chaos, the lawless vacuum was filled by a toxic mix of entrepreneurial warlords, Al-Qaeda-affiliated groups like Jabhat al-Nusra, and so-called Islamic State (ISIS or *Daesh*). The consequences of the rise of ISIS and Islamist extremism have been catastrophic for the Syrian Revolution, and for Syrian moderates. Members of the international community, perceiving the terrorist threat and galvanised by scenes of desperate Yazidis fleeing up Mount Sinjar, coalesced in August 2014 to run thousands of US-led coalition air strikes against ISIS first in Iraq, then in Syria. Meanwhile the Assad regime, held in place by Iranian and Russian militias and air support, has been allowed to continue killing and imprisoning the moderate Syrian opposition forces, branding them all as "terrorists".

In certain rural areas the struggle against ISIS has given way to Arab–Kurdish antagonism, where local Arab residents feel the majority Kurdish-led Syrian Democratic Forces (SDF) are intent on changing the demographic balance in favour of the Kurds. By 2017 the newly proclaimed Democratic Federation of Northern Syria— known as "Rojava" or Western Kurdistan, and dominated by Kurds— had seized most of the property of Sunni Arab populations in over fifty villages in northern Syria. Kurds from Turkey and Iran moved in. Decades of persecution by the ruling Ba'ath Party came to a head after the 1962 census showed a 30 per cent rise in the Kurdish population of Hasakeh province. In an attempt to deny their growing presence in an area that even then was recognised not only as a fertile agricultural region, but also as rich in potential oil and gas fields, 120,000 Kurds were stripped of their Syrian citizenship. Many had arrived as refugees from the Turkish revolt in 1915, and the French had granted them citizenship during the mandate in return for their loyal service in the army as auxiliaries recruited to help crush the 1925 Great Syrian Revolt. Under the Assads, the Kurdish ID card simply said "Foreigner from Hasakeh". Now it was the Kurds' chance to turn the tables, to retaliate for past grievances by barring regional Arabs from voting for the new Kurdish-led federal parliament of Northern Syria, only permitting them to vote for local councils. Unsurprisingly then, most Arab tribes do not trust the Kurds and their main Syrian political party, the left-wing PYD. There is mandatory conscription into the SDF for both Arab and Kurdish youth, but there are constant Arab defections.

Meanwhile the Assad regime has continued to vie for support from tribal leaders, hoping to use these links to regain control from ISIS in Raqqa and Deir ez-Zour. For the Kurds, for the regime and for ISIS, all of whom have been fighting for control over the natural resources in Syria's northeast, dealing with the tribes poses challenges. The tribes have become too fragmented and fraught by internal rivalries and divisions to be reliable allies, and their leaders frequently switch their allegiances in their own self-interest. Many tribal leaders have lost the respect of their tribes and are viewed increasingly as proxies for outsiders. Even the once respected older shaikhs have been unable to provide for the security and material well-being of their fellow tribesmen, and are therefore no longer worthy of deference.

The term "Syrian Revolution" is used less and less, in favour of more neutral expressions like the "Syrian uprising", the "Syrian crisis" or the "Syrian conflict". Many feel the revolution has failed, in the same way the Great Syrian Revolt of 1925 against the French Mandate failed after two years of fighting. Syrian state media uses the term al-azma, "the crisis", just as they euphemistically dubbed Lebanon's fifteen-year civil war al-ahdath, "the events", a phrase reminiscent of Northern Ireland's euphemism, "the Troubles". Most Syrians refer to their own government under Assad as al-nizam, "the regime". Only state media outlets continue to use the term "the Syrian government."

After seven years of conflict, the Syrian battlefield has become exceptionally complex, with nearly half the countries of the world involved directly or indirectly, their interests not only irreconcilable but often at loggerheads. Syrian territory has become fragmented and fallen under different zones of influence, each with its own networks of procurement and supply chains, supposedly at odds, yet in practice all trading with each other according to need. The country's pre-revolution population of 22 million is estimated to have dropped to about 17 million; the remainder have fled, been killed, or "disappeared". Over half the pre-war population has been internally or externally displaced.

The Assad regime is holding on to the most populous parts of the country: the main inland cities of Damascus, Aleppo, Homs and Hama, together with the Mediterranean coast, what is sometimes termed "useful Syria". This accommodates about two thirds of the country's remaining population, including virtually all the minorities—the 'Alawis, the Druze, Isma'ilis, Circassians and Christians—not necessarily because they support Assad, but because these areas are safest and have the most functioning infrastructure. So-called "useless Syria"—the northern and eastern provinces—is divided between the Kurds and other heavily fragmented opposition groups, including the remnants of ISIS. While these regions only hold around 4 million people, they are far from useless, containing all of Syria's oil and gas fields, the Euphrates river and the country's largest reservoir, Lake Assad, together with the biggest hydroelectric dam and the most fertile wheat and cotton fields. When ISIS extremists were displaced from Raqqa and Deir ez-Zour in late 2017, the Kurdish PYD and its YPG fighters expanded their control from the northern provinces of Jezira to include all the country's dams and all its larger oil and gas fields. Other opposition groups, a mix of Free Syrian Army–affiliated moderates and Al-Qaeda–affiliated Islamists, are scattered between the southern areas around Dera'a and the northwestern province of Idlib, where about 2 million people have been internally displaced. In the areas they control, all the various opposition groups have established their own councils, legal systems, schools, hospitals and even universities. There are four curricula in operation across Syria, as well as three currencies. A third of public consumption was outside regime control by late 2017.

In Idlib province, there has been a construction boom. New housing is urgently needed to accommodate the displaced people who have arrived from Aleppo, Homs and Wadi Barada. Iron is needed in large quantities, and is brought in by truck from factories in Turkey when the borders are open. Whoever happens to control a crossing or checkpoint levies taxes on trucks passing through, or takes bribes to waive them. Competing warlords abound, but no one monopolises the market. Anyone can make a contract with the Turkish iron companies and importers, including armed groups, who sometimes store amounts of iron to sell on at a profit as the price rises. Smuggling between regime and opposition areas is widespread, though not in the case of iron, since it is so heavy to transport, and since the regime can source iron cheaply from Russia and Ukraine via Lattakia's port. Metal trade between opposition areas and regime areas is therefore limited to scrap metal like aluminium, copper and chrome, often procured through looting each other's homes and offices. Sometimes traders even recognise a piece of decorative metalwork, from their own or a friend's house, being resold.

The Syrian government puts pressure on checkpoints to manipulate prices and tariffs on goods passing into rebel areas. As a rebel in Idlib province put it: "The strong eat the weak, and there's no law—much less any security apparatus—to do anything about it. The ones who have the power and influence here are the ones who kidnap and steal." Still, new deals between traders in different regions are struck on a daily basis to bring in whatever is required via whichever border crossings and checkpoints are the least expensive in transit fees. It is a gigantic and ever-changing maze, as the path of least resistance is constantly sought out.

The regime's "starve or surrender" sieges, for example, are big cash generators for those with the right connections. In besieged Eastern Ghouta on the edge of the capital, a dairy farmer took advantage of the blockade to grow a vast cheese and milk business. The set-up was so widely known it was even reported by various media outlets. The regime took a cut of the profit from the dairy farmer's lorry drivers at what became known as "Million Crossing", a checkpoint thought to generate $5,000 per hour in bribes. Blockaded residents saw him as "a kind of Robin Hood character, the only one bringing in food" in exchange for "exporting" their milk and cheese into Damascus. Before the war, the farmer had owned twenty-five cows. By summer 2017 he had become "the cheese king" and lorded over a herd of 1,000 cattle, a private militia of about 500 men and a workforce of 1,500, who were paid far more highly than regime or rebel fighters.

Many accuse the PYD of having a tacit partnership with Assad, a kind of marriage of convenience. In summer 2017, a five-year deal was announced under which the Syrian regime and the Kurdish PYD share oil revenues from the northeastern fields in Hasakeh province, with the regime taking 65 per cent and the PYD 20 per cent, the remaining 15 per cent going to "the Arab forces who are responsible for protecting the oilfields." Hussam Qaterji, the regime-affiliated middleman who brokered the deal, had previously worked on oil deals between the regime, the PYD and ISIS, a role for which he was rewarded by being "elected" to the Syrian Parliament, as representative for the city of Aleppo. The Aleppo and Damascus Chambers of Commerce are likewise full of new faces, unknown before the uprising, men who have built up their wealth from war-related activities. At the end of 2016 a deal was announced under which a Russian company receives 25 per cent of all oil and gas collected by the regime in areas cleared of ISIS militants by Russian forces, in a barter deal to pay for Russia's military support. A Russian engineering company has also been awarded rights to develop Syria's phosphate mines, previously awarded to Iran. Syria has some of the largest phosphate reserves in the world, in the desert near Palmyra.

Even in regime-held areas like Tartous where there has been no fighting throughout the conflict, there are nevertheless competing local power brokers who are increasingly acting independently of the regime, challenging Damascus' authority. These include leaders of government-backed and Iranian-financed National Defence Forces (NDF) who, though in theory just "volunteer" militias fighting "to defend the security of the state", fund themselves further through kidnapping locals, looting their homes and demanding extortionate "taxes" at checkpoints. Widely feared and hated, they also use their powerful presence on the ground to gain revenue by blocking or controlling the distribution of humanitarian aid supplied by the UN or other international NGOs.

However difficult the circumstances, people still need homes, schools and hospitals, and if these have been bombed and destroyed, they need to be rebuilt. Despite the turbulent conditions, new institutions have grown up, such as the Free Syrian Lawyers Association and the Violations Documentation Centre, which, however imperfect, are forming the beginnings of a civil society independent of the Syrian state. Many of these call themselves Local Coordination Committees (LCCs), self-governing councils which have spontaneously evolved in opposition areas to defend themselves against immediate threats, like air raids or barrel bombing, and to organise ways of sharing the essential sources of drinking water, fuel and electricity after infrastructure has been destroyed. Instead of imposing rule from the top down, like the previous state institutions, they govern through voluntary cooperation. The best known are the White Helmets—volunteer doctors, engineers, teachers, journalists and more—who rush to the scene of an attack to provide emergency medical help and retrieve civilians from under the rubble. Their efforts have been internationally recognised, and in 2017 a documentary celebrating their work even won an Oscar award.

One of the first to write about the work of LCCs was 'Omar 'Aziz, a Damascus intellectual who believed that people should not wait for regime change, but should take charge of their own governance. Psychologists have described a state of mind called "learned helplessness", a condition in which repeated threats to one's safety render a person docile and compliant, in order to avoid further danger. For 'Aziz the antidote to this helplessness is for people to initiate change for themselves, a solution recognised by the World Health Organisation, which prescribes self-government as the best cure among populations who have been victims of war or natural disaster. For people who have experienced trauma, as many Syrians have, the support of a social group is essential, so that communities can solve the problems which they are facing collectively. Once a community has a shared vision for its future, the bonds between individuals strengthen, developing resilience and leading to better cooperation and communal healing.

Bashar al-Assad understands this well, and has therefore been determined to prevent communities from rebuilding on their own terms. His method has been either to crush his opposition with overwhelming military force or to lure local elites back into his orbit with bribes and other incentives. This has made it virtually impossible for opposition groups to unite, especially when they have been unsupported by a vacillating and indecisive international community. The uprising began spontaneously without any central leadership, and so the Syrian opposition was localised and fragmented from the start. The regime continues to provide bread, health, education, and intermittent water and electricity to the areas under its control, and it also still runs two countrywide networks: mobile telephones and the banking system. Both mobile telephone networks, Syriatel and MTL, are run by regime supporters and both have seen big rises in revenue during the war thanks to the increased usage. Most Syrians own a mobile phone and the signal coverage extends to 96 per cent of the country. Syrian Air continues to run internal flights to Qamishli Airport by agreement with the city's Kurdish administration. The train network was an early casualty in the war, but buses have never stopped travelling around the country between the major cities, with drivers warning passengers who controls each checkpoint so they can adjust their clothing and wallets accordingly.

Throughout the war the regime has been at pains to maintain an image of normalcy, sometimes called the "Syria is fine" mentality. It has made a point of continuing performances at the Damascus Opera House, even if only through folkloric dances or Christian choirs to show support of the minorities. The SANA state media website has maintained its cultural and even touristic drop-down menus, with new content appearing at regular intervals, however minor and absurd, to keep up the appearance of ongoing activity. Tourism revenue is down by 98 per cent from pre-war levels, yet in summer

2016 the Ministry of Tourism launched a "Syria is beautiful" TV advertising campaign, showing footage of white sandy beaches on the Syrian Riviera as though there were no such thing as the Syrian war. The Central Bank of Syria has no independence to manage monetary policy, and the Commercial Bank of Syria, the largest bank in the country, has strong links with regime officials and is therefore under US and EU sanctions. Other banks came under pressure to close their branches in non-regime areas, meaning that many non-state employees have been excluded from the financial system for years and forced to convert instead to a cash economy. Major Lebanese banks, like Bank Audi, BLOM and Byblos Bank, have withdrawn from the country and started writing off their Syrian investments and assets. Official Syrian trade with Lebanon is at its lowest level in fifteen years, and most bilateral trade between the two countries these days comes under the "informal" sector or black market, just as it did during the Lebanese Civil War.

Western sanctions and the EU oil trade ban have meant that the government has lost its main source of income. To compensate, Iran began to bring in illicit oil supplies via the port of Banias, while offshore companies were established in Lebanon and the rest of the world to evade sanctions. Many businesses were relocated from the war-torn suburbs of Damascus to the safer city centre, while Aleppo businesses relocated to the coastal region or to cities in southeast Turkey like Gaziantep. Most businesses that moved to Turkey, Egypt, Jordan and the UAE still served the Syrian market, creating cross-border commercial networks. When Russia entered the war in September 2015 the regime also established the Russian import-export village in Lattakia's port, from which regular shipments were made to Russia of Syrian agricultural products. A new port at Lattakia is under discussion with Iran. It is only through this support that the regime has survived economically.

Foreign investors, donors and even Syrian businessmen bringing funds into the country for its future reconstruction will find that economic conditions and inequality are even worse than pre–2011. Corruption is still rampant, possibly even more entrenched than before. Consumers are at the mercy of sellers, who in the absence of government oversight can sell basic consumer goods at exorbitant prices. In 2016, a regime MP even denounced the fact that officials responsible for diesel distribution to households had been registering fictitious names in order to sell the diesel on the black market at inflated prices, yet no action was taken to rectify the abuse of power. Without a proper system of externally regulated oversight, there is a real danger that reconstruction will simply rebuild the old faultlines, as the regime pumps foreign donor cash into projects exclusively in its own areas. Throughout 2016 and 2017 UN aid money has been financing 50 per cent of the Syrian state budget, since the UN charter obliges it to send aid through a country's official government. The Syrian government in turn only permits reconstruction work funded by the UN. By late 2017 $19 million had been allocated to clear rubble, build emergency shelters and provide water, sanitation and education within regime-held areas. The civilian population in areas outside regime control gets no UN support whatsoever.

While the Syrian state will need to bring back investment from wealthy Syrians in the diaspora, those who stayed in Syria will want preferential treatment. Since 2011, many will have benefited from massive high-end government contracts, often funded by UN agencies and international NGOs. International sanctions and a shortage of supplies have provided them with the perfect opportunity to strike exclusive import deals and engage in smuggling rackets spawned by the war economy. The government has increased the price it pays to tobacco farmers by 260 per cent, for example, to reward the 'Alawi heartlands for their support. In contast, Syrian investors who have fled have fewer ties to the regime. Many come from the urban Sunni middle classes, whose wealth is based on their capital investment and is not dependent on state institutions. In cities like Aleppo, those that stayed behind, often the poor and elderly who refused to leave their homes, have been forced by the destruction of state infrastructure to pay by the hour for generator supplies of electricity, thereby channelling more money into the pockets of the exploitative wealthy elite. Only the rich can afford generators, so it a process reminiscent of Ottoman tax-farming, where the elite can recoup their initial outlay many times over. The gap between Syria's rich and poor has grown even wider than it was before 2011, a fact that does not bode well for the future.

Meanwhile both Russia and Iran—the regime's chief backers—are facing economic problems of their own. A steady stream of high-level Syrian officials has visited Moscow, seeking funds for reconstruction. Russia has provided no loans to the Syrian government during the crisis, but in summer 2012 flew eight planeloads of banknotes, newly printed in the highest Syrian pound denomination in Moscow, into Damascus, to enable Bashar al-Assad to continue paying army and civil service salaries. Syrian banknotes used to be printed in Austria before 2011, but the EU blocked the three-year contract as part of its European financial sanctions package against Syria. The regime has since invited Chinese companies to work in Syria "at all levels in all sectors." Syrian Air has leased an Airbus A340 that can fly non-stop from Damascus to Beijing, in readiness for the expert personnel and essential equipment the regime hopes China will send for Syrian assistance. So far, Iran has been the only ally to have provided Syria with loan aid during the conflict.

In return for its government's support, Iran has been rewarded with asset deals: by late 2017 an unspecified 5,000 hectares of land for crops, 1,000 hectares for cattle breeding and 5,000 hectares for oil storage and reservoirs had been promised to Iranian companies on a lease basis. By openly accepting these assets from the Syrian government, Iran has signalled that it will be a major player in Syria's future economic, military and security affairs. The balance of power is delicately poised at present, with Russia "advising" the Syrian defence ministry and Iran "supporting" the key intelligence and security departments. An Aleppan businessman described Bashar as "like a man with two false legs, one Russian, one Iranian, hopping from one leg to the other because the ground he is standing on is very hot."

SYRIAN REVOLUTION AND THE WAR ECONOMY

As the war rages on, the business of people-smuggling has thrived on the chaos, though the tightening of Turkish borders in early 2016 has made the process harder. Many who cross become smugglers themselves, helping friends and relatives to cross the same way, via back roads that border guards do not patrol. Plunder and war booty have also become rampant. In December 2016, after intense weeks of fighting, Aleppo was recaptured by the regime and residents were finally allowed back into their quarters to see their houses. On their return most were overjoyed to find their homes, which had been held under rebel occupation for over four years, relatively unscathed. The next day, the regime closed off the area again, saying they needed to clear away safety hazards and check for mines. When the area was reopened three days later, the owners returned to find their homes ransacked from top to bottom, their furniture and possessions gone. Convoys of trucks were seen openly queuing on the roads leading out of Aleppo, piled high with looted furniture destined for sale in so-called "Sunni markets". Armed militias with powerful patrons in the regime had been given licence to pillage and steal war booty in return for their support during the siege. Profits from stolen property tend to trickle upwards, so while the regime might make a show of protest against looters, in practice they are given free rein.

The same technique applies to reconstruction efforts. Ministers appear regularly on the state media and quote statistics. The health minister announces that he is reopening health centres in east Aleppo, while the housing minister announces he is building 6,000 new homes. The electricity minister promises electricity and the water resources minister promises water. The tourism minister even promises tourist attractions, posting videos in June 2017 of whirling dervishes dancing in front of the Damascus Umayyad Mosque as part of Ramadan's nightly celebrations. The source of the funds is unclear.

Rival groups controlling different parts of the country have also made arrangements to profit from Syria's cultural heritage, nowhere more so than in Palmyra. Even before the revolution began in 2011, when the archaeological site was under the control of the regime, looting was extensive. Tourists were offered coins and Roman statuettes at larger classical Syrian sites like Apamea and Palmyra. At Apamea this was a veritable industry, and a factory there churned out conterfeit artefacts that fooled many a gullible visitor. When ISIS captured Palmyra in May 2015 the plundering continued, only more openly, with ISIS taking a 20 per cent commission on all looted items before they were sent north into Turkey to be offloaded onto the international art market. When items in situ were too big to be smuggled abroad, these "symbols of idolatry" were blown up for propaganda purposes. The plunder and bribery did not stop when Syrian and Russian forces recaptured Palmyra in March 2016. "The illegal excavations have flourished despite the change of the parties controlling Palmyra," says Cheikhmous Ali, head of the Association for the Protection of Syrian Archaeology (APSA). "The antiquities trade in Palmyra continues to be conducted by the same looters, who have been able to deal with ISIS, the regime and the Russians. They bribe some officers and soldiers to turn a blind eye."

As the Syrian economy began to falter and splutter, the contrast between the fate of its textile industry and the success of Hield Brothers in the UK could hardly have been any starker. From its stable base in Yorkshire, the Chamsi-Pashas' textile firm controlled the mills, the factories and the supply chains, and was thriving in world markets. In Syria the textile industry, which pre–2011 had accounted for 63 per cent of the industrial sector's production, was increasingly exposed to sabotage and destruction. War had forced most governmental and private textile factories to stop their activity, whether partially or totally. Of Aleppo's original 40,000 factories, only 1,200 were still operational in 2013, though by summer 2017, six months after the city fell back to the regime, the number had risen to 10,000. Before the war the textile sector had been the second most important source of income for the Syrian economy after oil and gas, accounting for around 12 per cent of GDP and 20 per cent of the labour force. Syria used to export billions of dollars' worth of textile products—yarn, fabric, and garments—but current economic sanctions make it impossible for Syrian manufacturers to access European markets.

In early 2016 some 100 Syrian textile merchants, both men and women, attended a trade fair held in Beirut to showcase their wares. Many of them were still functioning out of small workshops, after their factories on the outskirts of Damascus and Aleppo were destroyed by bombardment, and were determined to show their businesses were still alive. Most of the 500 buyers who came to the fair were from the Middle East, and were drawn by the regional reputation that the Syrian textile industry enjoys. "I buy Syrian textiles because of their quality. It's better than Turkish or Chinese merchandise and almost competitive price-wise," one Egyptian textile merchant explained. "I like how Syrian manufacturers create a unique mix between Eastern and European styles." European buyers were absent at the fair, deterred by the sanctions. "Buyers used to come from all around the world, but the war has scared them," said a businesswoman whose factory had been in Harasta, north Damascus. Other businessmen were quick to point out: "It should be in Europe's interest to facilitate trade, otherwise Syrian workers without jobs will want to go to Europe."

In addition to the loss of European buyers, the industry workforce has been seriously depleted. "We had 100 employees, today only thirty of them are still working for us," explained the woman from Harasta. A businessman from Aleppo agreed: "Most of my employees emigrated because of the situation and some because they were forced to join the army for military service." Some Syrian textile workers who fled to Turkey have found themselves exploited as cheap labour in rival Turkish textile factories. Many are children working illegally, not going to school. "I will go back to school in Syria after the war," said one twelve- year-old boy who worked full-time in a textile factory in Istanbul. Much of the clothing made in these factories, ironically, is destined for the European market.

Syria's biggest lingerie and pyjama factory still employs 450 people in Damascus and survives by keeping its workers indoors during flare-ups in the fighting, sometimes even overnight. "I had seventy-two workers sleeping at the factory at one point," said the owner, surrounded by multicoloured bras and cotton sleepwear in his stall at the Beirut fair. "They started at six in the morning, worked until eleven, then slept. They would only go home to their families from Thursday night to Saturday morning."

The president of the Syrian Exporters Association confirmed that over 70 per cent of textile factories were closed or destroyed by the war. In the ensuing lawlessness, machines that survived the bombing were stolen. The owner of Aleppo-based Dream Girl Lingerie company lamented: "Thieves took them to Turkey. I had 220 machines before, now I only have ten." Many factories moved from Aleppo into the city's old Turkish hinterland, to cities like Gaziantep, but would move back if new business regulations for Syria's entrepreneurial middle class make it sufficiently attractive for them to return and reinvest. Some host countries of Syria's refugee businessmen want them to stay, after seeing the positive effect on their economies. Egypt has created a new special industrial zone for Syria's refugee textile makers, who inject 10 million garments per month into the Egyptian market.

As in all sustained conflicts, the war economy in Syria has developed to fill gaps in the market, and as expected unscrupulous entrepreneurs have seized new opportunities. The economy is fragmented but has not halted, as people still need food, wood and other essentials. Regime loyalists are rewarded with special contracts and concessions—by acting as middlemen they can then make profits of $2–3 million in three to four months. "In a war economy, only the poor are really poor," Abu Chaker's sons explained. "Lots of people benefit. In Lebanon during the civil war the warlords were awash with dollars."

"It's one of the ironies of war that money is concentrated in the hands of even fewer," they said. "In Syria it's no different, with the rebels, the Kurds and *Daesh* selling oil back to the regime, or sending it off to Turkey from the thousands of makeshift refineries all over the eastern desert. The Russians are making a fortune from their armaments sales and showcasing their weaponry for other foreign sales. All over the country illegal homes are being built, which is why wood, cement and iron are being imported in such big quantities—there is a building boom, with five-storey buildings suddenly appearing on agricultural land, as there are no checks any more." They told me about a Turkmen from Lattakia they had met on a flight to Europe, who had been on a trip to buy second-hand agricultural machinery to import back into Syria. The harvest would carry on, so the man planned to sell the tractors and other machinery at twice their usual price, either to the regime or the opposition, depending on where he was. "There's money to be made, if you're minded that way. Lots of people have an interest in the war continuing."

16

RETURN TO HOMS AND FINAL DISPLACEMENT

Think much, speak little, write less.

(Arab proverb)

When Abu Chaker resettled in his beloved Homs in 1999, he was an old man of seventy-eight. In his flat in London's West End, he could not help but miss Syria and its land. In London he had no farm, no animals, and no connection with nature—his balcony plants, Regent's Park and London Zoo were a poor substitute for the Syrian countryside. And so it was hardly surprising that towards the end of his life, Abu Chaker felt a pull to return to his roots, to his home soil where he felt a true sense of belonging. He started spending most of his time in Syria, returning to London only for periodic health check-ups. His sons remained in the UK and took care of running the business.

Even after his move to the UK in 1975, Abu Chaker had never cut ties with Syria and Lebanon and had continued to make regular trips back. At first, he had needed to return to collect payment for sales made in Beirut, especially since his warehouses and all their stock had been lost to fire and looting in the Lebanese Civil War.

He called on his customers in person, collected the money he was owed and then took the bundles of cash to money transfer firms that sent it to the UK. Later on, in the 1980s, Abu Chaker travelled regularly not just to Lebanon but also to Syria. His continued business links with the region even led him to set up a Nissan distributorship in Lebanon in partnership with his friend Shaikh Hassib Rasamny, a Druze from Lebanon, and Albert Bahna, an Orthodox Christian from Homs. Wherever he was, Abu Chaker was always alive to a business opportunity. By the 1990s he conducted most of his business from the UK, and had begun handing over the reins of power to his sons.

Instrumental in his decision to return to Syria was Abu Chaker's surprising but enduring friendship with one of Hafez al-Assad's top intelligence chiefs, an 'Alawi army general, 'Adnan Badr al-Hassan. This friend, known to his family and friends as Abu Sulayman, had also grown up in Homs. Like Abu Chaker he came from a devout Muslim background, and had been sent to a *kuttab* in his childhood to be taught the Qur'an by a shaikh. After school he had attended the Homs Military Academy, risen to the rank of major general and become commander of a tank battalion. He went on to fight in the 1973 Arab–Israeli War, performing well in the Golan Heights, for which he was decorated. He earned Hafez al-Assad's trust and was rewarded in 1987 with the position of chief of the Political Security Directorate (*al-Amn al-Siyasi*), one of the top five appointments within the Assad regime's *mukhabarat*.

Abu Sulayman was unusual in living a frugal lifestyle—another reason that Hafez al-Assad, himself abstinent and ascetic, felt he could trust him. Part of his job was to read the files of those businessmen who had been involved in the early days of Syria's economic liberalisation. He was therefore familiar with all the skeletons in the cupboards of the regime elite, and was not impressed. "Not many make their first million cleanly," Abu Chaker's sons explained, "but Father did."

The two men had first encountered each other in Homs, where Abu Sulayman knew of Abu Chaker as an honest trader in the souk, and had grown up with immense respect for him. He recalled that Abu Chaker had possessed the "true mentality of a Syrian merchant, a worthy descendant of Syria's Silk Road trading empire from across the centuries." He spoke admiringly of his friend's piety: "Abu Chaker's Islam was mercy, love, the real Islam. He had no education, no foreign languages, no studies or qualifications—he learnt his lessons from living." As Abu Chaker's business had grown, he had been able to buy three houses in Homs. "But he always lived a modest lifestyle, never flashy," explained Abu Sulayman. "He was a self-made man, he distinguished himself thanks to his own merits, not through aristocratic birth. He was never a big landowner, just a normal trader working out of his father's shop."

His friend described the seeds of Abu Chaker's connection to the land: the small farm that he had run on land his family had inherited from the Ottomans. "He grew to love nature and the products of the farm. In fact he was obsessed with old farm food and used to bring food products as gifts, like yellow *samneh* (sheep fat), 50 kilograms of honey, or truffles from Homs, very high quality." He loved sweet things above all, and while the men ate, they would discuss the next meal, talking about the wonders of Homs pie and a dish called *maqlouba*—a casserole of fried vegetables, rice and meat, cooked in one pot and turned upside-down on serving. Homs was known for the best aubergines in Syria, and almost every Homsi dish was prepared with the noble aubergine in some shape or form. The two friends' sons, who were similar in age, used to complain about aubergine overdose. Umm Chaker, as Abu Sulayman called Rihab, taught the maids how to make these dishes, and if the food was not up to scratch, Abu Chaker would sometimes scold her. It would be difficult to overstate the cultural importance of food. Despite difficult circumstances and the threat of indigence, many Syrian refugees who have fled to Europe continue to go to great lengths to provide food and hospitality to guests.

Abu Chaker would listen to Abu Sulayman's jokes and together they would rock with laughter until their sides ached. The two men would reminisce over shared memories from childhood—walking the cobbled streets in Homs or wading through mud to get to school. Though they shared the same background they lived in quite different worlds, but this did not stop them enjoying each other's company. They never discussed each other's work or money, and Abu Chaker never objected if Abu Sulayman drank alcohol.

When Abu Chaker first started coming back to Syria in the 1980s, his friend had helped him pass back and forth easily across the Lebanese border, at a time during the Syrian occupation of Lebanon when such movements were strictly controlled and required special passes. He had wanted Abu Chaker and Umm Chaker to come back to Syria more often and would say so quite openly, but Abu Chaker had felt he was better off in London where he could live a comfortable life free from state interference. In Syria he hated being hassled by the authorities, and the fact that at any moment he could get a knock on the door and be told, "You are a rich man from abroad, we want this or that," or be dragged away for questioning, never to be seen again by his family. Yet protected as he was by a high-profile figure, he soon realised he could have relative peace of mind.

In 1992 Abu Chaker was invited back to Syria, along with his eldest son, as part of the very first delegation from the Syrian Arab Association in the UK (SAAUK). The invitation was part of Hafez al-Assad's policy to tempt members of the diaspora back to Syria to encourage them to invest in its economy. The delegation consisted of about twenty-four city professionals and bankers, and they were treated like royalty. A small plane was specially chartered on arrival in Damascus to fly the delegation east to Deir ez-Zour, where they were shown the new oil installations, and to the Tabqa Dam on the Euphrates to see the hydroelectric plant built in the 1970s with Soviet assistance. They were also taken to Quneitra in the Golan Heights, and were told to keep one day free when they would meet Hafez al-Assad himself.

Abu Chaker and his son decided to skip the cultural part of the tour and go instead to Beirut, to see if their block of flats in Al-Haazimieh was still standing. During their visit they were treated like lords, and were even met by Ghazi Kanaan, the long-term head of Syria's intelligence apparatus in Lebanon, an 'Alawi and distant relation of Hafez al-Assad's wife, Anisa. Kanaan later replaced 'Adnan Badr al-Hassan as head of the Political Security Directorate and became the most feared man in Lebanon, with the power to arbitrarily arrest anyone he chose. He died of a gunshot wound to the head in 2005 after being questioned about Rafiq al-Hariri's assassination, in an incident declared by the Syrian authorities to be suicide, though it was widely suspected that those same authorities had orchestrated the shooting themselves. In addition to Kanaan, Abu Chaker and his son were subsequently met by the Lebanese prime minister, the speaker of the parliament and the president. In Syria the meeting with Hafez al-Assad never materialised, but in Lebanon the Chamsi-Pashas received the full red carpet treatment.

Abu Chaker had returned once before to see his Beirut block of flats, in the late 1980s when the Lebanese Civil War was still ongoing. He had been escorted by men specially appointed by Abu Sulayman to protect him. When they arrived they found a Maronite Christian family had taken refuge in the block, after their home had been destroyed in central Beirut. Terrified, the refugees began to cry when they saw Abu Chaker's Syrian military escort, but Abu Chaker assured them they could stay for the time being. Though they had broken into the building they were now taking good care of it, and had carefully packed up the Chamsi-Pasha family's personal belongings into cartons, which they had stored in the loft space above the bathroom. When the war ended Abu Chaker went through the courts to get the property back legally, and the refugees were never punished.

Thanks to the *wasta* or influence of his military friend, Abu Chaker was spared the hassle of dealing with authorities in Lebanon and in Homs, and gradually began to see the beautiful side of Syria once more, as opposed to its sinister politics. Hafez al-Assad's policy to draw back the diaspora was working, and Abu Chaker was slowly reconciled with Syria. He now knew his life in Homs would not be plagued by harassment, so he started returning more and more often, until in the late '90s he was spending four months a year in Homs and eight months in London. Then in around 2006 he reversed the order, living in Homs for eight months a year and in London for just four.

Right to the end of his life, he remained aloof from the politics of his country. He never joined the Ba'ath Party, even though he was frequently courted by Ba'ath Party officials. On one occasion the local Ba'ath functionaries in Homs published his name in the newspapers as one of the top donors to charity that year. Abu Chaker was congratulated publicly in the streets for his beneficence, but instead of being taken in and feeling flattered, he simply laughed and denied the accolade, saying they had made a mistake. Meanwhile he continued to give generously to the poor discreetly, in ways that could not be traced by the authorities. He gave regular monthly stipends to institutions for the poor, such as an orphanage in the outlying Homs district of Al-Waer, by asking a member of staff from the orphanage to come and collect the money or sending one of his own workers there. He also made a habit of donating a lot of fabric from his shops to charities in Homs before the two 'Eids, the two major public holidays. It was up to the charities to decide whether to sell on the cloth or use it for making clothing to keep themselves warm. By keeping his distance from the political establishment, he maintained his independence and freedom of manoeuvre.

For all his disdain of his country's political system, its cruelty and corruption were not enough to keep him away. Like many other honest Syrians, he knew that if he was careful, he could still live well in his native Homs. Having generated his own wealth as a merchant, not beholden in any way to the Syrian political system, he was free to do things his way. An example of this independence can be seen in the story of the old Arab well in his house in Homs. The well had dried up, leaving Abu Chaker dependent on the at-best intermittent government-supplied water, which he had to pay for. He enlisted the services of local workmen to build a new well. After digging a full 60 metres into the ground, the men had found nothing. Abu

Chaker would not give up and told them to dig deeper, and with the help of special equipment and pumps, the men finally succeeded and found water. To this day the house is supplied by water from this well, making it independent of the government supply. The free drinking water dispenser he installed outside his gate continues to function, like a modern-day version of an Ottoman drinking fountain, following in the tradition of his ancestors.

Over their fifty-year rule, the Ba'athists had turned Homs into the ugliest city in Syria. Once ancient Emessa, sitting on the crossroads of important trade routes from the Mediterranean coast east to Palmyra and beyond, its agricultural oasis of gardens and orchards was destroyed. Instead the city became an industrial hub whose oil refineries and chemical plants processed hydrocarbons and phosphates from Syria's underdeveloped but resource-rich eastern provinces. A car park was created by bulldozing chunks of the Old City, while an ill-considered dam on the nearby Orontes reduced the river to a dirty stream. The noxious fumes from newly built factories were blown into the city by prevailing winds.

Abu Chaker escaped this hell by creating his own oasis. He knew the Ba'ath would never agree to his ideas for town planning, and that they would in any case make sure that construction contracts were awarded to their own preferred companies whose vision did not extend beyond their own bank balance. With the help of his sons, he employed his own people and embarked on a project to build a caravanserai on his own land beside his beloved farm. In one of the Ba'ath Party's many "modernisation" schemes, the Chamsi-Pashas' original courtyard house in Bab Dreib had been due for demolition, and so, as the only way to save it, the workers had dismantled the walls, numbering all the blocks carefully to be reused in the construction of the new caravanserai.

Together they painstakingly recreated the design of an Ottoman *khan*, a building whose purpose historically had been to offer merchants, their livestock and their merchandise shelter on their travels, with high defensive walls to protect from brigands. Inside was a large open courtyard surrounded by arched and vaulted rooms.

The Seljuks had originated the system as long ago as the eleventh century to facilitate commerce along trade routes, and it was continued by the Ottomans. Usually positioned a day's ride apart, they offered the weary merchants a range of sleeping quarters, baths to revive aching limbs, cafés for refreshment, a blacksmith and leatherworker to do repairs and even musicians to relax and entertain. Stabling was offered for the donkeys, horses and camels with doors of varying height to suit each animal. The strong gateway was the only external architectural feature, on which all decorative effort was concentrated.

Most remarkable of all was that these services were offered free, funded by taxation. During the two centuries of their rule the Seljuks evolved an advanced welfare state, laying down the foundations for commercial prosperity, education and the arts. Universities, observatories, mosques and hospitals were built; medical schools were linked with the hospitals; orphanages, poor-houses, mental homes, baths and religious schools were set up, all offering their services free of charge. Ten centuries later, the state in Syria has reverted from altruist to extortionist.

Abu Chaker's own *khan* was perhaps an unconscious hark back to his ancestor's first *khan* in the Damascus souk, Şemsi Pasha's Khan al-Joukhiye for precious broadcloth, and he saw no reason why the authorities would wish to take it from him. He was a highly respected and wealthy member of society in Homs, and was not dependent on bribery and corruption to get what he wanted. People knew he had a business based in the UK, though few realised the extent of it. He kept himself deliberately low profile, dressing in a worn suit and driving an old Fiat out to the farm just north of the city every morning at dawn.

When he returned from the farm, Abu Chaker would enjoy a freshly prepared breakfast of fruit, yoghurt, vegetables, eggs and bread, accompanied by hot sweet black tea. When his grandchildren were visiting, he would encourage them to come with him to the farm, so that they could appreciate a breakfast afterwards feeling that they had earned it together. His grandchildren remember being reluctant on most mornings. It was their summer holidays, and they wanted to sleep in rather than follow their grandfather's timetable of rising at dawn.

After breakfast he would visit his shop in the souk, arriving just as everyone was opening up. Pinned on the notice boards on the shop walls were many postcards from around the world. They were addressed simply: Chamsi-Pasha, Homs souk. In Syria's third largest city, that was enough. Abu Chaker would sit out front on an old wooden chair in the alley, smoking his pipe and watching the passers-by. Just as he had as a young man, he would go to pray at Al-Nouri Mosque next door, while his Christian neighbours minded the shop. When his grandsons accompanied him to the souk he would make them sweep the shop floor and the alley in front of it, teaching them to spray the ground with water to dampen the dust and keep the heat at bay, just as his sons had been made to perform the same ritual. They didn't mind for a day or two, but the novelty soon wore off and thereafter they preferred to stay at home watching TV or playing computer games. Once, his eldest granddaughter had wanted to come to the souk and take photos. She had been wearing a loose shirt and trousers, which she had thought perfectly suitable for the heat. "Why are you wearing your pyjamas? Go and change," her grandfather had instructed.

Abu Chaker often spent his evenings in the enclosed garden of his home in Homs, smoking his *arghile*. The house, on a quiet residential street in a western suburb of the city, was a modern apartment block built in the same style as the Beirut house, and each son had a private apartment on a floor to himself. A high wall surrounded the block on all sides, with vehicle access via a double gate. Abu Chaker and Rihab lived on the ground floor, which also had the home's main reception and dining room for both guests and the family. Breakfast and dinner were often served on shaded parts of the terrace, where the cascading jasmine tumbled over the concrete walls. Lunch was eaten indoors at the great dining table, which was large enough to seat sixteen people. It was rare that the entire family—Abu Chaker and Rihab's sons, daughters-in-law and grandchildren—would all be visiting at the same time, which would have required seating for twenty-four. Nonetheless the table was often full with relatives or friends, from Homs and further afield.

Even in his old age, Abu Chaker preferred having guests and sharing the food from his table with them to visiting them for dinner at their homes. Hosting was a life-long custom that Abu Chaker enjoyed immensely. It was deeply rooted in the tradition of hospitality, and was born not of a desire to display his generosity or affluence, but rather of a delight in sharing with others. Abu Chaker did not talk much at these occasions but focused instead on making sure his guests were passed the full variety of dishes on offer, urging them to eat more and often even putting food on their plates before they could protest. In usual Arab fashion, all the dishes, both hot and cold, were served in one go, and there was no established or correct pattern of what to eat first. This freedom allowed such occasions to be very informal, since everyone could eat at their own pace and help themselves to whatever they preferred and in whatever order. The food would be the event's main focus and often the primary topic of conversation—the texture of the aubergines, the freshness of the mint, the ripeness of the figs. *Sidr Knafeh* was always served at the end, a syrup-soaked sweet cheese pastry served hot on a large flat metal dish, the proud creation of local pastry-maker Zarrouf who had been supplying the family's pastry since Abu Chaker's father had been alive. The food that remained after guests had eaten their fill was distributed to others in the neighbourhood, those who could afford it less. Nothing was ever wasted; that would have been an abuse of God's beneficence.

Among the people Abu Chaker socialised with in his retirement in Homs was his old friend and colleague Albert Bahna, a Christian resident of Homs with whom he had done business in Beirut in the 1970s and 1980s. They had been partners in the Nissan car distributorship and had known each other for fifty-six years. Displaced from Homs by the outbreak of war in 2011, Albert moved to Lebanon to live with his wife in the Christian district of Jounieh, north of Beirut. In his eighties, physically frail and recovering from a stroke, his mind was still very sharp. With tears in his eyes, he produced his iPad and showed me pictures of his home in Homs, a large gabled property in the district of Al-Mahatta. His neighbour in Homs had sent him the photos, to reassure him that the house was still fine. It was empty now, he said. Albert spent much of his time reliving those days in Homs, and had no difficulty recalling many details of that life. He had last seen Abu Chaker in 2013, when Abu Chaker had visited Beirut with one of his sons and his wife. They had met each other in Verdun Street in Downtown Beirut, and both had a sense then that it might be the last time.

Abu Chaker was famous in the souk of Old Homs, Albert said, and was highly respected. He himself had been born in 1937, sixteen years after Abu Chaker, but he still recalled buying cloth from him in the souk. He explained how Abu Chaker had kept his old shop in the souk for sentimental reasons, as a symbol and reminder of his humble origins. "Abu Chaker was kind to the poor," he said, "with a strong sense of duty to look after those who were not well provided for. He would arrange for money to be paid to Islamic charities. I would give the money and he would pay me back later," he explained. If he had died in Homs, said Albert, there would have been a very big funeral. He did not know that in London, Abu Chaker's funeral had in fact been a very big affair, probably even bigger than it would have been in Homs, with processions of ex-ambassadors and business chiefs calling to pay their respects.

One such ambassador was Jihad Mortada, the Lebanese ambassador to the UK. Now retired and living in Beirut, he was twenty years younger than Abu Chaker, and had known him in London for the last ten years of his life. He talked with deep nostalgia of the passing of tradition. Abu Chaker was, he explained, the last of a generation of Syrian Sunni merchants who had believed in trust and honesty in business. For these merchants, crime was unthinkable and would have brought great dishonour. "We are losing this war," he said in 2014, "Syria is being destroyed."

Another life-long contact from Homs with whom Abu Chaker had enjoyed over fifty years of business and friendship was Hajj

Choueib Rifa'i. Their relationship had been based on total confidence in each other's honesty. A quietly spoken man in his eighties, now living in Beirut, Hajj Choueib still dresses smartly in a suit and remains highly active. He had been a graduate of Aleppo University in civil engineering and had known Abu Chaker in Homs, where they had both lived in the same district, just a short walk apart from each other. The two men had worked with each other for decades, and had even built houses and bungalows together in Bradford. His own children, two sons and a daughter, completed their university studies in the United States.

Hajj Choueib returned to Syria in 1985 during the beginnings of liberalisation under Hafez al-Assad, when he said there were more business opportunities. As a building contractor in Syria he had been involved in the construction of five refineries in Homs, industrial plants, a water refinery, a fertiliser plant and a power plant in Banias. Even when I met him in March 2014, he was still returning to Homs regularly. "The safest way to travel to Homs from Beirut," he said, "is to go by Pullman [bus], with thirty to forty other passengers." His eyes misted over as he described what it was like returning to his home town. "Over half of it is destroyed now," he said. "It looks like it did three to four hundred years ago. The eastern part of Al-Nouri Mosque is destroyed, and half of Khalid ibn al-Walid Mosque is destroyed. It has been looted, even right down to the wiring and the cabling."

The cost of rebuilding would be at least $25–30 billion, he said, giving his professional estimate. The richest residents had left for abroad; about 200,000 had gone to the USA alone, especially Christians. In Damascus the western suburbs where wealthier people had lived were now empty. There were checkpoints every 200 metres at that time, making the city feel "like a big prison". As a result it took one and half hours to travel from Malki to the Shami Hospital, a journey that used to take just ten minutes. At the checkpoints themselves, the soldiers were impolite, and were mainly Iranian or from Hezbollah. "We are not fighting each other," he told me, "this is not a civil war. We are fighting Hezbollah and Iranians, under the cover of religion."

Abu Chaker's wish to live out his days in Homs with his friends like Albert and Hajj Choueib was thwarted. After the Syrian Revolution began in March 2011 in Dera'a and in Damascus, it spread quickly to Homs. At the time, everything had depended on whether the army, carefully structured and organised by Hafez al-Assad, would stay loyal to its Ba'athist leaders, or break away and side with ordinary Syrian people.

His sons back in England monitored the news anxiously. In August 2011, they decided it was time for their parents to leave Syria. The Chamsi-Pashas' youngest son flew to Damascus and travelled by car to Homs, a journey that was still possible at that stage. Abu Chaker did not resist. The fighting smelt to him like the start of the Lebanese Civil War. He knew the politics of the region too well to think that things would resolve quickly. Together with his son, Rihab and the two maids Eva and Johnette, Abu Chaker gathered his important documents, packed a few possessions and made arrangements for the house to be looked after. The departure was neither emotional nor sentimental. As a man of eighty-nine Abu Chaker knew that he was leaving for the last time but that he was one of the lucky ones. He never once complained. The family travelled to Damascus and flew back to London to take up residence once more in their West End flat.

He continued to follow the situation in Syria from London, and knew that friends and relations in Homs were finding it ever harder to make ends meet. With the right phone calls, money could still be sent to help them, legally routed by international bank transfers or Western Union into Lebanon, Dubai or Jordan, where it was picked up by one trusted contact and carried in the vehicle of another into Syria. Foreign currency held its value, enabling people to eke out their food purchases much more efficiently. For those without access to such cross-border networks, barter systems evolved instead, making cash irrelevant.

As the value of the Syrian pound began to slide, Abu Chaker recognised all the signs of a financial crisis. Inflation had spiralled out of control, and with it the prices of food and ordinary essentials. The Central Bank of Syria was determined to maintain a facade of normality and continued to issue economic statistics for eleven out of Syria's fourteen provinces, excluding only Idlib, Raqqa and Deir ez-Zour. International banks, on the other hand, were refusing to transfer funds to banks in Syria, causing investment projects to falter or fail. Inside the country currency exchange bureaux were forbidden to exchange US dollars and it was illegal to change money on the street. International credit and debit cards were rejected, both at ATMs and in retail outlets, except in a handful of top five-star hotels like the Dama Rose, where people like the UN and pre-authorised visiting journalists stayed; exceptions to the rules are always available to the elite. State sector employees like civil servants and teachers, whose salaries continued to be paid out from ATMs across the country, saw the real value of their wages fall week by week as the Syrian pound weakened ever further, eventually losing 90 per cent of its pre–2011 value.

The environment too has not been spared. The beautiful countryside Abu Chaker loved so much has been devastated by war. Forests everywhere, especially in the northwest Kassab region, have been burnt by accidental fires caused by aerial bombardment, and even cities like Homs have lost their trees, as desperate people chopped them down for wood to use as fuel for heating. Oil fields and pipelines that were deliberately broken and tapped have caused untold damage to the landscape and to the habitats of Syria's wildlife. Still, even as the situation deteriorates, NGOs and private companies run by a handful of committed Syrian environmentalists have been working on projects, often with the Ministry of the Environment and the Ministry of Agriculture, to try to salvage what remains and to invest in eco-tourism.

Wealthy individuals with plenty of inherited land have been able to overcome financial difficulties by selling off parcels of land. All over Syria people are selling their land for money to live on, of course at much lower prices because of the war. There is always a buyer, despite or even because of the uncertainty. The worst that can happen to a buyer is for cheap land they have acquired to be bombed or taken away from them. Many speculators take the view it is worth the risk.

Nowhere in Syria can return to what it was before the war. "Beirut," Abu Chaker's sons explained, "never went back to what it was, because you can never get it back to how it was, even if you rebuild all the souks in Aleppo or Homs or anywhere else." They told me about their neighbour's shop in Homs which was destroyed in the bombing. His family had owned it for 150 years. "It was on the corner and was just two metres wide and one metre deep. But even if the war stops today and you go back and rebuild it, how can it be reconstructed exactly as it was before? We can rebuild a new unit but it will never be the same, without the old materials, the old seasoned wood which had absorbed the soul and spirit of the souk. All the land registry records have been burnt so it's impossible to revive it as it was. It's good that Father stopped following the news after a while. We used to show him pictures of the souk destroyed but it was very difficult for him to take in."

What had concerned Abu Chaker most was the businesses of the people who could not leave Syria, how they would survive if their livelihoods were lost and how they would support their families. Many times over, under the French Mandate, under the Ba'ath and in the Lebanese Civil War, he had witnessed how war played havoc with people's lives, how when ruthless politicians and military men put their own ambitions above everything else, it was always the ordinary civilian populations who paid the price. Yet in spite of all the corruption and ugliness he had witnessed and experienced in his lifetime, Abu Chaker, like so many other Syrians, never lost his humanity. It was the secret of his success. In business he could be tougher than anyone when the situation called for it, but he was gentle as a lamb towards those who had fallen on hard times.

On 13 October 2013, Abu Chaker died in a London hospital at the age of ninety-two. His grave in Mortlake Cemetery remains unmarked with no headstone. When circumstances permit, his sons intend to take his body back to Homs, to be buried in Syrian soil, as he would have wished. All politics aside, he had loved his country deeply.

17

THE MERCHANT LEGACY
AND THE FUTURE OF SYRIA

All roads lead to the mill.

(Syrian proverb—on survival)

"Even were there no Syrian people, a Syrian problem would still exist," wrote Albert Hourani, one of the most highly respected historians of the Middle East. That was in 1946. This was not a claim that the Syrian people were historically difficult people—quite the reverse, for the Syrian response to the different currents that have crossed their territory has always been, wherever possible, accommodation and absorption. Hourani was recognising that Syria's location near the convergence of three continents has necessarily made it "at times a starting point, at others a terminus or a bridge" for the political and economic movements that have regularly flared up, waxed and waned on Syrian soil.

From the dawn of history the region of Syria has been a natural crossing ground for armies, caravans and traders, a place where competing interests are the natural order—perhaps nowhere more so than in Homs. Syrian people have reacted by becoming a mosaic society, adapting to the cultural, economic, political and

275

demographic currents that have swept in from Europe and the Mediterranean, from Anatolia and Central Asia, and from Egypt, the Arabian Peninsula and the vast deserts of Iraq and Iran to the east. When the region was one entity, Greater Syria, it was easier to withstand conflicting interests. Since being divided into the separate, far smaller states of Lebanon, Jordan, Israel, Palestine and Syria by the British and French governments, it has been far harder for each to ride the turbulent waves of history. As late as 1943 the British Middle East War Council realised the error of its ways, arguing for a kind of Arab Commonwealth, writing that "the problem of the Levant States cannot be treated piecemeal, for they are in all essentials a single unit."

The pieces of the Syrian mosaic—Sunni and Shi'a Muslims, 'Alawis, Druze, Orthodox and Catholic Christians, Syriacs, Armenians, Kurds, Turkmens, Circassians, Isma'ilis and, historically, Jews—are scattered across the country's diverse geography, its plains, mountains, valleys and deserts, in their various ethnic groups and sects. Sometimes they are blended in the cities, sometimes they live separately, but generally they have stayed in large extended families, which cultivated specific skills and specialisations that were carefully passed down through the generations. The glue of this mosaic society was trade, connecting all of the land's diverse elements, hence the high status of the merchant, the souk and the caravan. But Islam too played a broadly unifying role in creating a cultural homogeneity shared through prayer, fasting, pilgrimage and charity, even though the diverse Muslim population was characterised by differences in language, days of worship, diet, dress and leisure activities.

Looking back at the patterns that have afflicted Syria's socio-economic history since the fall of the Ottoman Empire, it is clear that as long as a government remains in place in Damascus that the majority of the Syrian population cannot respect, trust or depend on, conditions will continue to be ripe for warlordism and war-profiteering, be it by regime militia, Hezbollah, rebel opposition, Al-Qaeda affiliates, ISIS or simply merchants motivated solely by profit. The country as a whole can only prosper if it is built on a solid, inclusive commercial foundation where the motivation for wealth creation is shared benefit not personal enrichment. Otherwise it will simply sink into the same quagmire of corruption that all remember as the status quo before the war.

The Human Development Index in Syria has fallen back to the levels of the 1970s and current estimates reckon it will take thirty-five years for the country to recover its 2010 pre-revolution GDP level. The warlord mentality that now prevails inside Syria resembles that of the military *aghas* who were playing the same role in society in late Ottoman times. What will happen to today's Syrian warlords? Will they enter parliament in some future political settlement, as they have done in Lebanon? Will they end up inter-marrying with the offspring of the Assad regime, today's power-holders, just as the military *aghas* did with the notables, the elite of their time? It had been unthinkable as an outcome then, and seems unthinkable now, but perhaps it is part of an inevitable cycle, the result of an unstable society that needs to consolidate itself to survive. Northern Ireland's Martin McGuinness was the latest incarnation of a former paramilitary leader turned peace negotiator. A warm family man, he never denied his IRA background. It made him a stronger, more effective and credible politician and an essential player in the peace-making process. Syria needs many like him, from all sides.

This time however there is a complicating factor that did not exist at the turn of the twentieth century—the Islamist extremist organisations that have taken root and flourished in the lawlessness, such as the so-called Islamic State of ISIS and the Syrian Al-Qaeda-affiliate, still often referred to as Jabhat al-Nusra despite its various attempts at re-branding. These groups have arisen as a radical reaction to both the "immorality" of the West and the "irreligious" nature of governing regimes in Syria and the wider region, feeding on a poor and disadvantaged population ripe with resentment and hatred of their rulers. Such an ideology will continue to find fertile breeding ground among a brutalised and unemployed youth who have nothing to lose. As long as conditions on the ground remain unchanged, with a wealthy privileged elite exploiting a poor and disadvantaged underclass, flare-ups of violent conflict will continue and discontent will smoulder on, with deadly consequences for the rest of the world in the form of terrorism. Islamist acts of terrorism are also doing immense damage to international perceptions of Muslims and Islam. If there is no alternative on offer beyond the current Assad regime, even moderate Muslims may be driven to join the ranks of the extremists, making the future fight against them all the harder. Meanwhile the international community has failed to find a coordinated response.

The role of the merchant in this future Syria will continue to be pivotal. Without him and his ingenuity the outlook for the population remaining inside the country will be even bleaker. The danger is that the longer the current regime with its system of corrupt self-interest remains in place, the more honest merchants will leave in search of better opportunities elsewhere. The German and Turkish economies are already benefiting from a huge surge in start-up businesses from Syrian refugees. Given the choices that Abu Chaker faced, who can say he did not make the right decision when he headed west?

The Syrian Revolution and the subsequent descent into war have precipitated a massive social change, just as all earlier wars did. At the end of World War One in the death throes of the Ottoman Empire, trade stopped and it was estimated that a quarter of the Syrian population perished through poverty, disease or famine. Similarly horrific statistics are being repeated inside today's Syria. By the end of 2017 the human cost of the war was estimated at half a million dead, 2 million wounded, and well over 5 million refugees registered outside the country (3 million in Turkey, 1 million in Lebanon, 1 million seeking asylum in Europe and 655,000 in Jordan). The total number including unregistered refugees is of course much higher. Amnesty International has estimated that over 75,000 Syrians have "disappeared" following detention by the Assad regime, and a further 2,000 have been abducted by opposition groups. More than half the population is internally or externally displaced, 6 million of them children. 85 per cent of those who have stayed in Syria are living below the poverty line and life expectancy since 2011 has plummeted by twenty years. The UN Human Rights chief in March 2017 called it "the worst man-made humanitarian disaster since World War Two." Over 75 per cent of the deaths have been at the hands of the official government—the regime of Bashar al-Assad—and its allies, Russia, Iran and Hezbollah. ISIS and other extremist groups have killed about 6 per cent.

After World War One rural refugees in Syria fled to the relative safety of the cities. The resultant overcrowding then boosted housing prices in the urban centres, as in today's war, where real estate values within the walled city of Damascus have doubled or even trebled because the perceived safety premium has led to increased demand. Merchants who were threatened by harsh Ottoman tax penalties resorted to straightforward barter transactions to avoid losing more money, exactly as has been happening today across Syria, where the Syrian pound collapsed to just a tenth of its pre-2011 value. In areas outside regime control three different currencies are in use, just as in French Mandate times.

In July 2017 the Syrian government issued a new SYP2000 banknote, twice the value of the previous highest denomination and the first ever banknote to feature the head of President Bashar al-Assad. Worth about $4 in today's Syria before the war it would have been worth over $40. Its introduction is a tacit acknowledgement by the government of the colossal depreciation of the official currency, a devaluation which has meant that even the simplest of transactions made it necessary for people to carry round bagfuls of notes, far more than could fit into any normal wallet. The government hailed the new banknote as a return to more stable business activity, but it is also a symbolic move designed to show Bashar al-Assad reasserting his grip on the country, as are the ever-multiplying portraits of him on every shop, city square and street corner, and all along the main highways under regime control. The Syrian opposition refuses to use the new banknote, with some local rebel councils threatening a year in prison for those caught with it in their possession, saying it is a government ploy to flush out Turkish liras and US dollars from rebel areas to use as a war fund.

Some skilled but unprincipled traders, first in Ottoman times, then under the French Mandate, managed to grow rich from speculation, smuggling and selling supplies to the army, because they paid big bribes and kept on the right side of well-connected officials. Today's regime supporters have similarly enriched themselves from the war, often hoarding commodities. Unscrupulous grocers selling tea, rice, sugar and other basics into besieged areas have grown rich. Before the war they may only have had one simple shop. After years of war, they have several shops and their sons drive around in BMWs.

Desertion from the fledgling Syrian army in 1920 reached such high levels that even Faisal himself, first king of Syria, declared that more people seemed to be deserting than enlisting. In today's crisis, the Syrian army is similarly depleted by desertion and a refusal to answer conscription calls, many young men preferring instead to escape their country and even make the dangerous journey to Europe. It is the major reason why male refugees of military service age (eighteen to forty-two), most of whom currently live in the surrounding countries of Lebanon, Jordan and Turkey, are reluctant to return. Payment of the *badal* (exemption fee) is expensive: at least $8,000, far beyond what most Syrians can afford, unless they can call on regime connections.

At the time of the Great Syrian Revolt of 1925 the French brought in foreign mercenaries—mainly Senegalese and Moroccans from their colonies—to crush the rebellion. In the same way Iraqi and Iranian Shi'a mercenaries, together with Lebanese Hezbollah fighters, have entered the fight on Syrian soil to support the Assad government. The French used collective punishment of whole towns. The Assad government, with massive Iranian and Russian support, has been intent on doing the same, unleashing unprecedented brutality on its own citizens. After the suppression of the Great Syrian Revolt in 1927, the French established the internal security apparatus which was to become an enduring feature of post-independence government. The French, with their "divide and rule" sectarian policy, provided a model for Bashar al-Assad to follow and Syria today lives with the consequences.

The leaders of Syria's earlier uprisings largely betrayed their followers, abandoning them after first rousing them to fight. Echoes of today's rebel struggles in Syria can be detected, where rebel leaders started out strongly, only to disintegrate into bitter factional battles with each other, thereby letting down their honest and moderate supporters.

What will be left after the fighting stops? What will Syrian society look like, and could anyone like Abu Chaker ever fight his way through the chaos to emerge successful? Exploring his Ottoman background has given us clues, showing the complexities of the class system and how the various groups formed allies or rivals. It seems in some ways little has changed since then—only the groups are different, but the same cycles continue.

Homs, a city of such social cohesion in the first half of Abu Chaker's lifetime, has since the 1970s under Hafez al-Assad grown exponentially as an 'Alawi centre, becoming vital to the regime as the strategic gateway from Damascus to the coastal 'Alawi heartlands. It was one of the first cities to rise against the Syrian regime in 2011 and as such it provided the blueprint for the regime's four-stage strategy of siege, starve, destroy and transfer. As "Capital of the Revolution" it has been bombed into submission, to serve as a warning to other rebellious centres of what to expect.

Western international journalists have not been allowed into Syria to report on the uprising except under the strictest supervision, and even then only when the regime authorities invited them to cover a particular episode or phase that they felt reflected in their favour. Those journalists who attempted to come in without government visas met various grizzly ends, from being blown up by targeted regime airstrikes, like British Marie Colvin in Baba Amr, to being publicly executed by ISIS, like American James Foley. Syria has been the world's deadliest country for journalists every year since 2011. Russian, Iranian and Syrian state media journalists, on the other hand, have free rein inside the country, no censorship necessary. Russia's RT news channel had wall-to-wall coverage of the fall of Aleppo, all viewed from the western regime-held side of the city, presenting Russia and Putin as altruistic saviours of the Syrian people and the only international force truly fighting terrorism.

When Bashar al-Assad is questioned by foreign journalists about the tens of thousands detained without charge inside regime prisons, like Saydnaya and Mezzeh Military Airport, not to mention Hospital 601 just half a mile from his presidential palace, he denies the documentary and photographic evidence of torture and atrocities presented by Amnesty International and other human rights organisations, dismissing it as "fake news". Defectors like military police photographer code-named "Caesar" and survivors like Mohsen al-Masri corroborate each other's experiences independently. "We were swept into a system that was ready for us. Even the hospitals were slaughterhouses."

Cases filed in Spain in 2017 have begun prosecution of top Syrian regime officials, but the special UN Syria Commission, set up in 2012 to collect evidence of war crimes, has had its investigations repeatedly blocked by Russia's and China's use of their veto powers at the UN Security Council. Their refusal to allow cases to be referred to the International Criminal Court caused top war crimes prosecutor Carla Del Ponte to resign from the Commission in 2017 in protest at the inaction of the international community. Years of work spent conducting over 5,000 interviews and compiling thirteen reports have achieved zero results:

> In Rwanda and the former Yugoslavia I was able to pursue investigators, file indictments and arrest warrants [that led] to trials and convictions. But in this case nothing happens. It's a disgrace for the international community and particularly for the Security Council. It looks as if President Bashar al-Assad will escape justice because if we want to negotiate peace we will have to talk with him as we did President Milošević. But one day he will have to face justice. Justice must do its work because without justice there is no real peace. We know that from history.

MERCHANT LEGACY AND THE FUTURE OF SYRIA

Dictatorship comes in many forms, and ISIS too has had its own carefully manipulated "information dictatorship" in the areas under its control. At its peak in 2015 it had a massive social media footprint, posting 90,000 tweets a day. The French Mandate authorities' example was followed by the Syrian government in the early days of independence, when most Syrian newspapers were funded by a variety of foreign states, in return for which they span the required line in their editorials and fabricated or coloured their coverage of events inside Syria according to the cloth of their paymasters. Sometimes it was just a handful of articles with a certain bias, but at the other end of the spectrum entire newspapers were sometimes set up to peddle a certain angle from regional centres like Beirut. Foreign intelligence services set up clandestine radio stations broadcasting against Nasser, whilst posing as internal opposition groups. Everyone was at it. Yet interestingly, the Syrian coups that succeeded were not the ones backed by outside players like the USA, Iraq and Jordan, but rather the ones backed by Syrians such as Za'im and Hinnawi in 1949, and Shishakli in 1954. Foreign-backed coups were not sufficiently supported on the ground to succeed. Bribe money was routinely paid at elections for voting the required way. Saudi payments were made to Syrian army officers to "help" them oppose union with Iraq in the early 1950s.

Demographic change has been a consistent objective of the Syrian government since the start of the 2011 uprising, though some of it has been accidental, such as Syrians today accounting for one in every four members of the Lebanese population. The Syrian war has led to an accidental blending of the two countries, something that twentieth-century political leaders were never able to achieve. Lebanese official policy is now actively seeking to reverse the trend, by pressuring Syrians to return, denying them residency and refusing to renew their refugee status. Many of the refugees who might want to return home—men outside conscription age, women and children—will not be able to, because their homes have been destroyed or illegally sold on. Some will no longer be welcome in their former communities. Those who have found work in

Lebanon will be reluctant to give it up for uncertain employment prospects in Syria.

Any superficial union with Lebanon has only been with "useful Syria"—the major cities of Damascus, Homs, Hama and Aleppo together with the coastal provinces of Tartous and Lattakia. These are the parts controlled by the Assad regime, which wrap around Lebanon like a large belt and are under the control of Iran and its proxy militia, Hezbollah. In effect they form a security zone, though things are not quite that simple. Areas like the coastal regions of Tartous and Lattakia provinces were formerly seen as 'Alawi strongholds, but now play host to thousands of displaced Sunnis, tilting the demographic balance in those locations back towards a Sunni majority. Iran will find it hard to impose its presence there in the long run. It took ten years for Israel to withdraw from Lebanese territory after the Lebanese Civil War ended, while it took Syria fifteen years, in the years 2000 and 2005 respectively. Maybe it will take Iran and Turkey similar lengths of time—or longer—to withdraw from Syria.

The demographic changes resulting from the Syrian conflict have been comprehensively documented by the independent Washington DC-based Syria Institute in a 2017 report. The report was compiled from interviews with residents displaced from Homs since 2012, many now living outside Syria and most too frightened of reprisals from the regime to give their real names. It explains the deals brokered by Iran and Russia and with UN observation. Many residents mistakenly imagined that the UN presence would give them a measure of protection, not realising that the UN were simply bystanders and were powerless to control regime practices.

The Homs Land Registry office, says the report, was housed in a safe part of the city, not under siege, on the upper floors of a building whose lower floors were occupied by Syrian army forces. It was destroyed by fire in 2013. Then in 2016 Bashar al-Assad issued a decree for all Homs property records to be digitalised. Former residents were given four months to complain about the new digitalisation records, but most were not in a position to do so, being either in prison, in Europe or dead. Some original Homsis have been displaced internally more than once, deliberately targeted until they were eventually forced to leave the country.

Many displaced owners who have returned to reclaim their properties found their homes had already been sold on, using falsified documents. The new owners were without exception 'Alawi or Shi'a. Since the government controls who returns and to which neighbourhood, they are able to socially engineer the future demographic balance of Homs. It has not gone unnoticed that the areas singled out for the first reconstruction projects are either Christian or 'Alawi, while Sunni areas like Baba Amr and Khaldieh, site of the heavily damaged Khalid ibn al-Walid mosque, are still ghost towns, years after the residents were pushed out. Future *waqf* schemes, to rebuild communities as well as neighbourhoods, are crying out to be recreated.

The same pattern applies in Damascus, where construction projects have been given the go-ahead in the suburbs of Basateen al-Razi in the west, and a much larger area in the south including Darayya and Qadam. Informal housing in these areas, inhabited by communities broadly supportive of the uprising, has been razed to make way for seventy-floor-high skyscraper development, while similar informal housing areas in Damascus suburbs like Mazzeh 86 or 'Ish al-Warwar, inhabited by pro-regime communities, have been left untouched. The regime benefit is twofold: to punish its opponents and at the same time to enable its supporters to cash in on prime real estate assets in the capital. Basateen al-Razi has been renamed Maruta City, significant because *maruta* in ancient Syriac means "sovereignty" and "homeland". Presidential decree number 19 in 2015 allowed private sector investors, through officially approved joint ventures, to hold and manage assets that were public property or were expropriated. The move has given the green light to new well-connected individuals to make a fortune from development and reconstruction projects, like the business magnate Samer Foz from Lattakia, an unknown before the uprising but now Syria's most influential investor thanks to his links to Bashar al-Assad.

The example of Beirut and how it was reconstructed after its fifteen-year civil war provides a warning. One private company, Solidere, with Prime Minister Rafiq al-Hariri as its largest shareholder, was given the contract and proceeded to knock down more buildings than were destroyed during the war, erasing the past and turning it into a city of exclusion, with faceless skyscrapers and tax incentives to draw foreign investment. Hariri also owned Lebanon's largest private construction company. The rebuilding process was exceptionally lucrative for government members and their business associates. To finance the reconstruction, the country went deeply into debt, with interest payments totalling more than a third of the government's annual spending. However, since politicians and their families control a third of all Lebanese banking assets, they even reap rewards from the debt itself. The war economies that enriched the militia leaders have simply been transferred to the reconstruction process. During the Lebanese Civil War these militias engaged in drug-trafficking, pillaged the port and speculated against the Lebanese pound, amassing personal fortunes for themselves. There was no incentive for the war to end, unless they could gain similarly from the reconstruction.

Political reconciliation in Lebanon was sidestepped, as the former warlords became today's politicians, ministers and heads of government. They sit together in a parliament that rarely agrees on anything and has struggled for years to set a budget, as each member's primary concern is how to line his own pockets through a system of sectarian patronage. So far, state collapse and violence have brought them economic windfalls, so there is no hurry to become a stable country.

Meanwhile ordinary citizens of Beirut have had to suffer the chaos that results from such a government, like the months' worth of uncollected garbage piling high in the streets after a landfill site was closed in 2015. Civil society activists took matters into their own hands, organising the high-profile "You Stink" social media campaign, which finally shamed the government into action. Syrian refugees set up Recycle Beirut, a company organising rubbish recycling collections, providing both employment and a social service. "We can create job opportunities from something that was once a headache for the government," says its founder. A third of its employees are women. In today's Beirut the security presence is still shockingly heavy, with soldiers and blast barriers, concrete walls, barbed wire and checkpoints. The resulting tension and frustration is such that half of Lebanon's educated youth emigrate for easier lives elsewhere.

There are many lessons for Syria in Lebanon's fifteen-year civil war. When it ended in 1990 all the militias were disbanded except the powerful Iranian-backed Shi'a group Hezbollah. Christian General Michel Aoun's return as president in late 2016, nominated by the prime minister, Sunni Sa'ad al-Hariri, shows how Lebanese politics is trapped within certain patterns. Aoun was effectively Hezbollah's candidate, returning at the head of a "National Unity" government in which Hezbollah hold half the seats in parliament. The alliances are holding, for now, held in place by Iran behind the scenes, but even Aoun has realised that something has to change. In late 2017 he referred openly to the "Hezbollah problem", calling for the party to be assimilated into the Lebanese army and advocating "an economic common Levantine market." It was a recognition that only shared commercial interests could bind the region together, not politics.

All over Lebanon and Syria Hezbollah have networks of Shi'a-dominated intelligence outfits, and have made vast land acquisitions in key areas. While their opponents remain disorganised, Hezbollah's cohesion has made them a formidable force, and they have no problem accepting Beirut's multicultural glitz and glitter. They project themselves as a social welfare institution, operating free schools, hospitals, and low-cost housing, an image reinforced by their own TV station, Al-Manar (The Beacon). Hezbollah's deep involvement in the Syrian war across the border in support of the Assad regime is popular in Lebanon ever since a rash of suicide bombings in Beirut: "We are fighting to save Lebanon from Sunni extremists," goes the Hezbollah mantra. In Lebanon Hezbollah is everywhere—and is friends with everyone. They are careful not to impose their Islamist ideology on the Lebanese population, but control Lebanon's political and, to a large extent, economic future. The same may be true of Syria a few years hence.

Iran also provides grim lessons from its eight-year war with Iraq, when the clerics chose, at the war's end in 1988, to give the Revolutionary Guards a stake in the system's survival. Today the military role in Iran's economy is entrenched, controlling everything from telecoms to infrastructure construction projects. In the words of Iranian analyst Saeed Laylaz: "About 40 per cent of Iran's economy is not accountable to the government and does not pay taxes. The economy has been militarised." The similarities do not end there, as in Iran like Syria, the top 1 per cent, the gilded nouveaux riches, have stolen the country's wealth—more Porsches were sold to Tehran in 2011 than anywhere else in the world.

One of the few positives of the current Syrian conflict has been the strengthening of civil society groups. Mostly found in opposition areas, self-styled "Local Coordination Committees" took the running of their communities upon themselves after the state was absent. From high-profile groups like the humanitarian White Helmets saving people buried under bomb rubble, to women coming together to cook food or sew clothes for needy people in their neighbourhoods, there are now hundreds of civil society organisations that have evolved both inside and outside Syria, completely independent of the state.

Assad and his regime fear these organisations and their defiance, branding them all "terrorists". Backed by Russian air support, the regime bombed every single hospital in eastern Aleppo between July and December 2017, seeking to obliterate the opposition's essential infrastructure and make them give up the fight. But such organisations do not have affiliations with political agendas. Just as Haytham Al-Hamwi, now director of the Manchester-based organisation Rethink Rebuild, ended up in prison in Damascus for cleaning the streets, the organisations in Syria were the same. He explained: "They found people who fled without homes, so they built shelters. They found people without hospitals, so they built hospitals. They found unvaccinated people, so they vaccinated them. The regime forbids these organisations and sees them as terrorist organisations." In Syria under the 1958 Association Law, civil society groups became legally subject to supervision, requiring approval from the security services. In opposition-held areas too, such groups are routinely persecuted, particularly by hardline armed factions. Like the regime, they fear that such independent groups might grow to challenge their own authority.

But these civil society groups will not disappear once the war ends. They may well get a stake in the negotiations for peace, and some are already represented in the Civil Society Support Rooms at the UN headquarters in Geneva, set up through the agency of chief UN mediator for Syria, Staffan de Mistura. The precedent was in Northern Ireland, where civil society, especially in the form of women's groups, was involved in the peace process in the 1990s.

Abu Chaker would have approved of such people, ordinary citizens, taking control of their lives. He would not have known to call it "civil society activism", but by funding the setting up of things like schools and medical clinics, he instinctively supported his community, knowing that this was the way for people to thrive and prosper, not at each other's expense, but by helping each other. In London when he co-founded the Syrian Arab Association in the UK it was because the official institutions were absent. There were no diplomatic relations between Syria and the UK at the time, and so they had no embassies in Damascus or London, just like today. He felt the gap, the lack of any means for Syrians in exile to find each other and become a community.

What began as an aspiration to achieve a more just and dignified society with basic human rights has been hijacked into a highly politically charged agenda. Those who started the revolution did not think of themselves as political, but everything to do with Syria is political these days. Abu Chaker would have thought of them as naïve idealists. What he did in setting up SAAUK in London was never thought of as political. In a mature society such as the UK it was not regarded as a threat. There was no state-run intelligence service that would arrest him as a "preventive" measure, to make sure he didn't start a political party.

In Syria today life goes on in spite of the chaos and the warring factions. People have to survive. The country is blessed with much arable land, remnants of the Fertile Crescent, and remains a fundamentally agriculture-based economy, capable of self-sufficiency when properly managed. Even today in the war, agricultural business continues across the country, as crops still need harvesting and merchants continue to trade in agricultural produce wherever possible, often supplying not just their own territories, but also other parts of the country further afield. Trucks loaded with vegetables grown in the fertile Ghab valley of the Orontes have been routinely transported across ISIS-controlled areas, where taxes and dues are collected, then delivered for eventual sale in the northern Kurdish cantons. All over the country, trade of necessity continues, according to the local demand, often between rival communities. Throughout the war to this day the Aleppo merchants have made sure to maintain their ties with whichever group controls the cereals and cotton produced in the Euphrates Valley, determined to preserve their monopoly on exports, paying the necessary transit taxes to whoever mans the checkpoints, be they regime or opposition.

Always marginalised by the state, the eastern tribes felt excluded, making them vulnerable to ISIS overtures. Their land provided the agricultural and industrial powerhouse for the state-owned cotton, wheat, oil and gas industries that were dominated by well-connected regime loyalists from western provinces, yet in return they themselves were given little investment, no industrial infrastructure, no refineries—those are concentrated in Homs—and no training of skilled personnel.

The traditional tribal leadership in these areas of Syria's eastern desert, so weakened by decades of corrupt dependence and shrewd manipulation, first under Hafez, then under Bashar, found itself powerless to resist the ISIS onslaught. The fragmented tribal communities could no longer be mobilised by their shaikhs or unite against the new highly organised radical Islamists. The tribes account for at most 7 per cent of Syria's population, and their future in such a climate remains uncertain. It could still be possible that a strong individual leader from a shaikhly family might yet rise up to face the challenges, and play a role in future community building, especially given the complexities of the new Kurdish presence, now a factor in so many of the historic tribal territories. The fall of Raqqa, de facto capital of ISIS, requires much unity to fill the vacuum. As ever, the networks that have developed to get round the restrictions are based on contacts and trust—albeit sometimes misplaced trust, when greed outweighs morality.

Can Abu Chaker's legacy as the archetypal Syrian merchant give clues about the future of Syria? His story shows how the sectarian divisions that look so fixed now will slowly fade again once a measure of stability returns, just as they did after the French attempt to "divide and rule". A good merchant's role in this will be the same as his—to find partners who can be trusted, irrespective of their religion or ethnicity, to establish links between different communities, based on mutual benefit. In this Abu Chaker was a natural, a true professional.

Demographic change continues to be engineered or precipitated in today's war, as it has been throughout Syria's history. Centuries ago Sayf al-Dawla (Sword of the State), founder of the Hamdanid dynasty, relocated the entire Shi'a population of Harran to repopulate his capital Aleppo, after it had been ravaged by a Byzantine attack. After the end of the Crimean War, the Russians wanted to create a Christian majority, so they brought Christians in and by 1865 had pushed over half a million Muslims out into the Ottoman heartlands. In 1939 the French separated the Sanjak of Alexandretta from Syria and ceded it to Turkey, triggering the exodus of tens of thousands of Armenian, 'Alawi, Sunni and Christian refugees into northern Syria. In 1967 after capturing the Golan Heights in the Six Day War, Israel began almost immediately to settle Israeli Jews there, unilaterally annexing the territory in 1981. Israeli maps show it as Israeli territory, not as Syrian territory occupied by Israel. Official Syrian maps continue to show both the Golan and the Sanjak of Alexandretta (renamed Hatay by Turkey) as within the international borders of Syria. Future maps of Syria will no doubt vary according to who publishes them.

From 2012 onwards where opponents have been crushed, populations perceived as "disloyal" have been supplanted with "loyal" supporters under "starve or surrender/reconciliation" deals. By late 2016, after half Syria's original population had been displaced and citizenship granted to tens of thousands of Iranian mercenaries who had fought to keep him in power, Bashar himself boasted to a US interviewer that "the social fabric is much better than before." No amount of social engineering will succeed however in turning Syria from a 70 per cent majority Sunni country to a majority 'Alawi one, not even a wholesale exchange of populations on the scale of Atatürk's Christian–Muslim exchange between Greece and Turkey in 1923.

Ironically it has been the rise of the secular Ba'ath Party that has fuelled sectarianism inside Syria. Under the Assadist rule of the last fifty years, you have either been a Ba'athist or not—you are either with us or against us. The clientalism of the former "notables" was simply replaced with that of the Ba'athists. Loyal Ba'athists have been protected, be they Sunni, 'Alawi, Christian or whatever. Disloyal ones have been punished, through imprisonment, detention and torture. From early on in the war slogans like "There is no god but Bashar", "Do not kneel for God, kneel for Assad" and "Assad or we will burn the country" have been scrawled by regime militias on mosque walls and buildings everywhere. Backed up by a draconian network of seventeen intelligence and security departments, they crushed any free, independent political opposition that dared to raise its head.

Sectarianism in Lebanon and Syria has never been some ancient phenomenon rooted in age-old feuds. Abu Chaker's pluralism was not unusual. It was how most people functioned and such divisions as did exist between people were as likely to be within Christian or Muslim communities themselves as between the different communities. Lebanon's Christians are not one homogenous group—there are many internal divisions, just as there are within Muslim and Jewish groupings.

Regional sectarianism is a far more recent creation. French attempts to "divide and rule" under the mandate were not successful. It was not till after the Ba'athist revolution that sectarian sentiment in Syria began in earnest, when the sense of exclusion felt by many Sunnis led to the first real appearance of Sunni Islamist militancy in the 1980s. Matters were then made worse by the 2003 US-led invasion of Iraq, which resulted in huge destabilising rifts between Sunni and Shi'a across the region. Before the Ba'athists, religious and sectarian identities in the Middle East were numerous, but were only relevant at the social level and were not politicised or institutionalised. An important and potentially hopeful lesson emerges from Stefan Winter's careful study of four hundred years' worth of Ottoman archival tax records, executive orders and *iltizam* (tax farming) contracts, that 'Alawi relations with other groups in Syria were not historically determined by uniform animosity and inescapable oppression. Rather, as he puts it, they were "repeatedly characterized by accommodation, cooperation and trust." The Ottoman sources tell of fiscal exploitation, war and migration, but also of alliances between Bedouin and 'Alawis, of promotions to government office and of inter-communal friendships. The unlikely bond between Abu Chaker and 'Adnan Badr al-Hassan, an 'Alawi intelligence general, is a recent incarnation of just such a friendship.

The Syrian war has also triggered a revolution in the role of women, and half the population cannot be ignored. In Syria most women living in the cities, like Umm Chaker, wore Western dress and left their heads uncovered during the 1950s till the 1970s, when Western influences were prevalent. But in the 1980s the wearing of the *hijab* underwent a revival, partly as a result of the spread of Saudi Wahhabi practices, partly as a subtle protest against the secular Ba'ath regime of the Assads, so the government responded by discouraging the wearing of Islamic dress. Once the revolution started, the Assad regime relented on the headscarf, allowing *hijab*-wearing women back into government offices.

Many Syrian women have been involved in the revolution from the outset, either taking part in peaceful demonstrations on the streets in the early days, or voicing their cries for social justice, human rights and dignity through social media platforms like Facebook and Twitter, from the protection of their homes. As young men have either been killed or drafted into the army, or fled the country to avoid conscription or as refugees after their homes were destroyed, women have increasingly been left alone, either to look after ageing parents who refuse to leave, or to take on the jobs of men by keeping the country running, exactly as happened after the two world wars in European societies. One such woman took on her husband's job in construction, shovelling sand and cement, after he was injured. She was reviled by her male co-workers and taunted: "Do you think you're going to change the world? Do you think you're a man? You won't last long!" She stuck with it, in order to support her children and husband.

Syrian divorce rates have risen by 25 per cent between 2010 and 2015. Female refugees who leave and settle in Europe are increasingly questioning the patriarchal society they left behind, where religion has so often been used to keep women under the control of men. Of those women who stay in Syria, some want to break all taboos and challenge the entire patriarchal set-up, while others want to hold on to traditional conservative values. Some declare openly on social media that they do not want to be judged by intellectuals who see their *hijab* as a symbol of backwardness, while others proudly post photos of themselves without the *hijab*, declaring, "For 20 years, I was deprived of feeling the air touch my body and my hair!" For some the Syrian Revolution has been accompanied by the women's revolution, and one woman activist, named Batoul, posted her wish on the Facebook page for "The Uprising of Women in the Arab World", "to become the President of Syria, this is why I support the Uprising of Arab Women."

Many remain sceptical of the possibilities for real change, pointing out how in earlier revolutions in the region, such as in Algeria, women took an active role in the fight against oppressive rulers, only to end up again pushed into the background and subject to the rules of men. The blanket imposition of the *hijab* on the entire female population of Iran over the age of nine after the Iranian Revolution is the most obvious example. Even in Tunisia, where gender equality is in theory enshrined in the 2014 constitution, the reality is that the patriarchal mentality persists, with a Tunisian government study revealing that nearly half the country's women are still subject to physical, sexual or verbal abuse. In Tunisia, Jordan and Lebanon laws excusing rape if the perpetrator marries his victim were finally repealed in 2017. The Assad regime issued a decree in the same year saying that "wives of martyrs" would be guaranteed full-time jobs, a move designed to shore up loyalty, but that will also create divisions in society.

Financial hardship has also had an adverse effect on women's positions, with statistics showing an extraordinary rise in polygamy from 5 per cent in 2010 to 30 per cent in 2015. This has been a direct consequence of a shortage of men, where husbands have either been killed, gone missing or fled abroad, and where male relations, such as the husband's brother, takes on his brother's widow as a second wife in order to bring her legally into his household and protect her and any children she may have. Economic hardship has been cited by landlords who have taken their tenants as additional wives: "She couldn't pay the rent, so I married her. That way at least she is not out on the streets."

In other parts of Syria the scenario has been even worse, with women's rights going backwards by centuries due to the emergence of extremist groups like the Al-Qaeda-affiliated Jabhat al-Nusra and ISIS, the so-called Islamic State or *Daesh*. Their rise, ironically, has only been made possible by the destabilising effects of the Syrian Revolution, leaving lawless vacuums quickly filled by Islamist extremists, who then imposed their own antiquated version of Islam in which women, especially Yazidis who refuse to convert to Islam, are passed around as war booty. Guest-speaker imams were brought in to educate young girls on "Western misinformation about rape", explaining that these women were not raped, but rather were "given into the care of honourable *Daesh* fighters... to protect them."

Even in the Western-sanctioned opposition groups like the Syrian National Council, the men make the decisions and the women appear as window-dressing. One opposition activist said: "Women are like spices for men in the political opposition. They use us to add some flavour, but we do not affect the main ingredients. I refuse to take part in this cooking, as long as I am not considered an active participant." There is a very long way to go before women are acknowledged as equal stakeholders.

Abu Chaker's view on women was both traditional and progressive. His marriage to his first cousin quickly ended in divorce, but he accepted his second wife's Westernised dress and taught her how to drive. She had been the first woman in Homs to wear trousers. He encouraged her to be involved in his business and she supervised the construction of their blocks of flats. She is still hugely loved and respected by her sons, whose devotion to her is typical of Syrian society. The joke about the Arab man in a sinking boat with his wife, his daughter, his sister and his mother sums it up. He can only save one other person to stop the boat from sinking. All the others will have to be thrown overboard—who will he save? The answer: his mother, because he can get another wife, daughter or sister, but he can never get another mother.

The revolutionary gender-equal society envisaged by the PYD in the Kurdish-controlled areas of northern Syria would almost certainly have been a step too far for Abu Chaker. In their new semi-autonomous cantons men and women are supposed to be equal in work, education and all areas of life. In theory new laws have been passed, based on the Swiss legal code, banning polygamy and child marriage. Honour crimes must be tried with the same severity as murders, not just excused in the way they were before. Kurdish society has in the past been notorious for honour crimes within its heavily patriarchal framework. It is a massive societal change reminiscent of Atatürk's creation of modern Turkey, in the speed of its execution, with far-reaching implications, if it endures.

All across the Middle East women are actively engaged in a battle to be included on an equal basis in all aspects of education, political and social life, free from the discrimination so commonplace in patriarchal societies. It was not always so, and it is hard to imagine any woman further removed from ISIS sex-slaves than Palmyra's Queen Zenobia with her *mut'a* marriage to her warrior husband. In early Islam many women were involved in establishing educational institutions, such as Fatima al-Fihri who founded Kairouan University in the ninth century. During the twelfth and thirteenth centuries under the Ayyubid dynasty, set up by the sons of the ethnically Kurdish Saladin, twenty-six of the 160 mosques and madrasas built in Damascus were funded by women using the *waqf* system. Women could study and earn academic degrees (Arabic *ijazah*) as early as the twelfth century, if they were fortunate enough to come from learned and scholarly families who wished to give both their sons and their daughters the highest possible education. The twelfth-century Damascus historian Ibn 'Asakir, himself from a wealthy background, wrote that he studied under eighty different female teachers, and even Ibn Taymiyya, the controversial Sunni theologian and political activist whose views went on to profoundly influence Wahhabism, is documented as having four female teachers (and forty male teachers) during his studies in Damascus. True change in the patriarchal system will be a long time coming. Of late, under the influence of Wahhabi Islam originating in Saudi Arabia, societal gender equalities have gone backwards rather than forwards.

Good-quality education is the key. But that too will be a long time coming, with at least four different school curricula being taught to children across Syria, according to whether they have been in regime-held areas, Kurdish-held areas, ISIS-held areas or rebel opposition–held areas. Hafez al-Assad had grown up discriminated against at school because he came from the 'Alawi minority, but he benefited from an education instituted by the French with a more liberal and free-thinking approach. He watched rich Sunni boys getting top marks because the teachers did not dare upset their parents. When the Ba'athist educational policies dominated Syria, the same system applied in reverse, with Ba'athists getting an extra 10 per cent in exams by virtue of their party affiliation, then creaming off all the best jobs. Success in the authoritarian Ba'athist education system, both at school and at university, has been based for the last forty years on centralised rote learning, not of the Qur'an but of Ba'athist propaganda and the professor's notes, devoid of free critical thinking.

The Western media obsesses about ISIS-related terrorist attacks in Europe and about the handful of European nationals who went to Syria to join them. But only 0.09 per cent of the Syrian population joined the extremists. The focus logically should be on the 99.91 per cent who did not, but it is rare to read stories featuring groups like Syria's Girl Guides, who have been meeting every week throughout the war, learning how to change tyres and administer first aid. They are from all religions, celebrating 'Eid and Christmas together. "The war has made me stronger," says twenty-two-year-old Sham, "and helped me realise what I want to do in life. I know now that studying is the key to everything. We never talk about politics."

What will happen to the lost generation of Syrian children who are less lucky, now living in Lebanon, Jordan and Turkey, out of school for years, or forced into employment to support their families? Many of them will have forgotten what they learnt before the war, and many more will never even have started school.

Abu Chaker's example, deprived of education by his father's premature death, shows that it is possible to overcome such obstacles. With the requisite will power, faith and application, a person can still succeed. Some would even say the harder the struggle, the greater the rewards of success. Education, previously taken for granted, will be more treasured in future, with more effort expended to make up for lost time. The BBC reported in 2017 the case of student Mariam Hammad, dodging bullets and bombs in Aleppo to pursue an online degree in business with the US-based University of the People. Studying by candlelight, she said: "I hope that whoever sees my story will not be discouraged by difficulties they face. I believe that after every hardship comes a great rebirth, and in honour of every friend, neighbour and Syrian who lost his life due to this war, we must stay optimistic."

If Syria's children are not taught the skills needed to help rebuild their country when the war ends, they may find it harder to avoid being sucked into future further cycles of violence. But it is not a forgone conclusion. Only one in five schools inside Syria is closed because of the war, destroyed in the shelling or converted into refugee housing. Once the opportunity is there, children catch up very quickly, with the right motivation. What little formal education Abu Chaker had, under the nuns of Homs, was far removed from the rigid rote learning of the Ba'athists. A future Syrian education system where only merit, diligence and creative analysis were rewarded would transform society very quickly.

The hardest thing for young minds to overcome will be the deep psychological damage caused by witnessing so much bloodshed and violence. This is something Abu Chaker did not have to endure. As the only son and breadwinner for the family after his father died, he was excused from military service and never wore a uniform in his life. He never had to witness anyone he knew being killed, let alone was forced to kill anyone himself. Syrian teachers report how some children, having been exposed to so much violence, are now conditioned to respond in the same way, saying things like: "I'll shoot you if you talk to me like that!" Such mindsets will take longer to address than the time it takes to teach a child to read and write.

Abu Chaker, more than most in his own generation, understood and valued the importance of education. He was determined to make sure his own children gained the best possible education, so that they could ensure their own futures and get ahead. Despite his own truncated schooling, he knew that education and a caring attitude towards others were the crucial foundations for successful communities—plus the support of a loving family.

"If Father were alive today," said his sons, "he would have looked at the extremist groups in Syria with horror and have nothing to do with them. He could see the extremism developing—it didn't come out of nowhere. Even if he had been a much younger man when the Syrian Revolution broke out, he would not have got involved, even on the humanitarian side, he would not have gone to refugee camps in Turkey or crossed illegally into Syria. Rather he would have found ways of helping people in Homs, relations and friends, Muslims and Christians without distinction, getting money in to them to help them feed themselves and survive. Once foreign powers became involved he saw how little influence Syrians had over their own destiny. It was no longer a Syrian problem but an international one, dependent on the deals brokered between outside powers."

Abu Chaker's country is today overrun by multiple actors, using it as their stage to act out their rivalries and pursue their particular interests. He saw through all their usual devious tactics. For him it was just the way politics worked. He had seen from early childhood that politics was a dirty game in which loyalties switched regularly and unpredictably according to the latest set of interests. Ordinary Syrians who were not part of these machinations and power-plays had to survive as best they could. He warned all his sons to steer clear.

He learnt early on that in order to survive the turbulent world of politics, war and disaster, you had to seek out the constants in your life. For him those were first and foremost religious faith, then family and then commerce. In a country such as Syria no one could depend on the state. It had shown itself to be brutal, ruthless and exploitative to its citizens, utterly untrustworthy. It was up to the citizens to rise above the state and look after themselves.

In Britain he found a different system, one in which the state was largely benign. Bribery was not called for and corruption was not eating away at the apparatus of government. There were laws that were obeyed and people paid their taxes. If they did not, they were fined or sent to jail after a fair trial.

Abu Chaker's textile business went global while he was still alive, with markets extending from America to the Far East. From its simple origins in the Homs souk, it expanded first via Beirut, then via Bradford, into a multinational company producing not just the original broadcloth for suits on which its reputation was based, but also luxury upholstery materials, design and lifestyle products showcased from its Knightsbridge shop. The Queen and Prince Philip sit on Hield cloth in the royal Bentley. The discreet headquarters of the company remains in Briggella Mills, the last mill in Bradford whose looms are still producing.

How can that success be explained, and what does the future hold in Syria for the Chamsi-Pasha shop, burnt out and destroyed in the bombing of 2012? In summer 2016 the United Nations Development Program (UNDP) began funding a project to reconstruct the ancient souks at Homs, costing several hundreds of thousands of dollars and projected to take two years. It had several stages and began with an extensive cleaning up of the fire-blackened walls, pockmarked with shrapnel and bullet holes. Unexploded shells and explosives were carefully removed. Next came the documentation of the history of the souk, going back to its founding in the thirteenth century by the Ayyubids, the dynasty of Saladin's sons, and covering its subsequent extension under the Mamluks and the Ottomans. Finally there was the renovation and reconstruction, with the installation of a new roof and four new gates. About 200 shops out of the original 5000 or more that used to exist in the souk were to be re-opened. Some seventy people were involved on the ground in the project, led by a highly respected local architect, and its efficient running was much lauded in foreign media.

Then corruption struck. Midway through the roof installation, the head of the UNDP branch in Homs, an official from nearby Salimiyeh, derailed the construction by "arranging" for a vital support to be undermined. Three shops collapsed. The project came to a halt, leaving the official free to take matters into his own hands and thereby ensure his cut of the UNDP budget—a cautionary tale for would-be investors.

By the end of 2017 around thirty shops had reopened, despite the half-finished roof, keen to re-establish their businesses. One is a chocolate shop which used to have eleven employees, but now it is staffed just by the owner himself, a Christian who inherited it from his father. He started with only two or three customers a day, but slowly his old clients have been returning from as far afield as Damascus, Beirut and Tartous, once they get news that he is up and running. He is one of the privileged few who has passed the regime screening system, so has been allowed to return.

In a future Syria, years from now when the war is over and the Assad regime is long gone, schoolchildren will once again be able to take a detour from their walk home, just as Abu Chaker did in his own young and carefree days when his father or his sister held him by the hand. It will not be exactly the same as before, but will have been rebuilt using new materials and techniques, just as it was rebuilt with new materials and techniques from earlier ages after earlier destructions. But today's children will still wander through its shady alleyways, savouring the wonderful smells of the sweets wafting through the air, and refreshing themselves from the seasonal juice-stands, just like Abu Chaker did as a boy. The shops selling their wooden, copper and silver crafts, their fabrics and perfumes, will slowly revive again, turning the souks of Homs once more into the consumer centre of the city. In amongst them, his sons hope, there will once again be a Chamsi-Pasha shop, still selling the fine suit cloth manufactured by the British company of Hield from their own Bradford mill. Maybe it will even once again be staffed by a descendant of the faithful 'Ali, or in the summer months, by one of Abu Chaker's own great-grandchildren.

"Father spoke little of religion," said his sons. "He never quoted *Hadith* or verses [of the Qur'an]. He didn't have that database. He taught us to be pious by example. He set the tone by being the man we all wanted to be. He was especially averse to gossip and refrained from ever talking about anyone. Father was quiet in terms of opinion until someone needed his help. When someone he employed died, he would pay their family a proportion of their salary for five years, to help them get by. He gave away his wealth in his lifetime. He never discussed politics but always listened to whatever his guests had to say. He very seldom spoke in public or private unless you really pushed him."

On key issues in the Arab world and surrounding Islam that have arisen since his death, Abu Chaker's sons were in no doubt about what his views would have been. On the *Charlie Hebdo* controversy and the subsequent furore about the representation of human figures in cartoons, he would have laughed and said what a bunch of children all these extremists were. He would have bemoaned how their lack of education and their social exclusion made them vulnerable victims of radicalisation.

Where there were disputes, Abu Chaker was a known and respected mediator. Throughout his life people would come to him with their problems, seeking arbitration, just as people had sought out Hafez al-Assad's father. In another life, born into a richer family, Hafez would have become a doctor, just as Abu Chaker, given proper education, might have become a judge, a profession in which his instinctive common sense, his grounding in reality, and his natural inclination towards even-handedness and compromise would have been put to good use. But even without education, people still sought him out to help them solve their business disputes and wrangles. They were assured of a fair hearing and a sound decision.

On business techniques he taught his sons to negotiate hard with the supplier. He also taught them the overwhelming importance of trust. Your customer must trust you and your supplier must trust you. Even your rival must trust you. The sales director of Stroud Riley Drummond Brian Levi, son of Maurice Levi, who had known Abu Chaker as a customer and as a competitor for over fifty years, described him as "an absolute gentleman, scrupulously honest, a tough negotiator but very fair. When he said no, he meant no, when he said yes, he meant yes, no trickery, no games. We didn't even have to write an order down. Once we'd agreed a price, we knew he'd stick to it."

After retiring from Drummonds, Brian was persuaded to join the board of directors of Hield as a consultant. At their monthly board meetings, he would sometimes point out that large sums of money were outstanding from certain customers. "Abu Chaker and his sons would say, 'Never mind, we trust these guys.' They trusted a lot of people I wouldn't have trusted because I didn't know them like they knew them. He was one of God's gentlemen. Every single Syrian I met," he said, "through the father or through the boys, has been an absolute gentleman. Such charming people. I only hope one day they'll be able to say the same thing about us."

As for politicians and institutions of the state, mistrust in them has been the norm in Syria for centuries. Religion and trade, by contrast, have been constants, the two things on which earlier civilisations rested and which encouraged their innovative mindset. Something in that blend has given many Syrian manufacturers a deep, even mystical connection to their products, especially in the case of textiles. It is this exceptional sense of style and luxury, an awareness of texture, feel, colours and the emotions they evoke that make Syrian fabrics so distinctive. It is a quality that goes right back to ancient times, to the uniquely blended textiles of Palmyra, and is still, remarkably, to be found in Syria today, defying the tides of war and destruction. The urge to create something that is both useful and practical and an object of beauty in its own right is still alive in Syria, against all odds. Even the hand-made soaps of Aleppo, based on olive oil and laurel, scented with Damascus rose and jasmine, are still being made and sold in the souks, using the age-old skills and traditions.

All of Abu Chaker's sons share this vision, as do many young Syrians. The Ottoman inheritance runs deep and will not be erased by any war. He succeeded in passing on to them a fine sense of entrepreneurship combined with a close connection to the product itself. He taught them how to turn disasters into opportunities.

Future Abu Chakers, even those who have missed out on some years of education because of the war, will share his Syrian merchant heritage, his natural flair for innovation in trade and finance. Maybe they will be the first to devise new microfinance technology from their mobile phones, doing away with "the curse of cash" which can be abused by the rich and the corrupt. If money is just pixels on a screen available to all, financial transactions cannot be monopolised by powerful individuals and institutions. Abu Chaker would have approved of anything that cut out the middleman and spread benefit to the many, not just the few.

***

A month after Abu Chaker's death, I asked Yorkshire-born mill-worker Harold Chapman (1923–2015) about the Syrian owner of Hield. Harold had joined rival Drummonds Mill aged sixteen, worked there all his life and ended up as the overseas shipping manager. "Yes, I remember old Chamsi-Bacha," he said, "He didn't talk much, but you could tell he was a strong man. He used to buy a lot from us and I remember marking up all the crates of cloth for him, M.C.C.B., which stood for Mohammad Chaker Chamsi-Bacha."

When I mentioned Abu Chaker's charity work, Harold looked surprised.

"Really? We never knew he was involved in anything like that."

Both men lived to be ninety-two.

In the foyer of Briggella Mills is a photo of Abu Chaker planting a tree in the small flowerbed outside the entrance, alongside a photo of the mayoress of Bradford planting a similar tree in the flowerbed opposite.

Both trees are still there.

ACKNOWLEDGEMENTS

This book represents an enduring friendship, testament to the bridge that can exist between cultures. When their father died in late 2013, his sons—Chaker, Firas, Samer and Talal Chamsi-Pasha—asked me if I would write his story. During his own lifetime he had consistently refused any such attention, always urging them instead to get on with their own lives.

Now that he was longer in a position to object, they realised his life story could serve as an inspiration to young Syrians seeking sense and purpose in their country's tragedy. They have given me their fullest cooperation throughout, constantly inviting me to their homes, feeding me, arranging interviews with all the family members, including the many grandchildren, putting me in touch with more and more of their father's friends and colleagues, in Syria, Lebanon and the UK. His range of acquaintances was staggering, as befitted a man who had travelled widely and always maintained an open mind.

Above all, my many meetings with their mother, Umm Chaker herself, now well into her eighties, were always a delight, full of laughter and joy. "Thank you for making me remember my life!" she exclaimed at the end, clutching my hands with tears in her eyes.

In terms of structuring the book, I am deeply indebted to two people for their suggestions. My brother Mark Taylor, who has never visited Syria, patiently read my many drafts, his feedback forcing me to rethink many passages. He began by telling me I had no book, and ended up some years later by telling me I had two. He was the only person to see the manuscript before the publishers. Paul Chevedden, an American scholar and friend with strong Syria connections, hit upon the brainwave of a parallel structure. From across the Atlantic, his email assured me he had just read a book on Islamic law, where this had worked well.

My own family have been fully supportive throughout. My husband John McHugo, as a fellow Oxford Arabist, appreciates and understands my love for Syria. My children Chloë Darke and Max Darke confess to finding the extent of it at times baffling.

Michael Dwyer of Hurst Publishers immediately saw the intrinsic relevance of the book and accepted the manuscript in its entirety, for which the Chamsi-Pasha family and I thank him profoundly. He can rest assured that we will do our very best to carry its message to as wide an audience as possible.

GLOSSARY

'ajami—painted lacquer wooden panelling, usually eighteenth century, influenced by Persian styles.

'Alawi—follower of 'Ali, the caliph revered by Shi'a Muslims. 'Alawis belong loosely to the Twelver Shi'a sect of Islam, most of whom are concentrated in Iran, Iraq and Lebanon. Historically they were called Nusayris after their ninth-century founder Ibn Nusayr. Syria's population is estimated at 12–15 per cent 'Alawi, heavily concentrated in the western coastal provinces and the Ansariyeh mountains. Since 1970 Syria has been continuously ruled by two presidents from the 'Alawi minority, Hafez al-Assad and his son Bashar al-Assad.

'askeri—military (in both Arabic and Turkish).

'ulema—Muslim scholars, religious elite.

'umra—lesser pilgrimage to Mecca, can be undertaken at any time of year.

a'yan—the "notables", top layer of wealthy land-owning society, usually Sunni, because they formed the majority of the population, but also Christian, 'Alawi or Druze.

ablaq—patterned stone work of alternate black basalt and white limestone.

agha—military commander in Ottoman times.

arghile—Syrian water-pipe, also called hookah or *nargileh* in other parts of the Arab world.

ashraf—direct descendants of the Prophet Mohammad via Fatima.

Ba'ath—Arabic for "renaissance", name of the Arab socialist movement founded with Arab nationalist, anti-imperialist ideology; ruling party of Syria since 1963.

badal—military exemption fee to avoid compulsory conscription.

Badia—semi-steppe desert of eastern Syria.

bedestan—covered market hall for the sale of valuable goods.

caliph—from the Arabic *khalifa* meaning successor, used as the title for Muslim leaders who succeeded the Prophet Mohammad.

Daesh—al-Dawla al-Islamiyya fi-al-'Iraq wa-l-Sham, Arabic acronym for the extremist Islamist group "Islamic State in Iraq and Syria" (ISIS), which styled itself "The Islamic State" in June 2014.

Druze—a distinct religious community whose origins were in Shi'a Islam, mainly found in the mountains of Lebanon and Syria. They form about 3 per cent of the Syrian population.

'Eid—religious festival, always a public holiday.

fatwa—religious opinion issued by an Islamic scholar of jurisprudence.

Hadith—collected sayings of the Prophet Mohammad, as recorded by his Companions. The Hadith and the Qur'an together form the basis of Islamic law..

Hajj—pilgrimage to Mecca, to be undertaken at a specific time in the Muslim lunar calendar, at least once in the life of every Muslim; one of the five pillars of Islam.

Hajji—pilgrim who has been on the *Hajj.*

Hanafi—one of the four Sunni schools of Islamic law, named after Abu Hanifa (d. 767), son of a Persian slave. It is the oldest and largest by far of the four schools, accounting for about half the total number of Muslims in the world, and is the most liberal and tolerant. It insists on the right of judicial speculation, including analogical deduction and the role of reason. It permits female judges. Hanafi law applies in Syria's Shari'a courts. Most Ottomans were Hanafis (as are Turks to this day).

Hanbali—one of the four Sunni schools of Islamic law, founded by Ahmad Ibn Hanbal (d. 855 in Baghdad). It was the last and smallest of the four schools and is adhered to by most Salafis in Saudi Arabia, Qatar and small pockets of Syria. It is the strictest and most conservative school and rejected the principle of "consensus", insisting on uncompromising adherence to the letter of the Qur'an and the *Hadith*. It is considered by some to be the best for rulings on commercial transactions.

hara—small neighbourhood within a residential quarter.

haram—forbidden under Islamic law.

Hezbollah—Lebanese Shi'a militia and political party, led by Hassan Nasrallah, supported financially and militarily by Iran. The party currently holds half the seats in the Lebanese Parliament and its militias are considered more effective than the Lebanese army.

hijab—headscarf that covers a woman's hair but leaves the face uncovered.

iltizam—"tax farming", whereby the Ottoman authorities sold farms to local wealthy families, sometimes on a hereditary basis, who in turn collected heavy taxes from the peasant class and the agricultural produce.

Isma'ili—sect within Shi'a Islam; Isma'ilism has many offshoots including the 'Alawis and the Nizaris, whose titular head is the Aga Khan.

jihad—literally "The Party of God", nowadays contaminated by associations with terrorism, but literally "struggle" in Arabic. Jihad originally conveyed an individual's striving in the way of God (major jihad), but is also specifically used as a term for holy war against those considered non-Muslims (minor jihad).

jizya—poll tax on non-Muslims as stipulated in the Qur'an.

joukh—broadcloth, historically made in England from sheep's wool, known for its warmth and hard-wearing qualities.

khan—caravanserai, places where merchants could stay and trade their goods, often fortified for security.

kuttab—traditional mosque-affiliated school for Qur'anic teaching to young children.

mahalla—local quarter or neighbourhood.

mahram—male guardian for a woman.

Maliki—one the four Sunni schools of Islamic law, founded in Medina by Malik ibn Anas (d. 795). It is one of the smallest and earliest of the four schools and is dominant in Egypt and North Africa. It leans to the conservative side, but is not as extreme as the later Hanbali school.

Mamluk—slave soldier trained to be part of a military elite. The Mamluks founded an empire in Cairo that ruled Egypt and Syria from 1250 till the Ottoman conquest in 1517.

Maronite—the dominant sect of Christianity in Lebanon, named after a fifth-century saint called Maron. Some Maronites claim descent from the Phoenicians.

masjid—small, non-congregational mosque serving a local area.

Melkites—Syrian Catholics, sometimes confusingly also called the Greek Catholics. Today they are in full communion with Rome and belong to the Patriarchate of Antioch.

mihrab—prayer niche in a mosque indicating the direction of Mecca.

minbar—pulpit in a mosque used by the imam during Friday sermons.

muezzin—man who calls to prayer from the mosque minaret.

GLOSSARY

mukhabarat—the intelligence or security services, of which, in late 2017, there are seventeen branches in Syria.

mukhtar—literally "the chosen one", the person chosen to represent the quarter/local community to the authorities, like a kind of mayor.

muqarnas—"stalactite" decoration in wood or stone, used as an architectural feature to transition between the "earthly" and the "divine" and therefore often found where a dome transitions from straight pillar supports into a curved dome.

mutran—bishop.

niqab—full face veil, covering a woman's hair and face.

Orthodox—indigenous Syrian Christians of the Eastern Church (as opposed to the later Catholic arrivals who first came to the region at the time of the Crusades). They are the largest Christian denomination in Syria (accounting for 70 per cent of Christians in Homs). The Orthodox are not in communion with Rome and do not follow the Pope, but follow Constantinople and their own patriarchs.

Ottoman—Turkish dynasty with its capital in Istanbul, ruled Syria through appointed governors from 1516 to 1918.

Pasha—Turkish title of respect, an Ottoman honorific often given to the governor of a province.

qibla—direction of prayer towards Mecca.

Qur'an—literally meaning "recitation", the collected oral revelations from God to the Prophet Mohammad over a twenty-three-year period, written down after his death to form the Muslim holy text; the main source for Shari'a or Islamic law. It is considered "the word of God", so is only ever recited in Arabic, the language in which it was "revealed".

salat—ritual prayers performed five times a day; one of the five pillars of Islam.

sanjak—literally meaning "flag", used to denote an administrative district within the Ottoman Empire, a subdivision within a larger province known as a *vilayet* in Turkish or *wilaya* in Arabic

sawm—fasting during Ramadan; one of the five pillars of Islam.

Shafi'i—one of the four Sunni schools of Islamic law, named after the Imam Al-Shafi'i, born in Gaza (d. 820 in Cairo). It is the second most numerous of the four schools and is dominant in southern Syria and Damascus. It considers itself "the golden mean" between the more liberal Hanafis and the more conservative Hanbalis and Malakis who dominate in the Arabian Peninsula.

Sham—Arabic for both "Syria" and "Damascus", according to context; originally meaning "the North" or "the Left" (as viewed from the Arabian heartlands of Mecca and Medina).

Shari'a—the canon law of Islam, literally meaning "the road to the watering place, the clear path to be followed", derived from the Qur'an and Hadith.

shaikh—elder or head of a tribe.

Shi'a—the second largest Muslim sect, which accounts for under 10 per cent of Muslims worldwide. The sect split off from the Sunni orthodoxy, believing that the Prophet Mohammad's rightful successor was 'Ali, his cousin and son-in-law. Syria has some small pockets of Shi'a Muslims (who are not 'Alawi), such as the villages of Fou'a and Kefraya in the northern province of Idlib.

souk—market of stalls, bazaar.

Sufi—member of the mystical sect of Sufism, a tolerant and outward-looking form of Islam, popular with many moderate Syrian Muslims.

Sunni—the largest Muslim sect; they follow the Prophet Muhammad's "path" or *sunnah* and account for nearly 90 per cent of Muslims worldwide. Syria's population is estimated at 70 per cent Sunni.

GLOSSARY

Suryani—Arabic for "Syriac", which refers both to the indigenous Syriac Christians (also called Assyrians) and to their liturgical language, an ancient Semitic dialect of Aramaic, which was the language of Christ. The Syriac Christians are much smaller in number than the Syrian Orthodox today, who use Arabic as their liturgical language. Syriac was once the lingua franca of the region.

Tanzimât—literally "Reorganisations" of the Ottoman Empire that began in 1839 and ended in 1876, an extensive programme of reforms that sought to modernise or "Europeanise" the civil liberties of non-Muslim citizens, especially Christians.

tekkiye—a Sufi monastery, often with a school and hospital attached, together with a soup kitchen for free food distribution to the poor.

Wahhabi—very strict puritanical sect of Islam founded in the Arabian Peninsula in the eighth century by Mohammad bin 'Abdul Wahhab; it is still adhered to by the rulers of Saudi Arabia today.

wasta—a kind of patronage system; having connections in the right places, necessary for getting favours done in bureaucratic governments.

waqf—religious endowment, a system of Islamic trusts used to maintain a religious building.

waqfiyya—religious foundation deed for a *waqf*.

vilayet—Turkish word for an Ottoman province, also spelt *wilayat* in Arabic, a large administrative area with its own local courts and councils but no physical borders.

zakat—alms tax to the poor, as laid down in the Qur'an; one of the five pillars of Islam.

SOURCES AND SUGGESTED READING

Researching this book has been a difficult task. Political histories abound, but remarkably little has been written on the evolution of Syria's economic and social dynamics. My approach has been to combine oral history from the many interviews I conducted since 2013, together with archival research and ethnographic analysis, casting a very wide net to capture little-known facts. This triangulation of research methods has then been supplemented with first-hand knowledge gained from living in the country. Beyond the publications listed below, which I would recommend to those wanting to learn more, I have also incorporated information gleaned from radio, internet and press material over a number of years, from sources including the BBC, Reuters, Al-Jazeera, Al-Araby, Enab Baladi, All4Syria, The Syrian Observer, Syria Untold, the Carnegie Middle East Center, The Washington Institute, Asharq Al-Awsat, Cadmus European University Institute and The Syria Report. The latter in particular, with its weekly summary of economic data, was invaluable.

Much work remains to be done to illuminate the inner workings of Syrian society. My hope is that by contextualising how people live in modern-day Syria within a framework of how they lived in the past, the reader will come to appreciate the immense potential that exists for Syria's future, thanks to its mercantile tradition.

SOURCES AND SUGGESTED READING

Al-Sabouni, Marwa, *The Battle for Home: The Memoir of a Syrian Architect*, Thames & Hudson, 2015.

Antoun, T. Richard and Quataert, Donald, *Syria: Society, Culture and Polity*, State University of New York Press, 1991.

Bachich, Mariam, *Community-Based Rural Heritage Management in Syria: A Case Study of Dmenieh al-Sharkiya Village*, MA thesis, 2007.

Balanche, Fabrice, "Les municipalités dans la Syrie baathiste: déconcentration administrative et contrôle politique," *Revue Tiers Monde* 183, no. 1 (2008): 169–87.

————, *La région alaouite et le pouvoir syrien*, Karthala, 2006.

Ball, Warwick, *Rome in the Near East*, Routledge, 2007.

Barbir, Karl K., *Ottoman Rule in Damascus: 1708–1758*, Princeton University Press, 2014.

Barout, Mohammed Jamal, *Al-Takawwun al-tarikhi al-hadith lil-Jazirah al-Suriyyah* [A contemporary history of the Syrian Jazeerah], Beirut: Arab Center for Research and Policy Studies, 2013.

————, *Syria in the Last Decade: The Dialectic of Stagnation and Reform*, Doha Institute, 2012.

Batatu, Hanna, *Syria's Peasantry, the Descendants of its Lesser Rural Notables, and their Politics*, Princeton University Press, 1999.

Burns, Ross, *Aleppo: A History*, Routledge, 2016.

Butcher, Kevin, *Roman Syria and the Near East*, British Museum Press, 2003.

Chatty, Dawn, "The Bedouin in Contemporary Syria," *Middle East Journal* 64, no. 1 (Winter 2010).

Douwes, Dick, *The Ottomans in Syria: A History of Justice and Oppression*, IB Tauris, 2000.

Dueck, Jennifer Marie, *The Claims of Culture at Empire's End: Syria and Lebanon under French Rule*, Oxford University Press/British Academy, 2010.

Eltahawy, Mona, *Headscarves and Hymens*, Weidenfeld & Nicolson, 2015.

Gelvin, James L., *Divided Loyalties, Nationalism and Mass Politics in Syria at the Close of Empire*, University of California Press, 1998.

Hinnebusch, Raymond A., "Local Politics in Syria: Organization and Mobilization in Four Villages Cases," *Middle East Journal* 30, no. 1 (January 1976): 1–24.

Hitti, Philip Khuri, *Syria: A Short History*, Macmillan, 1959.

Hourani, Albert, *A History of the Arab Peoples*, Faber & Faber, 2013.

Khaddour, Kheder, "How Regional Security Concerns Uniquely Constrain Governance in Northeastern Syria," Carnegie Middle East Center, 2017.

Khoury, Philip, *Urban Notables and Arab Nationalism: the Politics of Damascus, 1860–1920*, Cambridge University Press, 1983.

———, *Syria and the French Mandate*, IB Tauris, 1987.

Lawson, Fred, *Demystifying Syria*, Saqi with London Middle East Institute at SOAS, 2009.

Lewis, Norman N., *Nomads and Settlers in Syria and Jordan, 1800–1980*, Cambridge University Press, 1987.

Meriwether, Margaret L., *The Kin Who Count: Family and Society in Ottoman Aleppo, 1770–1840*, University of Pennsylvania, 1981.

Necipoğlu, Gülru, *The Age of Sinan: Architectural Culture in the Ottoman Empire*, Reaktion Books, 2005.

Neep, Daniel, *Occupying Syria under the French Mandate*, Cambridge University Press, 2012.

Pipes, Daniel, *Greater Syria: The History of an Ambition*, Oxford University Press, 1992.

Provence, Michael, *The Great Syrian Revolt and the Rise of Arab Nationalism*, University of Texas Press, 2005.

Rathmell, Andrew, *Secret War in the Middle East: The Covert Struggle for Syria, 1949–1961*, IB Tauris, 2014.

Salaymeh, Lena, *The Beginnings of Islamic Law*, Cambridge University Press, 2016.

Scharrahs, Anke, *Damascene 'Ajami Rooms: Forgotten Jewels of Interior Design*, Archetype Publications, 2013.

Seale, Patrick, *Asad: The Struggle for the Middle East*, University of California Press, 1990.

Seifan, Samir, *Syria on the Path to Economic Reform*, University of Saint Andrews Centre for Syrian Studies, 2010.

Tripp, Charles, *Islam and the Moral Economy: The Challenge of Capitalism*, Cambridge University Press, 2006.

Van Dam, Nikolaos, *The Struggle for Power in Syria*: Sectarianism, Regionalism and Tribalism, 1961–1978, IB Tauris, 1979.

Velud, Christian, "French Mandate Policy in the Syrian Steppe," in *The Transformation of Nomadic Society in the Arab East*, eds. Martha Mundy and Basim Musallam, Cambridge University Press, 2000.

Weber, Stefan, *Damascus: Ottoman Modernity and Urban Transformation, 1808–1918*, Aarhus University Press, 2009.

White, Benjamin Thomas, *The Emergence of Minorities in the Middle East: The Politics of Community in French Mandate Syria*, Edinburgh University Press, 2012.

Winter, Stefan, *A History of the 'Alawis*, Princetown University Press, 2016.

World Bank, *The Economic Development of Syria: Report of a Mission Organized by the International Bank for Reconstruction and Development at the Request of the Government of Syria*, Johns Hopkins Press, 1955.

Culture Through Making
The charity supported by this book

As Syria seeks to reconstruct itself after the most destructive war in its long and turbulent history, there will be multiple challenges. The Syrian identity is still there, bruised and battered, in need of nurturing. Now is the moment, therefore, to support charities of a different kind.

Culture Through Making is an initiative that offers hope. Centred on craft, identity and education, with a focus on rebuilding lives, it is a transformative educational skills and training programme for Syrians inside Syria and in neighbouring countries. It offers the chance for those who have suffered trauma and violence to turn their energies towards creating objects that are useful, practical and beautiful, a process that is healing and therapeutic, bringing communities together.

Syria's traditional craft skills are rich in culture and identity, passed down from one generation to another. Textiles, ceramics, wood and glass are natural products, readily available on the ground, and these are the fields in which the Syrian sense of style, colour and design have excelled across the centuries.

When used in schools **Culture Through Making** has the immediate ability to support cultures of sharing and creating, to nurture a sense of community that may have been lost or damaged through the war. Long term it can be extended to adults, men and women, giving them "portable" skills which will have the double benefit of keeping Syrian creative cultures alive whilst also giving them a means for sustainable employment. Abu Chaker was helped to help himself, in a strong community where people supported each other. This was for him, as a devout Muslim, the meaning of charity.

A recent **Culture Through Making** project held across schools supported by **Syria Relief** in Syria was inspired by tiles from historic

321

mosques in Damascus, many examples of which can be viewed in London's Victoria and Albert Museum. Children made their own tiles. True to the Syrian flair for experimentation and design, they absorbed multiple influences, creating their own unique hybrid of motifs with swaying leaves and arabesques.

Even when it appears to have died, the vine can regenerate.

The **Culture Through Making** (www.culturethroughmaking.org) initiative supports the registered UK charity **Syria Relief** (no. 1143797), operating on the ground inside Syria since 2011, offering humanitarian support to the local population affected by the crisis. For more information about the charity please visit http://www. syriarelief.org.uk, or contribute to **Culture Through Making** by donating at www.syriarelief.org.uk/donate/culture-through-making.

The author is donating 50 per cent of her royalties to help.

INDEX

INDEX